The Earth Is My Patient

by
David F. Arieti

authorHOUSE™

1663 Liberty Drive, Suite 200
Bloomington, Indiana 47403
(800) 839-8640
www.AuthorHouse.com

First published by AuthorHouse 09/15/05

ISBN: 1-4208-3227-1 (sc)

Printed in the United States of America
Bloomington, Indiana

This book is printed on acid-free paper.

We appear to be a species out of control, setting in motion processes that we do not understand with consequences we cannot foresee.

Lester Brown

...for although our destiny is not entirely in our hands, we ourselves are among the important forces in its creation.

Silvano Arieti

ACKNOWLEDGEMENT

Writing a book like this one takes the help and cooperation of many people. Many of the people listed applied their talents in many ways in order to help me write this book.

The list includes those who gave me advice on what not to say as well as say in blunt terms so as not to offend too many people even though some people have to be offended if we are to save the planet.

I have to thank Steve Blithos and Deborah Lottman from the Columbia College, Chicago Writing Center who spent countless hours with me going over every single word of the manuscript. Dr. Jacob Nieva for compiling Appendix III regarding diseases associated with climate change. Caryl Danguilan for reading the manuscript and checking for errors. Judy Banicki for typing parts of the appendices. A heartfelt thanks go out to the following computer lab personnel at Oakton Community College who helped me write when I had computer problems.-Syeda Ahmed, Darakhshan Ahmed, Hammad Ahmed, Samuel Pudi, Manish Varma, Jigar Shah, Farrukh Ahmed, Rupa Vallabhapurapu, Sandhya Vallabhapurapu, Julia Gray, and Valeriu Gava. A hearty thanks to Anita Lathrop from Columbia College, Chicago. A truckload of thanks to J.J. Murray and his wife, Kristine Batey also from Columbia College, who helped inspire me. The library staff at Oakton Community College was very instrumental in getting me books that I needed for reference. The wonderful librarians at Oakton include Gretchen Schneider, Rose Novil, Merl Nadick and Trisha Collins. I also wish to thank Doug Jones for his suggestions. I wish to thank Merle Tuntland and John Ponzo from Waubonsee Community in Sugar Grove Illinois for their immense help in supplying pictures. I would like to thank Jim McCarthy for his superb legal advice. I also appreciate the ideas given to me by Norman Zaghi.

THE OPINIONS AND IDEAS
EXPRESSED IN THIS BOOK ARE
SOLELY THOSE OF THE AUTHOR

TABLE OF CONTENTS

DEDICATION

For Maggie, Amiel, Aviva, the memory of my parents Jane and Silvano and to all the bacteria, fungi, protista, animals, plants and viruses (both good and bad) and the Planet Earth

PREFACE

In late August of 2005 Hurricane Katrina (category 5 then 4) struck the Gulf Coast of the United States. Tens of thousands of people were left homeless, thousands died and flooding destroyed much of New Orleans and other areas. Damage is estimated to be in the billions of dollars

Was the intensity and the destruction of this hurricane an act of God or did humankind have a hand in making it this bad by adding millions of tons of heat trapping carbon dioxide (CO_2) by burning fossil fuels and causing destruction of natural barriers along the coast line by building casinos and other structures?

Whatever the case it will be wise to err on the side of caution by eliminating fossil fuel use (oil, coal and gas) and change to solar or some other environmentally friendly energy source.

Katrina may be a warning of worse catastrophes to come if we as a species don't change our environmentally abusive ways. It is wise to heed the warning!!!

It is for this reason that I write this book.

SYMPTOMS

The patient's condition is serious. Symptoms are multiple. His breath is noxious. He has a fever, higher than ever before. Efforts to bring it down are not working. Poison has been found in body fluids. When symptoms are treated in one area, more pop up in other body parts. If this were a usual patient, doctors would be inclined to declare the multiple sicknesses as chronic and terminal. Not knowing what else to do, they would just take steps to make the patient as comfortable as possible until the end came.[1]

CHAPTER 1
INTRODUCTION

If the environment goes, we all go.
David F. Arieti

After teaching environmental science for more than 23 years and being involved in research, I have come to realize that there are many real causes of Environmental pollution. We can equate this pollution as if the Earth were a sick human being.

We all know that both factories and cars pollute and rain forests are being chopped down, but do we pay attention to the real causes of these activities? Well, it is here that I intend to dwell upon this problem. With much thinking and discussion with many people I have come up with what I believe to be the real causes of environmental pollution.

Before discussing the real causes of environmental pollution, let's define pollution. The first two definitions come from a children's joke book (Smart Alecs, 1987)[2]. The third is my own. These definitions are as follows:

1. *The contamination of Mother Nature by human nature.*
2. *The effluence of affluence.*
3. *The contamination of an ecosystem by either the addition of something or the removal of something. (My definition)*

An ecosystem is the area containing living and non-living factors. Living components include fungi, plants, bacteria and animals whereas non-living components include the air, sunlight atmospheric pressure etc. By addition of something, we mean the addition of some non-natural chemical like polychlorinated biphenyls (PCB's) or pesticides which poison the living organisms on the planet. By removal of something I mean the loss of soils, destruction of the tropical rainforests, over hunting and over fishing which lead in many cases to total devastation of the local ecosystems as well as elimination of many species.

One of the most important aspects of our environment is its biodiversity. This is the fact that we have a tremendous variety of organisms (any living thing) on this planet. There are roughly 1.8 million organisms identified thus far which include bacteria, fungus, single celled organisms called protists, animals and plants.[3]

All organisms have specific functions on the planet. The functions can be called "**Natural Services**" These natural services include the following:

ECOSYSTEM SERVICES AND FUNCTIONS
1. **Gas regulation**
2. **Climate regulation**
3. **Disturbance regulation**
4. **Water regulation**
5. **Water supply**
6. **Erosion control and sediment retention**
7. **Soil formation**
8. **Nutrient cycling**
9. **Waste treatment**
10. **Pollination**
11. **Biological control**
12. **Refugia**
13. **Food production**
14. **Raw materials**
15. **Genetic resources**
16. **Recreation**
17. **Cultural**

According to many investigators the value of the Earth's natural resources and services are approximately $18-54 trillion per year.[4]

Now let's look at the real environmental problems facing all of us today. Human beings face the same sort of environmental problems no matter what part of the globe they live on. The following is a list of problems facing the planet Earth today:

1. **Water pollution**
2. **Air pollution**

3. Noise pollution
4. Light pollution
5. Land pollution
6. Greenhouse effect and its role in climate change.
7. Comeback of diseases like Tuberculosis and the introduction of new diseases.
8. Animal extinctions
9. Bleaching of coral reefs
10. Soil erosion
11. Ozone depletion
12. Acid Rain
13. Eutrophication
14. Bioinvasions
15. Lack of adequate space
16. Algal blooms
17. Oil spills
18. Estrogenic effects of chemicals in the environment
19. Salinization
20. Garbage
21. Environmental racism
22. Eco-Tourism
23. Environmental refugees
24. Disrupted nitrogen
25. Sea Life Loss
26. Chemical leaching
27. Deforestation
28. Topsoil loss
29. Sickly animals
30. Radiation Contamination
31. Environmental illness
32. Loss of natural pollinators
33. The end of males

The above is just a partial list of damage caused by humans, which can be prevented, as we will later see in the chapter entitled *"Solutions."* From looking at the above list we realize that almost any human activity causes pollution. It is my intention to define the real causes, which are basically socially motivated. In fact, some topics like over fishing, which is found in the chapter titled *"Greed"*, (Chapter 11) might just as well be placed under the chapter dealing with **Ignorance and Stupidity** (Chapter 12). Each chapter of this book is devoted to one of the following REAL CAUSES:

Agriculture

Attitudes

Capitalism, American Way, and the Pursuit of the American Dream

Apathy

Because it's there

Business

Communism

Convenience

Corruption

Greed and Human Values

Ignorance, Stupidity or Both

Impression

Low Status of women

Perception that Nature doesn't exist

Overpopulation

Paradigms

Respected, Disrespected, and Pious Individuals,
with Idiotic Ideas Including Politicians, Talk-show
hosts, misguided Environmentalists etc. etc.

Poverty and Affluence

Search for the Perfect Pear, Apple Peach etc.

The Need for a Monstrous defense Budget

Tradition

DIAGNOSIS AND SYMPTOMS OF THE EARTH'S ILLNESS

A BRIEF DESCRIPTION OF POLLUTION AROUND THE WORLD

The following is a brief description of the types of environmental pollution that are currently on the planet. The reader is encouraged to consult other environmental textbooks for more details.

1. WATER POLLUTION.

Throughout the world we keep hearing about water pollution. There are seven major contaminants involved in water pollution. These are the following: sediment, sewage, disease causing organisms, organic chemicals, inorganic plant nutrients, inorganic chemicals, thermal (heat from power plants and other sources) and radiation.

1. Sediment covers bottom dwelling organism.
2. Sewage pollutes waterways with fecal material as well as adding pathogenic organisms. Diseases like cholera, typhoid fever, and schistosomiasis (a disease which is caused by worms living in the veins of humans) are rampant in many countries because of water pollution.
3. Organic chemicals poison the waters
4. Plant nutrients lead to eutrophication (overnutrification) of lakes and other bodies of water which will eventually lead to solid ground.
5. Inorganic chemicals also cause pollution problems because many are toxic to organisms living in the waters.
6. Thermal pollution comes from cooling condenser water, from powerplants and may increase the temperature of the waters thus causing havoc with many aquatic organisms which live there.
7. Radiation winds up in waters from many sources.

WATER SHORTAGES

Many countries don't have enough water for both industry and their people. In Africa, women spend a great deal of time getting water which is increasingly polluted and scarce. In other areas, lakes are drying up due to human greed and stupidity. The quintessential example of this is the Aral Sea, located in the former Soviet Union which is no longer the fourth largest lake in the world (see chapter 8). In America, developers are creating water shortages by over-building homes in formally unoccupied areas such as deserts such as those that surround Las Vegas.[5] Some individuals in the wealthier countries must have their swimming pools and human made lakes so that they can enjoy themselves at the expense of the world's environment.

2. AIR POLLUTION [6]

There are six major priority pollutants especially associated with big cities with lots of car traffic. These are the following: ground level ozone (O_3); Carbon monoxide (CO); Sulfur dioxide (SO_2); particulates (particles of lead from leaded gasoline and dust from coal); Nitrogen oxides (NOXs) -these include Nitrogen dioxide (NO_2), Nitrous Oxide N_2O and Nitric oxide NO; and VOC's (volatile organic chemicals). Each year Americans spew out over 150 million tons of air pollutants. This amounts to almost one half ton per person including every man, woman and child   Air pollution is a serious problem in many cities worldwide and is responsible for many diseases such as the increase in asthma.

3. NOISE POLLUTION

For those of us who live in cities we are familiar with the constant din of noise almost 24 hours a day. This is especially true with cities where there is lots of traffic. Noise is a problem especially in the 21st century due to bigger planes, especially jets, which contribute to airport noise; industrial noise in factories which sometimes gets to be unbearable; and during construction.

4. LIGHT POLLUTION

Those of us who live in big cities are familiar with light pollution. It is hard to see the stars on a clear night because of all the lights. For those of us lucky enough to live in the country we see the beautiful sky with its stars and planets. However, for those who live in big cities the only thing we can see on a cloudless night is the full moon. Nature is obscured.

5. LAND POLLUTION

Land pollution include garbage, hazardous waste, and other things such as paper and pure junk. Americans produce 3.5 pounds of household garbage per person, per day, and roughly the equivalent of one metric ton of hazardous waste per person, per year. Hazardous waste includes substances that poison the land and organisms that live there, and also contains reactive and corrosive chemicals that can catch fire readily. We see this all over the planet due to the demands of human overpopulation. In fact, we have even polluted the moon. We have used cars, cameras and other items up there that the astronauts left behind on their many trips.

With our affluent way of living we also add more garbage to our environment. Approximately 41% of our garbage in the developed countries is mainly made up of paper. The rest of the garbage includes plastics, metals, cloth, wood, food and other materials. These are part of the waste stream of affluent countries.

We in the Western world produce lots of garbage. According to one source it is estimated that the United States produces the equivalent of 174.8 million metric tons of household garbage per year.[7] When viewed another way it could be viewed as the equivalent weight of 33 Egyptian pyramids of which I can assure you are quite heavy. It is not hard to see how we can generate so much garbage not only in the United States but in most of the developed nations on the planet. Most of the garbage is composed of paper followed by yard waste which gets composted in the United States. This is a major reason to reduce paper consumption.

6. GREENHOUSE EFFECT AND CLIMATE CHANGE

Perhaps one of the biggest problems we have on the planet is the greenhouse effect brought about by our insatiable appetite for oil: The greenhouse effect is caused by the build up of gases such as carbon dioxide (CO_2) and methane (CH_4). These gases allow solar energy to enter the earth's atmosphere but prevent heat from leaving thus causing a heating affect much like that of the greenhouses where flowers are grown.[8] Carbon dioxide is caused by burning coal, oil and gas. Methane comes from rice paddies, and animal digestive tracts such as cows and termites that's right, termites, (those little buggers that like to eat wood.) There are single celled organisms living in the gut of termites which gobble up the wood.

Although the temperature has increased slightly, it is enough to cause disruption in the world's weather patterns as we have seen in the violent hurricanes and storms that have inflicted billions of dollars of damage. In fact many insurance companies have gone bankrupt due to high claims caused by storms.[9] We have exacerbated the problems by humans cutting the world's rainforests. Forests and other vegetation absorb the carbon dioxide by the process of photosynthesis. This is the mechanism whereby plants produce oxygen. By cutting down the rain forests we are destroying the "sponge" which soaks up the CO_2.

The year 2002 set world records for windstorms, rain intensities, floods, drought and temperature increases. Economic losses approached $53 billion. Nearly 8,000 people died in storms, floods, droughts, heat waves and cold. Severe weather events didn't just affect the poor countries but countries like Germany, where floods caused 108 deaths and 450,000 people were forced to evacuate their homes. Extreme cold in Moscow killed 300 people in December and January. Bolivia's capital, La Paz was hit by the most powerful storm in its history receiving almost a gallon of water per square foot in an hour. In June of 2002, Southwest Asia sweltered in temperatures as high as 50°C (122°F) where more than 1,200 people died. In June of 2003 more than 1,000 citizens of India died due to heat waves where temperatures rose to 52°C (125°F). All over the world we are seeing catastrophes. In August of 2003 over 3,000 French people died due to a heat wave.[10] See Table 1.

TABLE 1
COUNTRIES IN 2002 WITH CATASTROPHES
Countries with various environmental catastrophes in 2002

FLOODS	DROUGHTS	HEATWAVES	EXTREME COLD
Germany	United States	India	Russia
China	Australia	France	Peru
Bolivia	China		Bolivia
India			Argentina
South East Asia			
Japan			
South Korea			

It should be pointed out that total losses to insurance companies in 2002 amounted to $53 billion. Losses in the 1990's exceeded those of the 1980's by three times and five times the 1970's losses and eight times the losses of the 1960's.

The following is a list of possible consequences of global warming due to too much fossil fuel use:

Temperature changes of 1.5-5°C

This temperature change does not seem to be a lot but it should be pointed out that even slight changes cause environmental effects. I remember when I was going to graduate school in Long Island, New York in the early 1970's. We missed getting snow by one degree Fahrenheit.

Diseases like malaria and viral outbreaks showing up in unusual places.

With increases in temperatures mosquitoes that carry diseases such as malaria and yellow fever might infect areas of the planet that were never exposed to them such as Chicago, New York and other cities.

9

Droughts

With global warming we can see increases in droughts. Areas of the planet that once had plenty of rain are now getting less rain. Formally dry areas are getting more rain. Kind of topsy-turvy, isn't it?

Floods

With increases in temperatures we can see increases in rain. Remember the flooding of the Mississippi River a number of years ago?

Flooding of coastal cities and island Loss

With increase in temperatures not only will ice caps melt, but due to thermal expansion of water many cities on the coasts as well as islands may be eliminated due to flooding.

Crop disruptions and loss of food security

If temperatures change in certain wheat or corn growing areas maybe we won't be able to grow those crops in areas that were formally used for those types of crops. This could have disastrous implications since the U.S. is the breadbasket of the world. Crop production may be hindered which may lead to political instability and warfare.

Loss of Biodiversity including extinction of certain species of organisms

Temperature changes can cause hormonal disruptions in organisms and thus cause changes in metabolism and physiology. We can also see disruptions in migration patterns which can cause food imbalances. The world may lose important species of organisms which cannot adapt to changing environments.

Disruptions of ecosystems

With increased temperatures ecosystems can have their whole physiology changed thus causing imbalances between animal, plants, bacterial and fungal species.

Gulf Stream disruption

The Gulf Stream keeps Europe at a constant moderate temperature. Global warming has the potential of causing elimination of the Gulf Stream. All or some of the disruptions mentioned above may cause total havoc.

Weather pattern disruptions

Severe weather disruptions may occur if we continue with temperature changes. Hurricanes and tornados will get worse thus, causing more physical destruction which will undoubtedly raise insurance premiums.

Brush and forest fire increases

As we have seen, there have been increases in forest fires such as those in Indonesia due to tree felling and burning. The climate was changed thus, preventing the annual rains from putting out the fires. In October of 2003 brush fires in California consumed over 1,100 homes and thousands of acres.

Animal behavior disruptions

It is very possible that animals can have their behavior changed if the outside temperature changes. Animal behavior can be disrupted. We can especially see this in bird migration patterns. I noticed this during the last few years while living in the Chicago area. The geese who normally head south for the winter seem to be staying in the Chicago area for extended periods of time. This could be my imagination, but I really believe it's happening.

The possibility of other dreaded diseases that we can't even think of may be lurking around the corner due to global climate change.

During the last few years the world has witnessed the emergence of dreaded diseases such as the Ebola virus and the Hanta virus, both of which are deadly. These could have arisen because of humankind's interference in the environment of which the greenhouse effect is a prime suspect.

Increase in respiratory diseases in both animals and humans.

Good examples of these are asthma and cardiovascular disorders.

Heat wave deaths

During the 2003 summer season, Europe, India and other places suffered from intense heat which caused thousands of deaths. During the summer of 1995 in Chicago over 700 senior citizens succumbed to the heat. It is evident that since the 1990s heat waves are getting more intense and deadly.

End of winter as we know it?

If we have global warming on a scale unprecedented in human history, then winter may be a season of the past. Now many of you may seem to think that this may be good. However, if you have relatives who are snowbirds, they may decide to stay up north all year round. Generally it appears that winters are much milder in the Northeast and Midwestern parts of the United States. Snowfalls are rare and when they do occur they melt almost immediately much to the dismay of schoolchildren.

Melting glaciers all over the world

Glaciers are melting all over the world due to global warming. For a partial list of melting glaciers see Table 2.

TABLE 2
MELTING GLACIERS WORLDWIDE

Location	Name	Number or percentage gone
Alaska	Columbia	Retreated 13 kilometers
Montana	Glacier national park	100 of 150 melted since 1850
Argentina	Upsula	Retreated 60 km/year
Peru	Quelccaya Ice cap	Retreated 30 meters per year in the 1990's
Spain	Glaciers	14 of 27 Disappeared
Mt Kenya	Glacier	92% lost
Central Asia	Tien Shan Mountain	22% of volume since 1960's
China	Duosuogang Peak	60% since 1970's
Arctic	Ice	Thinned by 40% since 1970's
New Zealand	Tasman Glacier	Thinned by 200 meters since 1970's

Source: Worldwatch Magazine November-Dec. 2000. Vol 13, #6 p. 5-7

According to Bill McKibben when economies grow so does energy use.[11] The reason that economies grow is because there is an increase in populations. McKibben mentions that in places like Thailand and Tijuana for every 10% increase in economic output there is a 10% increase in fuel, which means more carbon dioxide in the environment and the possibility of environmental disaster because of the greenhouse effect.

7. THE COMBACK OF TUBERCULOSIS AND OTHER DREADED DISEASES WITH A VENGENCE

Diseases like Tuberculosis are coming back with a vengeance, especially in countries like Russia. Many of the diseases are resistant to drugs. Other diseases like the Hanta virus, Legionnaires Disease in Europe, Anthrax, Cholera, Dengue Fever, Pneumonic plague and Hong Kong Flu are just a few of the returning diseases.[12]

Other diseases such as the following are likely to spread due to global warming: Malaria, Schistosomiasis, Filariases, Onchocerciasis (River Blindness), African sleeping sickness, Dengue Fever, and Yellow Fever. For details of these organisms, see appendix III.

8. ANIMAL AND PLANT EXTINCTIONS

Those of us who read the newspapers and study environmental science are increasingly aware of the fact that due to increased hunting and destruction of habitats all over the planet, plants, animals, fungi and other organisms are either extinct or on the verge of extinction. The list so far includes hundreds of species which were known to exist during the past four centuries, but due to human activities have become extinct.[13] Examples of these are the Dodo bird, the Dusky seaside sparrow, Abingdon tortoise and the Greek auk just to name a few.[14] Added to this list should be marine organisms, plants and other species. There are probably species that we never knew existed that have already become extinct.

9. CORAL REEF DISEASES AND BLEACHING

Coral reefs are dying throughout the planet. The reasons could be pollution and diseases. Coral diseases such as blackband, yellow blotch and whiteband are becoming more common.[15] This may have serious consequences for the rest of the planet because corals help spawn many other organisms. This destruction prevents the birth of marine organisms, which act as a protein source for much of the world's human and non-human population. Approximately 11% of the world's coral reefs have been destroyed due to humans. [16]

In addition to the above mentioned diseases, bleaching, which involves the death of photosynthetic algae also occurs. The algae give corals their color, hence the bleaching if they die.

Destruction of coral reefs is also due to coral mining, waste dumping, vessel collisions, inland deforestation and farming.

According to the Worldwatch Institute, the Indian Ocean has the largest percent of destroyed or dying reefs with 59% of them gone followed by the Middle East with a 35% loss.

Reefs are very important for oceanic biodiversity. Thousands of living organisms live around the reefs from the small bacterium to large fish.

10. SOIL EROSIONON

Topsoil is the stuff that food is made of. We need this soil to grow our food and feed ourselves as well as the animals that we eat such as beef and foul. However, due to our poor practices of managing the soil all over the world we are losing it to erosion. In the United States alone we are losing about 4.6 billion tons per year.[17] Imagine what it's like in the rest of the world especially now that cropland per person is shrinking because of overpopulation.

11. OZONE DEPLETION

Ozone (O_3) is a gas containing three oxygen atoms in a special arrangement that filters out Ultraviolet Light (UV) from sunlight. This ozone layer not only protects animals from cancer-producing UV light, but also protects plants. When ozone gets too thin in the stratosphere, its normal location in the atmosphere, UV light can harm animals by giving them cancer and interfere with photosynthesis from plants.

12. ACID RAIN

Normal rain is slightly acidic but acid rain is more acidic. Most normal rain has a pH of 5.6. Acid rain, which has a pH below 5.6, is a problem worldwide such as in the United States and Germany. It is caused by emissions of Sulfur Dioxide (SO_2) and nitrogen oxides coming from tall smokestacks. These gases mix with water and form acids, which cause erosion of buildings and monuments as well as cause leaching of chemicals out of the soil.

13. EUTROPHICATION

Eutrophication is the process where lakes get overnutrified and which eventually turn into dry land. This is a serious problem because the nutrients are released into waterways by human activity. This process also depletes dissolved oxygen which causes fish kills. The water also turns turbid (cloudy) and has low biodiversity.

14. BIOINVASIONS

This is a term that sounds like something out of a science fiction movie. Bioinvasions is the introduction of non-native organisms in an area that is not accustomed to them. Examples of bioinvasions are plentiful. Some good examples are the following: the invasion of the Leidy's comb jelly (*Mnemiopsis leiydyi*), an organism similar to the jellyfish, which occurred in the Black Sea in 1982. These organisms originally came from the east coast of the U.S., but were introduced accidentally into the Black sea from ship ballast water. The weight of these organisms was estimated to be 900-million tons in the Black Sea. This number of tons was ten times the annual fish catch worldwide. These organisms are no bigger than a person's thumb. It doesn't take much imagination to understand the severity of this problem or its consequences.[18]

Another example is the invasion of the Zebra mussel, an organism related to oysters and clams. These organisms were introduced into the Great Lakes region and they caused havoc by clogging water intake pipes. To show you how prolific these organisms are it is estimated that a single female can produce up to 5 million eggs in one year. It's no wonder that they reproduce so fast.[19] Some other common examples of bioinvasive organisms are plants such as water hyacinths and purple loosestrife.

Disease organisms like malaria and the Ebola virus can also be examples of invasive organisms. One of the most recent organisms to affect the Chicago area is the invasion of the Asian Long Horned Beetle (*Anoplophora glabripennis*). Due to its life cycle many trees had to be cut down in the city of Chicago.

15. LACK OF ADEQUATE SPACE

For those of us who live in big cities, (I used to be one of them) the place of choice is in tall apartment buildings literally on top of one another. In one respect it is good because people will take up less space. However, one drawback to that is the fact that here in America many people have cars even though they live in big cities. The example I will give you is Lefrak City, an apartment complex that lies near the Long Island Expressway. Those buildings are big, crowded and there are many cars. One day I visited my cousin and I almost choked after getting off a bus because of all the cars coming and going. The people may have lived in big apartment buildings, but pollution from the cars was atrocious.

16. ALGAE BLOOMS

Algae are microscopic plants which are incredibly important for the planet because they produce immense amounts of life giving oxygen and they help feed billions of organisms such as fish, which are eventually fed to humans. Blooms occur when lots of nutrients such as nitrogen and phosphorus contaminate waters where algae live. These organisms (algae) multiply like crazy and cover entire areas with their mass. This leads to lower light penetration and die offs of organisms.

17. OIL SPILLS

Who hasn't heard of the Exxon Valdez incident that took place in 1989? This was the spill that caused havoc in 1989, at Prince William Sound. As long as oil still powers most of the planet we will still have oil spills. That is why we have to consider other energy resources such as solar. There are many incidents like the Exxon Valdez but not of the same magnitude. In fact some spills can be greater than the Exxon Valdez as we have seen during the Gulf War of 1991 when Sadham Hussein spilled millions of barrels of oil into the Gulf. Another documented case occurred off the coast of Mikuni ,Japan, in January of 1997 when a Russian tanker, the 13,157 ton Nakhodka, split and sank leaking fuel oil into the sea causing lots of damage to the seaweed and shellfish industry.[20]

18. ESTROGENIC EFFECTS
OF CHEMICALS IN THE ENVIRONMENT

Estrogens are natural chemicals manufactured from cholesterol by women's ovaries, and circulate within the blood stream. It is eventually eliminated in the gut leaving most body cells unaffected. However, certain tissues contain estrogen receptors, which cause cell proliferation. Cells of the female sex organs such as the vagina, uterus and breast all contain large numbers of estrogen receptors which result in ovulation, breast development and pregnancy. A set of chemicals called *"xeroestrogens"*, (literally strange estrogen-like compounds) mimic the effects of real estrogen in the body thus causing havoc in the body. They may enhance the effects of normal estrogen by causing cancer and other hazards to people. [21]

19. SALINIZATION

Salinization is the deposition of salt due to too much irrigation water on fields used for crops to feed the increasing human population. Mineral salts such as sodium, calcium, magnesium and chloride and others occur naturally in rainwater, rivers and groundwater. When this water is being used in the large amounts as is used by farms, salts tend to be deposited on the ground thus causing the fertility to be reduced. Ten thousand tons of water is used for each hectare of crops, which is a typical irrigation amount. It should be pointed out that for every 10,000 tons of water used there are between 2-5 tons of salts.[22]

20. GARBAGE

Here in the United States the average person throws away about 3.5 lbs (1.59 kg) of waste per-person, per-day. When added up to include other waste we get the following horrific numbers:

1. Every year we generate enough paper to make a wall from Los Angeles to New York, 12 feet high; every week we cut 50,000 trees to make newspapers which include the 2/3 that never get recycled.
2. Every year we throw away enough iron and steel to constantly supply the nation's automakers.
3. Every two weeks we throw away enough glass to fill the 1,350 foot tall towers of the World Trade Center in New York City. (Prior to September 11, 2001)
4. Every hour we throw away 2.5 million plastic bottles many of which don't get recycled.[23] Garbage, especially here in The United States contains lots of stuff other than paper and plastics: it may include yard waste, metals, wood, food and rubber products. This is mainly a huge problem with affluent countries because they are able to generate more waste because they have lots of money to buy, buy and buy which generates garbage. Lots of it. Let me give you another statistic.

Americans throw away seven million tons of aluminum cans each year. This amount is enough to rebuild the entire commercial air fleet over 25 times.[24] Think about this on a world scale. That's why the garbage business is a good line to get into because business is always picking up.

21. ENVIRONMENTAL RACISM

Every major city in the United States contains pockets of urban blight which are spacious wastelands, deprived of development and dignity. Urban sites are lucrative places where corporate giants make their millions and vanish into thin air. A new substance has invaded the land of the disenfranchised poor: it is called Environmental Waste Products.

Toxic waste facilities are often located in communities that have high percentages of poor, elderly, young and minority residents. An inordinate concentration of uncontrolled toxic waste sites are found in black and Hispanic urban communities. For example, when Atlanta's ninety four uncontrolled toxic waste sites are plotted by zip code areas, more than 82% of the city's black population compared with 45.2% of its white population were found living in waste site areas.

The same is basically true here in Chicago. There is a community called Altgeld Gardens which is located on the south side of Chicago. Short distances from the community are chemical plants, steel mills, illegal dumps and heaps of rotting garbage. Many of the areas residents are sick with cancer, asthma, heart problems, etc. The list goes on and on. In fact, in 1987 a book entitled, The Toxic Cloud, by Michael Brown devotes a chapter to the plight of Altgeld Gardens.[25] He describes in depth the health problems of some of the residents. Hence, environmental racism is rampant in areas with people of color and little clout.

22. DESTRUCTION BY TOURISM

There is a new type of tourism called" ecotourism". Tourists from all over the world like to visit species-rich areas like the rainforests and islands along the equator. These tourists place a burden on the fragile ecosystems for the following reasons. mainly from the west these tourists like to have the ameneties of home like swimming pools and objects which require plug in electricity such as, razors, coffee pots and hair dryers and of course golf courses.

23. ENVIRONMENTAL REFUGEES

Perhaps one of the least considered aspects of pollution is the displacement of millions of people worldwide due to environmental mishaps which make areas uninhabitable for local residents. We have seen this over the years in cases of flooding of Bengladesh and in the Sudan in 1988 and in mudslides in Medelin, Columbia, in 1987, in which deforestation caused rain soaked mud to kill 500 people in an avalanche and leaving hundreds homeless. Even in the United States there are environmental refugees, as in the case of Love Canal, a now-famous toxic dump in a suburb of Niagara Falls, New York. Hundreds of residents were slowly being poisoned by years of unregulated dumping of chemicals by a chemical company.

The list goes on and on. This trend will not stop at least in the foreseeable future if we continue with our wasteful ways. Drought and warfare caused by humans have caused millions of refugees in Ethiopia, Somalia and in other places around the world.

If the environment in which many people live gets destroyed many refugees in search of a better life are created. Environmental disasters, which are caused by human stupidity, may include loss of fertile land due to poor farming practices and search for fuel wood;[26] avalanches, mudslides floods, and chemical contamination. [27]

24. DISRUPTED NITROGEN

What exactly does disrupted nitrogen mean? Nitrogen makes up 78.09% of an unpolluted atmosphere. However we humans keep adding nitrogen in the form of fertilizers, nitrogen fixing crops, fossil fuels, burning of biomass (wood and other substances from living organisms), manure from millions of farm raised food animals such as cows and pigs, wetland drainage and land clearing. All together we are adding 400 million tons of fixed nitrogen to the planet.[28] Fixed nitrogen means the nitrogen which is formed chemically to be used as fertilizer. Although the atmosphere contains over 78% nitrogen, plants can't use atmospheric nitrogen so they have to have it in a form that is usable such as nitrates (NO_3). When added to the soil in manure it causes nitrogen clouds in the soil, and if the manure gets into waterways due to flooding, little organisms like the dinoflagellate, *Pfiesteria pisicicida* can multiply and cause fish to die and illness in humans.[29] (See APPENDIX III)

Too much nitrogen can add to the greenhouse effect in the form of nitrous oxide, which is better known as laughing gas whose formula is N_2O. (49% of the major greenhouse gas is carbon dioxide (CO_2)). Nitrous oxide is 200 times more effective in retaining heat than CO_2 is.

Too much nitrogen in the water and in the air can cause odors, miscarriages in women, algal blooms and ozone loss. Ozone absorbs Ultraviolet light, which may cause human skin cancer if it is allowed to penetrate. To sum it all up, too much nitrogen (human made) can be toxic to the environment and those organisms which depend on it such as us humans, animals, plants, fungi, and bacteria.

25. SEA LIFE LOSS

With the increase in pollution and the world's population and new satellite technology we are over fishing the world's oceans. We are also taking bycatch (unwanted organisms) by the millions as well. Plus with the added burden of pollution the life in the oceans is diminishing. Some examples of this is the decline of Cod from 1970 with 3.1 million metric tons down to 916,000 metric tons in 1991. Similar declines are recorded for Atlantic redfish, Western Pacific Yellow Croaker, herring and Mackerel.[30]

26. CHEMICAL LEACHING INTO GROUNDWATER

Leaching is the dissolving of chemicals in water due to rainfall or some other means. When water leaches through soil or when water runs through landfills leaching occurs and may contaminate groundwater.

27. DEFORESTATION

Deforestation is another activity that is facing the world's forests, especially the tropical rain forests. Thirty one million hectares of rainforest are being lost every year which is equivalent to the size of Poland.[31]They are being destroyed yearly in order to build roads, ranches for cows, golf courses, fuel wood for cooking and to get oil. I should like to mention that many of the rain forested countries of the world are facing this situation.

28. TOPSOIL LOSS.

Topsoil is the major soil that is used for raising crops. Worldwide 26 billion tons are lost, 85% of which is lost due to live stock rising. This could be devastating to the world's food supply. Topsoil not only helps raise the crops but contains many of the organisms that help keep the earth fertile.

29. SICKLY ANIMALS

Due to the increase in pesticide use and dumping of chemicals, animals are becoming sick and deformed. This is especially true with the use of chemical pesticides such as deformed beaks of birds and reproductive problems which was exposed in the book, Silent Spring by Rachel Carson. A few years ago many seals in the North Atlantic were found dead in the belief that chemicals in the environment disrupted their immune systems thus making them susceptible to disease. We have also seen this in Lake Apopka in Florida where the alligators have reproductive problems; birds are found with deformed beaks from PCB contamination as well.[32]

30. RADIATION CONTAMINATION

Radiation in the environment is on the increase. Although much radiation is a result of natural radiation, it found naturally in our food, the earth, air and water. However, large amounts are emitted by our activities which included fallout from above-ground nuclear explosions in Nevada[33] [34] and in other places by other countries; radiation has also been found in devices left by Soviet researchers such as in X-ray machines and other medical machines which are also implicated in radiation exposure. Radiation has also been used in fluoroscopy machines which were located in shoe stores to see how shoes fit.

In a recent article from *Smithsonian Magazine*[35] it was reported that in many continents throughout the world there was "hot stuff" (radioactive) littering the landscape. Some examples include the following: in 1997 several Soviet recruits began to suffer intermittent bouts of nausea, vomiting and weakness and rapid loss of weight. It was later diagnosed as radiation poisoning from tea-kettle sized containers of Cesium 135, a gamma ray emitter.

In December of 2001 a group of men gathered near a river in Northern Georgia (Russia) and encountered a pair of paint-can sized canisters. The men gathered around these canisters because they noticed that they were hot to the touch. They didn't know that the canisters contained Strontium 90, a beta and gamma radiation emitter. Needless to say they received radiation burns. Each canister emitted a total of 40 times the output of a radiation therapy machine.

But perhaps the most devastating incident occurred in Brazil in 1987 when a metal scavenger took a radiation therapy machine from a deserted clinic and sold it to a junk dealer. There was a powdery material in the machine which was taken out. The material unfortunately contained three ounces of cesium 137. A six year old girl played with the dust by coating her hands with it. The end result was that she died shortly thereafter from kidney and lung problems.

31. ENVIRONMENTAL ILLNESS

What exactly is environmental illness? Environmental Illness (EI) is a disorder where people who get exposed to minute substances such as gasoline fumes, perfumes, cat dander, pesticided strawberries and other things both natural and unnatural react by getting symptoms like headaches, confusion, welts, etc. Fortunately there is an organization called "The American Academy of Environmental Medicine"that deals with this problem. The physicians that treat patients with this disorder are called clinical ecologists. Their website is www.aaem.com.

32. LOSS OF NATURAL POLLINATORS

Bees and other pollinators are in decline due to human made causes such as pesticides, habitat destruction and many other reasons. Without organisms like bees we would not be able to have apples, broccoli, avocados, cherries, cucumbers, melons, carrots, oranges, pears, pumpkins, squash, blueberries, grapefruits, macadamia nuts, raspberries, plums, onions and others.[36] At the present time we are pollinating many of these crops with managed bees. These bees are raised by humans who found a need for them because we are destroying the territories of natural pollinators due to conversion of their natural habitats to agricultural land and roads.

33. THE END OF MALES ON THE PLANET

Why mention this as an environmental problem? Simple. Between 1970 and 1990 the percentage of males compared to females dropped from 51.5% to 51.3%.[37] Even though this appears to be a small drop it does raise some eyebrows. This drop may be due to pesticides, drugs and alcohol, pollution, radiation or something more ominous that we don't really know exists. Not only are male births declining but there is ample evidence to suggest that sperm counts have decreased by as much as 50% in the last ten years.[38] The conclusion to this fact if true is obvious. There are fewer births period. I will leave the implications of this fact to the reader. I recently spoke to a Gynecologist/obstetrician who just confirmed this finding by stating to me that among his deliveries, 60% are females.

THE CAUSES

CHAPTER 2
AGRICULTURE

...my thoughts kept returning to how rich the soil had looked when I was a kid. It didn't look like that any more. Now it crumbled in my hands. It was as thin as sand. There were no worms in it After all the tons of herbicides and pesticides and chemical fertilizer...the soil looked more like asbestos.[39]

The nation that destroys its soil destroys itself.
Franklin D. Roosevelt (1882-1945)

INTRODUCTION

Let's take a look at one of the most important activities that has taken place throughout the history of the human race. The human race has been increasing since the middle of the 19th century and so has the need to feed themselves. As mentioned earlier the world's population is increasing at the rate of 80 million per year which is four times the population of the continent of Australia or the New York City metropolitan area.

Now it is true that we have to eat, but let us take a look at what we eat, how we grow the food and what methods we use to produce the food.

It is obvious that we expend a lot of energy to feed people in agriculture. Before the industrial revolution began, about 12,000 years ago, there were less than a billion people on the entire planet (Now there are more than six times that). The people, at that time, were hunters and gatherers. These were people who survived through "Earth Wisdom" (Miller, 1995). [40] That is, they were able to live off the land without cutting, chopping and digging and devastating their environment. If you were to look at countries like China[41]

23

you would see that they are doing severe damage to their environments so that they live like people in Western culture or wealthier countries.

CONCEPT

Agriculture and the way it is practiced in the United States and in other places leave much to be desired. It is true that without agriculture we would not be able to eat. However, we overdo things. Let me give you some examples. If we were to read the book by John Robbins, **Diet for a New America** and other sources we would learn the following: 90% of the soybeans and oats grown are eaten by livestock. Another statistic is the following: 20,000 pounds of potatoes and 165 pounds of beef can be grown on any one acre of land. As a matter of fact 56% of U.S. land is being used to raise livestock. It should be pointed out that in the world there are about 16.1 billion domesticated animals, or roughly a one to three ratio of edible animals to people. The animals that we eat are mainly vegetarian (plant eaters).

Figure 1. A typical grocery store in The United States. Note the wide range of products. All food items are associated with agriculture in one way or another. (Photo by author)

Today, things have turned around 180 degrees due to the fact that the planet has more than 6 billion people. In order to feed these people we have to grow more food, which places a strain on our environment. However, because of the fact that we cannot be hunters and gatherers anymore, we have to find more ways to feed our ever-growing earthly population. In order to do this we have to cut, chop and dig like no time in history. Modern agriculture has increased food supplies immensely, and inequitably, I might add, because of our disproportionate economic systems between countries such as China and the United States; hence the differences between the West and the Third World's developing countries.

Here in America we are seeing the devastation brought to our farmland by the use of fertilizers and pesticides. In his wonderful book "America, the Poisoned" Lewis Regenstein mentions how pesticides have had a very devastating effect on cropland.[42] It seems that the same amount of food is destroyed by pests now as has been lost to pests in medieval Europe with 35% and 30% respectively. [43] We have also seen many pest species gain resistance to common pesticides.[44]

We have to feed not only humans on the planet but because of rising affluence, we have to feed the 16 billion domesticated animals the very same grain that we should use for humans. Animals, especially larger ones such as cows and pigs produce methane, which accounts for 19% of the greenhouse gases. Carbon Dioxide is the number one greenhouse gas at 49% of the total if we don't include water vapor.

PROBLEMS ASSOCIATED WITH AGRICULTURE

1. **Water shortages**
2. **Desertification**
2. **Pesticides, Bhopal syndrome.**
3. **Fertilizers-nitrogen**
4. **Waterlogging**
5. **Salinization**
6. **Land conversion**
7. **Soil erosion**
8. **Nitrogen clouds**
9 **Patented seed varieties**

WATER SHORTAGES

`Water tables are falling all over the world, and ultimately, if we keep increasing our human population we will run out of fresh water. We see this now as reservoirs are drying up which is exemplified by Mono Lake, which supplies water to Los Angeles, in California[45]. In addition, countries are at odds with their neighbors over water rights, as is the case between Israel, Jordan and Syria. Millions of gallons of water are wasted by inefficient use of irrigation techniques.

DESERTIFICATION

Another problem with agriculture is that it promotes overgrazing. When cows and sheep eat without end they tend to denude the area of needed plants, which stabilize the soil and tends to make it hotter and drier. Those plants, which need more water don't survive and thus drought tolerant plants take over . As occurs in the rainforest there is less water to evaporate and add to the clouds, which come down as rainfall, hence the name "Rainforest". The process where water evaporates from the leaves is called transpiration. The process of denuding the area of both grasses and trees leads to deserts, hence the term desertification.

PESTICIDES AND THE BHOPOL SYNDROME

Perhaps one of the most misunderstand parts of agriculture is the use of the pesticides. We are told that without pesticides we would not have crops and perhaps diseases like malaria will make a gigantic comeback, even in countries like the United States. It wasn't until the end of World War II that pesticides really took off. However, pesticides cause cancer, immune system disorders, endocrine and neurological disorders and other problems. In addition they also kill pollinators such as bees and birds and poison water supplies used by animals and humans, especially groundwater. Something even more insidious is the fact that pesticides are used on cash crops (these are crops that have no real food value but are grown because they bring in a lot of money.) Many of these cash crops are luxury items used in developed countries like the United States and Western Europe. These include coffee, bananas, cotton and others.[46]

The majority of the world's pesticides are mainly divided up into three categories. They are herbicides (kills weeds) , insecticides (kills insects) and fungicides (kills fungi). But there are others which include a whole range of organisms in various stages of development. See Table 3

TABLE 3

PESTICIDE[47]	TARGET
Acaracide	Mites
Algicide	Algae
Avicide	Birds
Bactericide	Bacteria
Fungicide	Fungi
Herbicide	Weeds
Insecticide	Insects
Larvicide	Larvae but mostly mosquitoes
Miticide	Mites
Molluscicide	Snails, slugs, oysters etc.
Nematicide	Nematodes (small unsegmented roundworms)

PESTICIDE[47]	TARGET
Ovicide	Eggs
Pediculicide	Lice
Piscicide	Fish
Predicide	Predators
Rodenticide	Rodents
Silvicide	Trees and brush
Slimicide	Slimes
Termiticide	Termites

The world uses over 400 million kilograms of pesticides annually with a financial value of $13 billion in 1983.[48] As of 1986 the United States alone used thousands of pounds of pesticides. Approximate numbers are as follows: 220 X 10^6 kgs herbicides (242,660 short tons); 62x106 kgs (68,386 short tons) of insecticides and 38 x106 kgs (41,914 short tons) of fungicides.[49]

Some countries where pesticides are unregulated such as those in South America are especially at risk because of the way that they use them. Some fishermen who can't read know that fish are killed with pesticides. So, what do they do? They throw pesticides into the water to kill the fish. It doesn't occur to them that if the pesticides kill the fish it may not be healthy for those who eat the fish. If I ever go to South America I will not eat fish unless I am 100% sure where it comes from.

The main source of food in the world is plants. There are thousands of diseases of plants caused mainly by fungus, viruses, viroids, rickettsias (intracellular parasitic bacteria) algae, weeds, parasitic plants, nematodes (unsegmented roundworms) and insects.

Pesticides are designed to disrupt various metabolic processes in organisms ranging from plants to animals, to fungi to bacteria. However, due to the fact that hundreds of pests are now becoming resistant to the various pesticides more and more pesticides have to be used. Some don't work anymore. Millions of dollars are now spent in producing non-chemical based pesticides. (See chapter on solutions to the types of pesticide substitutes.)

Our desire to feed ourselves combined with the greed of the chemical companies makes us use tons and tons of pesticides on our crops which eventually poison us and cause resistance to occur thus making us use more pesticides.[50] This use of pesticides causes health problems in non- target organisms as well as making organisms more resistant. [51] This is called the circle of poison.

Environmental Effects of Pesticides

Pesticides, including those associated with lawn chemicals are very bad for the environment. These problems are as follows: chemical pesticides and fertilizers are capable of contaminating surface waters such as lakes and rivers and ground water such as underground aquifers. They also can threaten the health of children and animals, including pets such as dogs and cats, local wildlife such as birds and squirrels and can reduce effectiveness of beneficial organisms such as plants, grasses and trees. When the local environments of these organisms are damaged then the ability of the land to perform their proper functions are limited. Bacteria, those little single celled organisms, perform vital functions like nitrogen fixation, (the ability to make nitrogen usable for plants) and decomposition of dead organisms.

Health Effects of Pesticides

Health effects of pesticides have been documented for the past half century. Illnesses associated with various pesticides and their uses are the following: muscle weakness, dizziness, malaise, sweating, headaches, salivation, nausea, vomiting, abdominal pain, diarrhea, neurological manifestations such as convulsions, bradycardia (slow heartbeat), and hyperesthesia (increase in sensation), paresthesia (abnormal sensations like burning, tingling, and numbness for no apparent reason), eye, throat, lung irritations, cell injury to tissues of the liver, kidney, nerve and other tissues, lethargy, delirium, cancer, coma, spasms, and shock just to name a few. [52]

Take the case of DDT. Rachel Carson discussed this problem in her famous book *Silent Spring* published in 1962. She helped launch the crusade against the use of this pesticide. Another prominent author, Lewis Regenstein also wrote a book about pesticides entitled, *"America the Poisoned"*.[53] How's that for an optimistic title. In the book he points out that herbicides and other toxic chemicals are being used for agriculture and that they wind up in human breast milk and in our food.

Another aspect of pesticide use is the[54] fact that greens keepers, those individuals who are responsible for maintaining golf courses, get various sorts of cancers from exposure to the chemicals that keep their golf courses green.[55]

Perhaps the biggest drawback of pesticide use is the possibility that another Bhopal-like incident might occur. This is not only my idea but in fact there was a whole book on the topic of pesticides and the dangers that their manufacture imposed on the workers and the public at large.[56] David

Weir, the author worries that a Bhopal-like accident might occur again in factories and in areas where pesticides and other chemicals are made. For those of you who don't know what happened in Bhopal on that fateful day in December, 1984, I will explain here.

In the early hours of December 3, 1984 the worst industrial accident in human history occurred. Methyl isocyanate (MIC)[57] , a very toxic substance used to make the pesticide Sevin leaked out of its holding tank causing the deaths of two thousand Indians and injuring over 100,000. The substance escaped from the Union Carbide Plant in Bhopal, India.[58] Many of the workers who were killed and injured lived near the plant in shanty towns. To this day there are still many thousands injured who never got compensated by Union Carbide. In fact, there is still a warrant out for the arrest of the former Chairman of the Board, Warren Anderson. Anderson was the Chairman of the board of Union Carbide at the time of the accident.

It is unfortunate that even until this day the effects of MIC and Anderson's inaction are still evident. Immediately after the accident Anderson stated that he would devote his whole life making right what had gone wrong for the victims. But within weeks after his handlers and lawyers got a hold of him he began to waiver by stating that "he had overreacted and then sought to limit compensation to the victims killed or injured. The reason why he made a correction is because if he really did what he first said he would, he would have jeopardized the company financially.[59] What a human being!!!

Methyl isocyanate was an intermediate chemical used to make the pesticide. The substance works by inhibiting cholinesterase activity, which is the enzyme used to break down acetylcholine (a neurotransmitter) in nerve cells. The physical and chemical properties of methyl isocyante (MIC) make it a very dangerous chemical to store and use.

The point that Weir is trying to make is the fact that accidents like that at Bhopal could happen anywhere in the world, even in the United States. With many companies making pesticides, similar accidents can happen again. Another problem with pesticides is that they tend to kill non-target organisms and thus kill beneficial organisms as well as those people who manufacture them.

Who knows how many people worldwide are sick because of pesticides. Not only do pesticide residues in food cause a hazard, but the farmers and agricultural workers who are exposed to them are at risk. According to Culliney et al, 65% of all pesticides in the United States are handled by farmers.[60]

Now you may ask, "Is it possible to grow crops without pesticides?" The answer is definitely, YES, YES and YES. Some of the alternatives are biological control, in which natural predators of pests are used to eliminate them. These attack the pests by eating or killing them. Examples of biological control agents include bacteria, viruses and other insects. Genetic control is currently being used to eliminate pests. This process involves insertion of genes inside plant cells.

Other ways of preventing pesticide use are the following: The use of heteroculture, in which many crops are grown side by side; crop rotation (where farmers change crops every year) which prevents pests from becoming established; and altering the time of planting are a few of the alternatives. If the reader wants more information on this topic I suggest that they go to the library and look up environmental science texts that are currently coming out on the market.

Figure 2 Here is a can of DDT, the most famous
pesticide of them all (photo by author)

FERTILIZERS

With our use of fertilizers to increase crop yields we are destroying the soil's natural ability to grow crops. By adding substances such as nitrogen (N_2) we are increasing nitrogen gases in the atmosphere which contributes to global warming. As we all know fertilizers are used to feed the crops. World fertilizer use increased from 14 million tons in 1950 up to 141 million tons in 2000.[61] That is ten times in fifty years.

But over the years we have been applying way too many fertilizers because we have depleted the soils of their natural ability to retain nutrients. Not only that, when we acidify the soil with acid rain, the nutrients tend to leach out and cause other catastrophes such as poisoning water supplies. This in turn poisons animals such as birds and mammals which drink the water. Of course the main beneficiaries who benefit from fertilizer use are the chemical companies which produce them. Now, am I advocating eliminating the fertilizer and pesticide companies? Not necessarily. What

I do advocate is a more natural based form of fertilizers and pesticides. But what about people's jobs being lost? Good question. Perhaps with all our American Know-How we can come up with solutions before the jobs are lost.

In addition, our desire for meat helps us heat up the planet and thus cause weather patterns to change as we are seeing as of this writing, July 1998, is purported to be the warmest July since records were being kept. How does raising meat contribute to global warming? Simple. Cows produce methane which is expelled from their intestines into the atmosphere. The more the number of cows the more methane. This methane thus winds up in the atmosphere and adds to global warming. By the way, 18% of the greenhouse gasses are composed of methane.

I think that people should realize that global heating will lead to disaster for all organisms on the planet.

WATERLOGGING

Waterlogging occurs when too much water is applied to the soil. If the soils are not drained properly water can rise to the surface and suffocate the roots of the plants .About one-tenth of the irrigated cropland is suffering from water logging at the present time.[62]

SALINIZATION

Salinization occurs when irrigation water accumulates in the soil and then evaporates. This evaporation results in salinization which is a buildup of salt in the soil. This can be detrimental to plants.

LAND CONVERSION

Lots of land all over the world is being converted from arable land to golf courses, industry and housing.[63] Since 1950 grain area per person from 0.24 ha down to 0.12 ha. (One Ha -hectare is equal to $10,000M^2$).[64]

SOIL EROSION

Around 4 million acres of topsoil are lost each year, 85% of which is due to livestock raising. All of the erosion is due mainly to human activity. In our quest to feed our meat loving society we are slowly degrading the very land that we depend on.

NITROGEN CLOUDS

Nitrogen clouds are produced when you have a lot of animals in feeding lots. Their excrement contains nitrogen and when you have such a concentrated mass of animals as in cows you will see lots of nitrogen in their feces. These animals are kept in areas known as CAFO's (Concentrated

Animal Feeding Operations.) It is obvious when you have hundreds or thousands of animals in a small area you will expect lots of nitrogen in the soil. Too much fertilizer, as is excreted out, will not help the land but destroy it. We all know too much of anything, with the exceptions of hugs, is bad, unless, of course, you are getting a hug from a live bear.

DIMINISHED SEED DIVERSITY
WITH INCREASED GENETIC UNIFORMITY

One of the problems with modern agriculture is the creation of genetically engineered seeds. These are seeds that grow into crops with increased resistance to pests, temperature changes and pesticides. This sounds perfect doesn't it? Just think of being able to grow crops with built in resistance to the various insults that are inflicted upon them on a daily basis. But, like everything else there is a down side. When we grow only one or two varieties of the same crop they are susceptible to an invasion of a fungus or some other pest. This is what wiped out the potatoes in Ireland during the 1840s. The potatoes were infected by a fungal disease called Late Blight. Millions starved and many Irish emigrated to the United States because of the famine caused by the blight.

The world faces a great danger if we continue to use genetic conformity. Just think, if everyone used the same genetic stock of seeds and an unexpected pest decimates it we will all starve. Hence, we will face a worldwide blight.

Due to the fact that we have 6.4 billion people, as of this writing that has to be fed, it is inevitable that the human race has to utilize every bit of arable land and more in order to accommodate the growing population. If we use foresight and intelligence by controlling our carnivorous (meat eating) appetite, the world's population could be sustained until the end of humanity. We will use less energy and pesticides, which can contribute to the death of humanity. By being more sensible in our eating habits the earth could remain green until the sun burns out.

CHAPTER 3
ATTITUDES

We live in society hagridden with ultra-wealthy and delusional fools who are fighting, tooth and nail, to defend their right to squander our lives and our planet[65]

Of course, as long as the global economy continues and the world is dominated by powerful corporations that are only interested in maximizing their immediate profits, the requisite measures will be extremely difficult to undertake.[66]

INTRODUCTION

Perhaps one of the major causes of environmental pollution are the attitudes that famous people have. People like Rush Limbough, Dixie Lee Ray,[67] the former governor from the State of Washington, Elizabeth Whelan and Norman Borlaug, the winner of the Nobel Prize for Peace, all poo poo the idea that the environment is degrading, thus allowing business to continue with reckless abandon their ruthless assault on the environment. It is these attitudes that help perpetuate the problem. These are discussed below.

CONCEPT

It is true that we are all bombarded with news about pesticides in our food, destruction of the ozone layer, overfishing of the oceans with drift nets, etc., etc. Now, if these environmental insults are not true how come whenever you go to a big book store like Walden Books or Barnes and Nobel you see a whole section devoted to the environment, many which are monographs dealing with only one environmental catastrophe; many of which are cited in this book.

If you listen to those individuals of high repute whom I mentioned above, you would think that all this environmental calamity talk is a lot of nonsense. But, if you will delve closely, you will notice that most are lobbyists or people who derive their income from businesses which actually cause contamination or they may actually be people who honestly believe that there really is no environmental danger.

One example of this extreme view was held by George Bush Sr., who vowed during his losing reelection bid in 1992 that he will allow drilling in the arctic national wildlife refuge despite the outcries of environmentalists. It did not seem to phase him that we could actually save the oil that would have been pumped from there (assuming that there was any), by conserving our energy back home by increasing the fuel efficiency of our automobiles or by better insulating our homes, or by installing energy efficient light bulbs. But it appeared that he was caving to the oil interests despite the fact that we all witnessed the catastrophe up in the Prince William Sound with the release of oil by the Exxon Valdez.

Even to this day I wonder how Bush lives with himself. His attitude just goes to show you that here in America we have the best politicians money can buy. There is no doubt in my mind that he was bought by the big oil barrens.

Dixie Lee Ray says in her book that many of our environmental fears are unjustified such as pesticides, radioactivity and asbestos. I must admit that the only real substance that is probably not so toxic is asbestos. I believe that this substance was much maligned and the fear to remove it was overdone.

Simply stated, many people just don't give a damn. Here in America the thing which is mostly on their minds are taxes, unemployment, minimum wages, the Dow Jones average, the dollar vs. the Japanese yen or Euro, etc. From reading the newspapers I got the impression that nothing but personal wealth is important. It is true that we have to try to make a living and that it is very difficult because of the greed of the industries upon which whose products we cannot live without, at least here in the United States. Electricity, clothes, food, medical care pharmaceuticals, books, college, etc., all these things we must have in order to live a decent life, are relatively expensive. So, if people only care about the bare necessities of life and not so bare necessities, how can they possibly care about the effects of their necessities on the environment?

Then we have people who help foster these attitudes, like Rush Limbough. With his constant bashing of the democrats, and, of course, his favorite whipping boy, Bill Clinton, it is no wonder that we have these attitudes about the environment and money.

In doing research for this book, I have found numerous references regarding how *great* Ronald Reagan was as president. Those references, however, only point to his economic achievements and foreign policy successes such as the downfall of the Soviet Union. Sure, The USSR finally collapsed. They were on the verge of bankruptcy because they had to spend money on their nuclear armaments while we spent money on them as well. We spent and they spent and the end result is more environmental damage, more crime, more homelessness, more malnutrition in the world, more children dying of starvation and disease, all of which could have been prevented if we spent all this money on humanity instead of trying to outdo each other militarily. Ask yourself how much damage was done just trying to test those weapons of destruction and how much nuclear contamination from radiation leaks occurred.

I actually blame Reagan and those who voted for him because, again, this stupid notion that we have to have a tremendous military while the very same people whom we are trying to protect and defend are, themselves, dying and getting sick because we spend the money on the military defense and not on defending them.

It is precisely because of these attitudes that we have these problems. We cannot go around with the attitude that *Homo sapiens*, the scientific name for human beings, are more important than anything else. In his book, "Extinction. The Causes and consequences of the disappearances of species. Random House (1981)", Paul Erlich dedicates the book with the following: "To *Homo sapiens* who without the other organisms will lead to its own destruction."

PESTICIDES VS.HUMANS

Have you wondered about the following: When a child is sick and is in pain and is suffering we call it parental anguish. When an animal is poisoned and squirming while dying, like a mouse, we call it pest control. Think about it. What have we done to demonize these poor creatures? We poison them, we zap them with electronic zappers, we trap them in leg traps, and we make them thirsty with specific substances that when these animals drink water they die because of the chemical reaction that takes place in their stomach. And we say that we are intelligent.!!! Yeah right. See more on pesticides in the chapter on Agriculture.

PAPER, MORE PAPER AND STILL MORE PAPER

Let's take a sheet of paper. What does a sheet of paper represent? Well I ask my classes that same question. IT REPRESENTS LIFE. YES LIFE. PAPER IS NOT A PIECE OF WORTHLESS GARBAGE. IT WAS ONCE PART OF A LIVING ORGANISM. WHAT ORGANISM? A TREE, YES THE TALL, STATELY TREE WHERE WE GET OUR OXYGEN FROM, WHERE BIRDS LIVE, WHERE LICHENS LIVE, THAT ALSO

PREVENTS SOIL EROSION BY HAVING LARGE ROOTS. YES, THE LIVING TREE. But, we consider a piece of paper just a piece of garbage.[68]

I teach at six colleges all in one semester. I have eleven classes and of course I have to give tests. For the past seven years I have given tests without paper. How you ask? Simple. I project the test questions on the screen by either using PowerPoint, Microsoft Word or by making transparencies. I also use one answer sheet for the whole semester because most of the questions are either one word fill-ins or multiple choices.(See Appendix VII) The first day of class I hold a sheet of paper up and show the class. I ask them, what is this? They, of course, say that it is paper. I ask them what does this represent. They say that it represents oxygen production, homes for animals, and soil stabilization (this is the function of roots). I know that I am a fanatic about this but if everyone was a little fanatic then maybe we would all have a better environment to live in.

Now occasionally I have a class that objects to doing the test my way. I tell them that I am trying to save paper. So, some students, many who are older than average students, say that at their workplace they have plenty of paper that is in the recycle bin. They suggested that they bring it in and that I could print the tests on the blank side. I agreed. Do you know that I had three students bring in about five hundred pages each with one side printed that wound up in the recycle bin? Now what is the significance of that? Simple. If I am able to get 1500 sheets of paper just from three people how much paper is lying out there in all the office recycle bins? Perhaps thousands and thousands of tons. All of it represents trees that have been killed just for making paper. Much of it is not used for reading and just winds up in the recycling bin. What a waste.

Figure 3 Here we see the author standing in front of a cart filled with paper from memos, advertisements for books to be used in classes, catalogues and other paper items placed in his school mailbox. Just think how much paper the author gets in all of his six of the schools that he teaches at. Now multiply that amount times the amount of paper that all teachers receive in the United States and you can see how much that adds up to be. Probably thousands of tons per year, metric or otherwise. (Photo by Merle Tuntland)

ENDOKE FOREST

Just what and where is the Endoke Rainforest? It is the Belgian Congo (formerly Zaire). The Endoke rainforest like other rainforests is under assault by poachers for food, trees and for wood. The wildlife is being devastated every year in order to feed and employ and keep certain individuals financially secure. However, the first time that I heard about the Endoke Rain Forest was on TV program called "Prime Time" with Sam Donaldson. There was about a 20 minute segment explaining how the Endoke Rain Forest was under assault, and of the naturalist, Mike Fay trying to save it. In the piece John Kinyonas , the reporter from Primetime, went on a trip with Mike Fay and discovered the largest elephant killing ground ever, 300 in all, including baby elephants. This was really horrifying. Now comes the clincher. After that segment was over with there was another segment dealing with how Fred Goldman won the wrongful death suit for the murder of his son Jeff and Nicole Brown Simpson allegedly by O.J. Simpson himself. Now what am I driving at? Well for one thing Mike Fay said he needed $600,000 to save the Endoke Rain Forest. How much money was spent on the O.J. Simpson trial? Many millions. Why spend the money on the O.J. Simpson trial and not on things which have a low profile such as the Endoke Rain Forest disaster? Because that is not a priority. Our priority is what will attract more attention no matter what it costs such as the O.J trial. Obviously there is more interest in seeing O.J. Simpson go down in defeat than the rain forest which can give life to the entire planet by providing us with medicines which can wipe out dreaded diseases such as leukemia and cancer.[69]

Let me explain to you, the reader, a story that happened to me about attitudes. When I was on one of my many project manager jobs at schools supervising asbestos removal we worked with a company that would have a book containing all the paperwork of each worker. In order for a worker to remove asbestos, at least in Illinois he has to be licensed. Not only does he need a license he needs a medial clearance allowing him/her to wear a respirator. He needs a respirator fit test which makes sure that he has no air leaks in his mask and he must have a current refresher certificate. The refresher certificate must be renewed every year so that the worker can get his/her license renewed. I was also given a list of the workers who would be coming for the duration of the work which would last for about one and a half weeks during Christmas break. I got the list from the foreman and I told my fellow project manager coworker that I would make copies of just the workers' paperwork. She wanted me to make copies of the whole book which contained about 100 sheets of paper containing the workers documentation (paperwork). She insisted that I copy the whole book because it would save time. I told her that I would only copy the paperwork of the workers who showed up on site. She then told me that it is more time efficient to just copy the whole book. I told her that we had plenty of time and that I felt it was a waste of paper to copy the whole book because only about 30% of the workers in the book were scheduled to show up. I insisted and I did it. I also told her that each piece of paper represented part of a home of an animal. Which, if you haven't guessed by now, paper does come from trees and trees are homes to millions of ANIMALS, PLANTS, BACTERIA, LICHENS AND A MYRIAD OF OTHER ORGANISMS. Here we see a clear example of how our attitude towards nature causes pollution. I would rather waste a few minutes of time rather than waste a few pieces of paper. But, I am sorry to say that here, especially in the western world we see paper as just another commodity without regard from where it came from. Those of you, who are reading this passage, think about what I said. Why waste even a single sheet of paper? Next time you think about wasting paper think about where it came from. Perhaps another way to look at this is as follows: Let's assume that you, the reader, own a house that has wooden frames. How would you like a bulldozer to ram through it and destroy it so that some company can make paper from it? Yes, that's right. You wouldn't like it one bit considering the price you paid for your home. Now, place yourself in the place of the insect, bacterium or fungus that lives on that tree or even an epiphytic plant. Do you get the point?

GEORGE BUSH AND ABORTION

There was a special session of the United Nations on children in May of 2002. Bush decided to set back efforts to provide reproductive health services for young men and women in other countries of the world. How? By eliminating funds for the United Nations Population Fund and by building an unusual alliance with the Vatican, Iran and ,yes Iraq of all places, in which references to abortion or reproductive services be eliminated . Instead grants awarded to schools, churches and health centers were geared for abstinence only.[70]

It never ceases to amaze me how people who are placed in high offices, yes, placed and not elected , (many of us environmentalists and professors believe in our hearts that the 2000 election could have best been described as grand theft) who in this case are so uninformed when it comes to matters of life and death for the planet. By this I mean issues such as overpopulation with its associated destruction of the planet and misery of billions of its human inhabitants.

It is a known fact that when women have fewer babies in developing countries their lives are much more secure and healthy. Those women who use contraceptives have fewer pregnancies and happier lifestyle. Ask yourself, has George Bush practiced abstinence? How come he has only one set twins (at least that we know of)? The answer is probably due to the fact that he used contraception which here in America is easy to acquire whereas in developing countries they may be hard to come by. He may have used devises that he preaches against. We can sum this up from a quote from Thoraya Obed, executive director of the UN Population Fund in which she says, "If we do not slow population growth we're only going to increase the number of people who are under the poverty line, who are frustrated, who have no employment, and no future".

WHO WEEPS FOR THE BACTERIA, FUNGI, ANIMALS, PROTOZOANS (SINGLE CELLED ORGANISMS) AND OTHER ANIMALS? For a look at the wonderful organisms that we have on this beautiful planet of ours check out books from the library on rainforest organisms.[71]

As of this writing our government headed by G.W. Bush (G.W. may stand for Global Warming) is heading toward a war with Iraq for reasons that are not actually clear. But, whatever the case, if we do go to war which results in actual fighting with guns and bombs we will be destroying billions and perhaps trillions of bacteria , plants and animals.

Figure 4 Place your own caption regarding family planning in third world countries.[72]

JOURNALIST IN AFRICA- READ ON RADIO BY MIKE MALLOY ON JULY 15, 2003

Mike Malloy is a talk show host now on Air America Radio who won the A.I.R award in 2005. In July of 2003 he was on the IEAmerica network .Mr. Malloy read a letter from an unknown journalist describing Bush's July 2003 trip to Senegal and of the humiliation suffered by Africans because of his visit which infuriated me because of the environmental destruction which preceded his visit. .

Dearest Friends,
As you probably know this week George Bush is visiting Africa starting with Senagal .He arrived this morning at 7:20 AM and left at 1:30 PM. Senegalese security forces were not allowed to come near the US president. Fourth, All trees in places where Bush will pass have been cut down. Some of them have more than 100 years (sic). Fifth, roads going downtown where are located hospitals, businesses and schools, all the roads from downtown were closed from Monday night through Tuesday.

Let's see now. Trees, many over 100 years old were cut down just so that they wouldn't be used as hiding places for potential snipers. Now, what about all the birds, fungi, bacteria, insects and other life living in those trees? Well, they don't count. An unelected American president who believes he is the master of the world comes by and that is the end of the life in those trees as well as the trees themselves. What about the displacement of the Senegalese people? Well you know they don't count. Go ahead reader, say that I am exaggerating. How would you like your home to be destroyed if the president of the US was passing by your home because it could harbor potential snipers? I assure you not good.

OUR NEED FOR LOW GASOLINE PRICES

Perhaps one of the attitudes that we in the United States have is that we are entitled to low gasoline prices. We have the largest car fleet in the world with over 125 million of them. Yet we also pollute the most also. Why? Because we have incredibly low gasoline prices compared to the rest of the world. Our prices now range around $2.50 per gallon while in Europe it is over $4.00 per gallon.

Figure 5 Here we see big expensive houses on what was once prime farmland. The right side of the picture contains corn stalks on what's left of farmland. (Photo by author)

CLIMATE CHANGE? WHAT THE %$#@ IS THAT?

The large oil conglomerates are king in America. They have immense political clout which means that they rule the world. They don't seem to care that the effluent, (in this case carbon dioxide) is destroying the earth's ability to support its human and non-human inhabitants by causing temperature change (greenhouse effect). We in the United States have 5% of the world's population but use 28% of the world's energy. In the fall of 2001, the (non elected or perceived as such) Bush administration recommended that funds for renewable energy be cut by 27% while funding into coal research increased by 813% even though coal produces more CO_2 than oil or gas. They know that CO_2 is on the increase, yet they tend to ignore it because money is more important than common sense. It should be pointed out that the oil industry is not alone in its uncaring attitude. The world's forests contain 400 billion tons of carbon and soils contain 1,600 billion tons. These are being degraded by logging companies and forest fires. [73]

It can be seen how attitudes of people play a role in shaping our environment. If these attitudes are fostered by millions of people even if they help destroy our environment then they are accepted. It takes people with guts to see that these attitudes are changed if the environment will benefit.

CHAPTER 4
CAPITALISM, THE AMERICAN WAY
AND THE PURSUIT
OF THE AMERICAN DREAM

A father and son were going to the Museum of Natural History in New York and they were viewing the way American Indians lived over 200 years ago. The boy turned to his father and asked, "Daddy, how could those people live without radios, color TVs, cars, computers, and fax machines? The father replied, "They didn't. That's why they all died."

INTRODUCTION

The purpose of this chapter is to show how the American Way and its associated materialism help influence the rest of the world. We can divide the American Way into three parts: **Consumerism, the American Dream, and the Hell with Everyone else.**

According to Ruth L. Sivard[74].... In the US the amount of wood and paper thrown away is enough to heat five million homes for 200 years. If statements like this are true then we should really be embarrassed and change our lifestyles.

Perhaps another astonishing fact that I discovered while researching this chapter is the following: at the height of the Ethiopian famine Britain imported 15 million pounds worth of linseed cake, cottonseed-cake, and rape seed meal from Ethiopia. These items were not meant for human consumption, but for animal feed. The author makes the point that instead of growing crops like these for rich countries why not have the Ethiopians grow their own food instead.? Good question isn't it?[75]

THE CONCEPT

Perhaps one of the biggest causes of environmental pollution today involves the American Way. Many of the things that we have here such as cars, swimming pools, and video recorders are things that other countries now have. Americans are obsessed with possessions and do not always care about their non-monetary costs such as environmental degradation.

One outstanding example comes to mind. This is the TV show, *Dallas* that at its peak, was shown in over 100 countries. It shows the good and bad times of a rich family, the Ewings. It had the effect of making the rest of the world want what they perceive as the good life that *Dallas* portrayed. It is obvious also from looking at magazines that the American Way of life is quite elaborate. When Emelda Marcos and her husband Ferdinand were whisked away from the Philippines to Hawaii, one of the reporters asked her why she looted her country. She said that she wanted to be like the people portrayed on *Dallas*.[76]

People in those countries who viewed *Dallas* think that we here in America have the good life because of all the materialism. They think that with all these high tech gadgets our lives are better. It is true that the machines add some enjoyment to our lives, but they also have negative effects such as environmental damage. This damage is caused by obtaining raw materials to make the goods. Since more people want and are able to afford the goods this places a strain on the Earth's natural resources.

At a lecture I gave at a meeting of The Ethical Humanist Society of Greater Chicago, I mentioned these facts and showed some pictures relating to this problem. Part of my presentation is a five-minute video, which I taped from a show called, *Inside Edition* hosted by Debra Norville. During this segment she mentions the fact that some dogs and cats have diamond studded leashes that cost as much as $100,000. This is an absurd use of resources.

Every couple of years I travel to Israel. On my way I pass through various European airports while changing planes. I am always astounded at the variety of things for sale at the airport. There are electronic items, liquor, watches, video cameras and other consumer goods. Everything, with perhaps the exception of various brands of perfume is obtainable in the United States. When I was an undergraduate at the University of Denver in the 1960s, I remember my sociology teacher saying: "If you want to go to Europe you had better hurry because soon Europe is going to look like the United States." He was right. Not only is Europe looking like the United States but Asia as well. If you look at pictures of Bangkok, Thailand, you notice that it looks just like any European or American city.

Let's take a look at what we have here in the United States that we take for granted. Here in America we need cars. We must have expensive sneakers that cost more than $100/pair. We must have lots of cheap hamburgers and meat products. We must have low gasoline prices. We must have large TV sets and we must have a high standard of living that the rest of the world envies. Now the fact that we have all these things is actually a mixed blessing. It is good that human beings can live well but in order to live as well as we do we ignore both the rest of the world's population and the environmental damage that we help inflict on the whole planet.

What effect does all this luxury have on the environment? Conceptually speaking, the more refined the end product the more unrefined material is initially required. If we want bigger homes we have to use more raw materials such as trees, ore and oil. If we want to eat more meat we have to raise cows on land that was once prime rainforest in some other country. If we want our Sunday newspapers we have to cut in excess of 75,000 trees just for one issue. Now here in America we have around 260 million people. Just think how much environmental damage would be inflicted if more than one third of the earth's six billion people have what we have.

I can say this because I lived in both Mexico and Israel. They may be considered developing countries but Israel can also be considered a developed country as well. In 1968 when I lived in Mexico I saw many heart-breaking scenes caused by poverty. Nothing is more painful then watching a mother beg for money to feed her small children. This was an all too common sight in Mexico. Here in America we don't see it as much, but we too have our poverty. What makes this so distressing is the fact that there are so many riches serving so few people.

Consider golf courses. The United States has more than 14,600 golf courses (Environmental Science M.McKinney 1996.).[77] Look at the environmental damage that golf courses do. They poison insects and birds, they give brain tumors to the greens keepers because of the pesticides and they take away prime farmland. In the Chicago area alone there are around 219 golf courses.

Let's look at businesses like McDonalds and Toys-R-Us. These are large corporations based in the United States; but their fastest growth has been overseas. Israel, for example, has both these stores and China and other Asian countries now have McDonalds. Is this good for the other countries? I suppose the owner benefits because he is the one getting in the money. If you have been reading news reports lately you can realize that going to McDonalds, for instance, is very expensive in other countries.

In an article by R.C. Longworth in the Chicago Tribune there is headline, *America's rally cry: Buy, Buy. It begins by saying the following:*

American shoppers, on a never-ending spree, are buying more than ever before. But the rest of the world, much of it sunk in recession, is buying less. The article begins by praising the American way of life and then putting a damper on it by mentioning rising deficits and job cuts.[78]

I would like to clarify a point. Materialism is not inherently bad. The idea of just accumulating wealth at the expense of everything and everyone else plus exporting this idea with TV is to say the least very immoral. Some people barely make enough money to eat much less to waste on non-essential consumer toys. Using scarce resources to promote a consumer centered ideal is a concept I find obscene.

CONSUMERISM

Americans exist in a consumer driven society. All we seem to care about are consumer goods whether they are appliances, electronic gadgets, toys and other necessary as well as unnecessary items such as large gas guzzling cars, private swimming pools, and 65 inch TVs. According to the C. Collis et al web site continuing to behave as if consumerism is the only conceivable choice contributes to the environmental destruction of the world.[79] To quote them... "in a world of limited resources, a system that advocates an ever increasing level of consumption and equates such consumption with personal well being, economic progress and social fulfillment is a recipe for ecological disaster."

I also want to point out that rejecting mindless consumerism does not mean we have to reject our basic needs, all technology or our life style. In America we have between 4% and 5% of the world's population and yet we consume 30% of its resources. We are responsible for more than 50% of the greenhouse gases. In the wealthiest nations we eat between 30-40% more calories than we need, certainly we could curb our use of resources without lessening our enjoyment of life.

UNFAIR TRADE PRACTICES

Unfair trade practices have kept the poor farmers poor because they usually don't have any leverage over how much money they can get for the crops that they grow. This of course leads to their dislike of our way of living as well as adding to environmental degradation by cutting, chopping, and digging in the pursuit of the holy dollar. Not only do the farmers suffer by their marginally controlled standard of living, but the very environment that the farmers live and work in is being threatened which will have a global effect by producing less food for the ever increasing population.

DEBT

Almost all Third World countries have huge foreign debts because rich nations encouraged them to borrow during the 1970's. Many of these countries are hard-pressed to meet their debt obligation. Emphasis is placed on paying back this debt. How do they do it? Yes, that's right by growing consumer cherished crops. As you have probably guessed, one solution to this problem is right in front of your eyes. (See the chapter on solutions).

I think that by now the reader gets the idea. It seems grossly unfair that we in the West are exploiting our environment, yes, our environment, even though we live in a land mass known as the United States. The rainforests, deserts, grasslands, mountains and water systems all belong to us Americans as well as to the rest of the world's population.

THE AMERICAN DREAM

During elections we always hear about the American Dream. Just what do politicians mean by the American Dream? According to what we hear on the radio and TV it appears that the American Dream is the idea that we must have a nice home, a perfect job and a comfortable life. But is this search an elusive goal perpetrated by politicians or homebuilders that are just after a quick buck or is it something like the pot of gold at the end of a rainbow? We will discuss its implications here and how it may lead to environmental pollution.

CONCEPT

Just what does it take to achieve the American Dream? Well for one thing you need money. Money buys the materials needed to make homes. Once you have money what is it used for? You need wood for the frame work, you need bricks, drywall, metal for wires, wood and or oil for roof shingles. Then the interior needs cover: a heater and air conditioner. The auto requires a driveway to the garage. The list goes on and on. Now I am not advocating giving up homes; just suggesting that the resources used have some relation to need. Certainly, we do not need a mansion. A nice moderate size home with a few bedrooms, two bathrooms, a living room and a dining room will do. This should be adequate for most families. Just because you have money does not mean that you should be overindulgent.

My idea of the American Dream is the idea that we should all live comfortably but not in excess. Have all our material needs met with a TV and/or radio for entertainment, maybe a small car for transportation and trips and if one wants to swim, a nice swimming pool to go to at the local community center or the health club. News reports dealing with terrorism or wars between countries like Israel and the Palestinians or between the Protestants and Catholics in Ireland would be few and far between. Why? Because the US will have used its energy in pursuit of peace instead of trying to give its citizens unlimited material goods. I believe that a revitalized United States will be able to solve these seemingly unsolvable situations.

Using our energy to cut, chop and dig just so that we can have more and more does not seem to be a worthwhile goal. By building bigger homes and wanting to live out in the suburbs we are making the inner cities ghost towns. Spreading out too many people will make the suburbs look just like the crowded cities that everyone wants to escape from. This is exactly what has happened in various suburbs such as in Denver, Colorado. It certainly has happened in the Chicagoland area like the city of Schaumburg, which used to be a quiet city. Now, it is home to one of the largest shopping centers in the United States, (Woodfield Mall). On occasion I traveled through the area fighting traffic but I always had the feeling that I am glad not to live there. I believe that there are many areas around major cities with places just like Schaumburg: a haven that started out being a nice place to escape to but developed the problems of urban life.

A good example of lifestyles of poor and rich is described in a CNN series, which is entitled, *"The People Bomb"* [80] in which two lifestyles are examined. One in Nepal, a country close to India, and one in Pleasant Hill, California in the United States. In the segment the narrator examines the fact that the Napalese family being highlighted had six children and lived in a small modest house basically consisting of one room made of mud. The American family, which was highlighted lived in the suburbs of San Francisco had a nice home, a nice kitchen with a microwave and other appliances and lived on a nice tree lined street. The difference between the two lifestyles was phenomenal, just like day and night.

Here in The United States life can be quite a challenge on its own. If you are lucky you work for a company that is in relatively good financial shape. Then maybe you don't have to worry about losing your job and health insurance, unless, of course, someone needs to spike the worth of its stock by laying people off. Many part-time professors, of which I am one, have basically no benefits with the exception of the job. This makes our lives much more interesting, (scary and insecure) because we are on our own when it comes to health insurance and other things that other employed people take for granted. For us enough money is the knowledge that you are able to save for odds and ends like retirement and perhaps a working computer, something that has become vital in the education field.

THE HELL WITH EVERYONE ELSE

Now that I told you about the American Way and Capitalism let me finish up this chapter with giving you some people's attitude, at least with some people here in these United States. One of the things that bugs me most is the fact that many Americans could care less about the plight of people in other countries.

A good example: In 1992, Hurricane Andrew hit the Southeast coast of the United States. Many organizations in the Chicago area set up collection centers to gather blankets, canned food, and other items that people left homeless due to hurricane Andrew needed. I volunteered to help collect the supplies. I happened to mention this to a friend of mine and asked him if he would take some time (which he had) to help. He said, and I quote," What did those people ever do for me?" Well, I was astounded and ticked off when he said this. However, I didn't take it to heart because I know this individual. But, unfortunately, there are too many like him here in America.

One of the things that I think about is helping the Haitians, those who live in Haiti, the poorest nation in the Northern Hemisphere. I say to my friends that if I had won over $20 million I would help the Haitians by having an architectural company design homes for them and I, myself, would buy the supplies for them and have the Haitians themselves build their own homes.

So when I mention this to my friends they say, "How come you won't help our own people here in America?" The answer that I give is as follows: I ask them, "Why doesn't Haiti have an atomic submarine?" They say because Haiti can't afford it and besides, they don't have the enemies that we have. Then I say, "We have lots of submarines and lots of poor people. Why don't we help our own citizens with the money that we use for the Submarines? It would go a long way in protecting our citizens from starvation, homelessness, and drive-by shootings and disease. How will drive by shootings be prevented? Easy. When kids have decent homes they won't be in gangs. Gangs are a large part of the reality which drives the "the drive by shootings."

I think by now the reader realizes that we can't just think of ourselves. If we are number one in the world then we have the responsibility to act like number one.

With the reckless pursuit of the media driven American Dream, the people in the West seem to be pursuing the "mythical pot of gold" at the end of the rainbow. The only way this should be achieved is if the rest of the world is able to achieve it without destroying its own environment.

CHAPTER 5
APATHY

What's the difference between ignorance and apathy?
Answer: I don't know and I don't care.

INTRODUCTION

Webster's Dictionary defines apathy as the feeling of not caring. Occasions for apathy present themselves all over, whether it is seeing a drunk lying in the middle of the sidewalk, an animal run over in the street, or we not giving a damn about what's happening in other countries like Somalia, Rwanda, Haiti, Cuba, etc. We have been so bombarded with human misery throughout the planet that we just don't care anymore. It's hard to pick up a newspaper without seeing some sort of human induced atrocity, whether it is mass starvation or the killing of people because of hatreds that were kept pent up for thousands of years. People are just concerned with getting through the day without worrying about anyone else's problems. Many people just want to go out and buy more luxuries in an effort to cope. There may be nothing inherently wrong with that if everybody in the world were equal, luxury wise, but these extravagances are costly to our environment. The effect of apathy on us and the rest of the world is a widely held phenomenon.

CONCEPT

Many people don't care what happens to the environment or they think nothing they do can help save the world. Yet, a few of us can save the world by using our influence to vote out of office those inept politicians who are just interested in getting reelected no matter what it takes. They will promise anything. More jobs...more cutting down trees, more of anything just to get reelected. Yes, and of course, LESS TAXES!! Apathy takes many forms, such as more waste (ad inserts) in the Sunday newspaper, buying big gas-guzzler cars (SUVS), building bigger houses just to impress a friend or neighbor or even buying 64 inch TVs. All this I place under apathy. The buyers feel that since they have the money they can do whatever they want. Many of the things that they buy are absolutely not necessary. They can get by with lesser amounts if they cared about the environmental consequences of continuously making things bigger, which includes using more natural resources which equals more environmental degradation.

Cases of apathy occurred on a street where I used to live. I lived near a forest preserve and every so often I would see animals dead in the road. One day I passed a dead raccoon by the side of the road. Behind me there was a woman talking on her cell phone. It occurred to me that she could care less about the poor dead animal. I immediately turned around and removed the raccoon from the road, placed him in the forest preserve and said a prayer for him. This was not the first time this occurred. Once there was a large deer lying on the side of the road. I stopped my car and noticed that his head was bleeding. I touched him with my foot and he got up and ran across the street. He ran into another part of the forest preserve. Again, I wondered how many people just passed him by. It was evident to me that the person that hit him could care less. Fortunately, he was able to run across the street himself. He just missed being hit by a car coming from the opposite direction. This goes on all the time and the result is just squashed animals whose remains are being eaten by birds and other animals.

What do you think causes this apathy? Well, for one thing our society fosters it. We don't instill values in our children like we used to because society fosters individuality over everything else. Politicians thrive because of these attitudes but avoid discussing serious issues because people lack interest. Why don't they want to hear them? Well, the answer is obvious: many people refuse to believe that dead animals or live ones for that matter have any effect on their lives.

Another example of apathy shows in our attitude toward other countries. As long as we sit here in America living the American Dream (which has never been adequately defined) and not caring about the rest of the world we are contributing to the planet's downfall. We want more and more, and meanwhile people in poor countries like Haiti have less and less and would just like to get by with enough food and a decent place to live. However, we in the richer countries could care less about them because of the old saying, "Out of sight, out of mind!" How many people really know what bacteria are? Perhaps many, perhaps a few...Do you think if our politicians really cared about organisms such as bacteria and plants, they would bomb countries like Afghanistan? Probably not, but the fact that we do bomb other countries, especially the desert areas of Afghanistan, indicates to me we could care less about other organisms who inhabit the planet with us humans. This is demonstrated during bombing campaigns which killed trillions of individual bacteria and millions of plants and animals. It is obvious that we humans, "in the name of defense" just don't give a damn! It appears that we don't care what happens to them because they are not here. They are not in our immediate consciousness because they are not emphasized in the local newspapers, despite the fact that they play an immensely important role in the Earth's eco-systems. Whenever we hear about house fires, we only hear about human's being killed or injured, but what about the bacteria in the house: the poor fungi (the plural of fungus), or about insects killed, like the poor cockroach, which everyone seems to hate. Maybe now is the time that we should all be singing (La Cuckaroacha, La Cuckaroacha!)

If the world's humans continue to just think that they are the most important organisms on the planet, then it is obvious that the world will continue to be plundered. It is in everybody's best interest to care about every single organism from the safest to the deadliest, from the most beautiful to the ugliest, from the most inspiring to the least inspiring because our lives depend on all of them.

CHAPTER 6
BECAUSE IT'S THERE

"Proud sponsor of OPEC "

Seen on a bumper sticker on a Hummer

INTRODUCTION

This chapter's purpose is to show that if we produce unnecessary items there will always be a market for them. Many of the things that we want and buy are totally unnecessary but they exist because someone imagined them. Ask yourself, "Why go to the bottom of the ocean?" Well, we have curiosity of course but the main reason that we go there is because it is there. Why go to Mars or the Moon or Pluto for that matter? Why? Because they are there.

CONCEPT

Why do people buy big cars that are gas-guzzlers, or big houses with two living rooms? What causes people to buy 64-inch rear projection TVs? Why do people buy Sunday newspapers that help destroy enough trees to build many houses? THE ANSWER IS BECAUSE THEY ARE THERE. It's obvious that if these things were not made there would not be any demand. By producing these products, manufacturers are creating demands. If those items were not made then we could not have them. You might also object that many jobs would be eliminated or missing if we didn't have those items. While this is true, maybe they would be replaced by jobs making smaller items such as cars, TVs and even smaller, more practical houses. At the rate we may be going there will soon be plenty of jobs available but no one left alive to fill them.

If human "ingenuity" did not invent these big gadgets then we wouldn't buy them. Perhaps those entrepreneurs out there may realize that inventing these new gadgets is not necessary for ones survival in today's world. Let's make a list of some things that people use and are bad for the environment but are there. **(See chapter 11 on greed)**

CARS

Consider Sports Utility Vehicles (SUV's) and Hummers (Bummers).

Why are they so big? Why are there so many? And why are so many bought? The answer is because they exist. If people want something and it doesn't yet exist two things will happen. Number one, someone will invent it if it seems that the item can make someone rich. Number two that item cannot be made because we do not yet have the technology to make it. What happened to the good old station wagon? Actually these days they may not be so good because many had eight cylinders when four would have done just fine. Four cylinder cars may have less power, but I think for most uses they will do. Sport utility vehicles have taken their place. Based on statistics 15%, or more of vehicles sold are sports utility vehicles. These make up 60% of industry's profits. [81] In addition if SUVs crash into small cars the drivers of the SUVs are virtually uninjured while those in the small cars are more likely to die of serious injuries. [82]

Using lots of raw materials in their manufacture, SUVs pollute the air because they run on gasoline and of course as stated above, they endanger the lives of people traveling in smaller cars.

Figure 6 Here we see a hummer (Left) and a bunch of SUVs at a swimming pool parking lot in Illinois. Do we really need cars this big in America or anywhere else for that matter? Can you even spot a non SUV in this picture?[83] (Photo by author)

After the Exxon Valdez [oil] spill, Exxon representatives commented that the grounding of the ship was unprecedented in scale. In terms of the amount of oil spilled, this was not true. Because of the nature of the area in which the disaster occurred this one spill appears to have killed more wildlife than any other oil spill in history: an estimated 100,000 to 300,000 seabirds, thousands of marine mammals, and hundreds of bald eagles. In villages scattered along a thousand miles of affected coastline, the spill devastated subsistence hunting, fishing and gathering -- essential parts of the rural economy and Native American culture. In terms of the volume of spills from marine or land-based sources however, the Exxon Valdez spill was not unusual. On average, a spill of a million gallons occurs every month.[84]

In my classes I ask if any of the students have SUV's and most of the time the answer is yes. Many of the students seem to like them.[85] When I ask them why they own one of them they tell me that it is convenient. I reply that they use too much gas and are too big. That argument does not seem to persuade them enough to buy something smaller.

In my opinion Hummers might better be called **Bummers** because of their low gas mileage of between 8-10 miles per gallon. I realized why they are called Hummers. Because the oil executives are going to the bank **humming** the song; "We're in the Money"!!!!

Sports cars

The same is true about small sports cars. What practical use does a small sports car have? Who needs one anyway? (I know - a playboy who wants to pick up girls or women.) In all fairness to women, when I was going to the University of Denver in 1963-67, I saw the reverse. I remember one female student who drove a sports car and some guy rode with her.

Again I asked some of my female students if they would go out with a guy because he is rich and drives a sports car. Some said yes and others, the vast majority said no.

If you look at one of these cars they are impractical in many ways. One, they are too small to add luggage especially if you are going on a long trip. Two, they go very fast, certainly faster than the 55 mph or 65 mph that we are allowed to go without getting a speeding ticket Three, they are also very expensive, especially the Mercedes Benz.

Large homes

How large does a home have to be? Good question. If a family contains two members do they need a mansion? Obviously not, unless the homes serve some function other than living. I think a nice house should have three maybe four bedrooms at the most unless a member of that particular household has some function like an office or something else. Extra space may be needed if the person is severely disabled or if the people adopted many children.

There are homes being built near where I live, which are outrageously expensive, between $300,000-750,000. I myself live in a modest three bedroom home with a basement and attic as a den where I get most of my writing done for school. The house is very small but I feel comfortable. All my physical needs are met with relative ease. I'm sure some people want to impress their friends, but let's look at this from an environmental point of view. It's obvious that the bigger the house the more environmental degradation occurs in order to get raw materials for building the house. Not to mention the accumulated waste in wood and brick and other waste products that go with home building. Utilities such as water, electricity, and gas should also figure in when discussing damage to the environment. Need I go further?

64 inch TV's

The other day I went to a friend's house and saw a big 64-inch TV screen. I asked myself, "Why does my friend need this?" The answer is probably, although I didn't come right down and ask him, "because it exists" and he could afford it. Now we have in my house a couple of small 15 and 21inch television sets. These are just fine for me. I figure that if I want a big screen I can always go to a movie theater.

This of course leads us to consumerism. As we shall see in the chapter on Solutions, one way to end this needless buying is not to make the things that we consume. It is obvious that if these things don't exist then we can't buy them. It's funny. We make things people absolutely don't need and yet we don't make things that people do need. A case in point: Let's look at plastic popcorn makers. Can we make popcorn without them? Yes, of course, by using a large saucepan and adding a little bit of olive oil or some other oil. We then put in the popcorn and let her pop. As for things that we do need and that can be made there are solar powered cars. We can certainly use them to cut down on pollution. Do we have them yet? No. Why not? Because our wonderful politicians are not interested. They feel that if we did develop these cars their oil buddies will not remain rich.

I think that you get the point. Of course, I like to buy things but I only buy things that are reasonably priced and reasonable in size. When I go to stores like Target and Wal-Mart I am amazed at how many things are for sale. I ask myself "Do I really need these things?" Sometimes I think about buying things that I don't really need, but then I think of all the poor people not only in America who have virtually nothing, all those people who live in the poorer parts of the world as well. Some of them barely get enough to eat. I think about the poor African children and those poor children of Afghanistan who when they get sick, cannot even go to a doctor. I think about the things they don't have. No large TV's, no cars, no bottles of perfume, no choice of sneakers, blue jeans, children's toys or just a small bottle of Coca Cola, or a picture of themselves on their parent's dressers (chances are many of the parents don't even own dressers.)

Then I think about what we have here in the Western world. We have literally millions of choices of everything. We are inundated with many choices for the same type of item whether it is cars, breakfast cereals, clothing, homes, or cameras. We should ask ourselves: Do we really need so many choices of each type of item? Certainly not! If something is being made no matter how ridiculous it is, it will be bought by somebody. If it is not made then it won't be there, and ultimately, will not consume environmental resources.

CHAPTER 7
BUSINESS

*Business is pretty bad. A kid recently walked into a store
and asked the owner if he had any empty boxes. The
owner said, yes, the cash register. Milton Berle*

INTRODUCTION

As we have seen, business dominates every aspect of our society. We
always hear the Dow Jones Average, The Standard & Poor (S&P) average
as well as other financial indices. I am not trying to knock industry just for
the sake of knocking something, but I want to point out that business *has
priorities* over environmental or other issues. Not only in America but in
other countries we see that building golf courses or other endeavors such as
shopping centers *take priority* whether they are needed or not which results
in environmental degradation. This chapter discusses these issues.

THE CONCEPT

As Paul Hawkins says in his book, *The Ecology of Commerce,*[86]
business does whatever it wants in order to do business. He also points
out that if business takes responsibility for the environmental damage
then it will do things that are less damaging. True, but we have to take a
look at business at its roots. First, we must ask ourselves, "What drives
businesses?" Well, it is obvious that they are out to make a profit. Yes,
the bottom line is profit, more profit and more profit, while selling their
goods or services at the price that the market will bear. In other words,

they want to sell their products as high as possible and make a profit while not alienating the public.

Of course, the consumer is also at fault. They want things at the lowest possible price because they feel that they are bombarded with taxes as well as high prices. Now, businesses also realize that if they start charging higher prices then they will lose business. Hence, cries of bankruptcy. "There goes the economy." This is the crux of the problem. We all know that if business goes, so does the economy. Now we have the politicians involved if it is politically advantageous. They will want to turn business around no matter what it takes and, yes, even if it takes environmental damage then so be it!

Again, it all boils down to the fact that we, the consumer, must learn to either pay higher prices or do without certain things that we can most assuredly do without. This may mean only one TV or radio in the house, two bathrooms instead of three, one video recorder instead of two or more, one car instead of two or three, one living room instead of two. The list goes on and on.

Now, remember that in order to have more than we need, production has to be greater. With greater production comes more business with their soaring profits, and, of course, resulting in more damage to the environment. We constantly see this. Wall Street will not agree with less production because they are interested in the Dow Jones Average and its ramifications either up or down. The lower the Dow the higher the anxiety of the investors. The higher the investors' anxiety the lower goes the Dow. One feeds on the other. Each stockholder forgets that he or she has to eat uncontaminated food, breathe uncontaminated air and live in an environment that keeps sustaining itself. If we cut down every tree so that business can reap high profits then business will eventually die like a parasite that kills its host: A parasite will die if the host dies. A good example of this is the book and animated movie entitled, "The Lorax" by Dr. Seuss.

If I am not mistaken, stockholders are humans that need the same life support systems as non-stockholders; but you may wonder if they realize that. Politicians, too, need a life-sustaining environment. Perhaps the worst case scenario to illustrate this point was the worst industrial accident in the history of the human race: The Bhopal incident where more than 2,000 people died and 200,000 or more people were injured. (See more on Bhopal in chapter 2 on agriculture). By the way, as of this writing, which takes place almost 20 years after the accident, many of the victims have not been compensated by Union Carbide, the owner of the factory that caused the accident. Union Carbide, by the way, is still in business as if nothing has ever happened. So much for morality...Business cannot be permitted to cut, chop, dig and burn as if they own the planet, although they act as if they do own the planet.

A corollary that comes with business is the same old cliché that we hear all the time. If we cut back on business, there go the jobs. Again, jobs are more important than the environment. For example, the massive Exxon Valdez oil spill in 1989 not only devastated the local environment, but also eliminated many jobs connected with the fishing industry. The only jobs available after the spill were temporary clean-up jobs and those that supported the clean up crews.

By using mass transit instead of cars, we can reduce petroleum consumption by half as well as lowering the risk of other Exxon Valdez accidents occurring. Businesses hold allegiance to their stockholders and not the environment. This fact was brought out in the TV movie, *Dead Ahead*, which was about the Exxon Valdez disaster in Prince William Sound in Alaska. John Heard, who plays Dan Lawn, the environmental specialist, makes the comment at the end of the movie that, "It is amazing that Exxon cares more about its stockholders than the land." [87]

Unfortunately, it is not just Exxon, but many companies that feel that way. We see this all the time when "Developers" (to me this is a curse word) get a hold of some land, especially near a coast or lakefront and develop houses so that those who have the large financial means can own a house there, while in many cases poor people cannot even approach the area because it is guarded by a gate or a security company. That same land used to contain swamp or marshland that helped keep the lake, ocean or estuary productive. By productivity, we in the science field mean capable of producing more life. Swampland and marshes are where the spawning of fish and crabs take place. By building houses for those fortunate few, we diminish the quality of life not only for the poor but also for the whole planet as a whole.

As I write this section, it is mid-November of 2003. Here in the Chicago vicinity the temperature is in the high 50's to low 60's. This is quite unusual for this time of year in this area. So far, we have had not one day below 32°C this month. Quite unusual you say. Perhaps, and perhaps it is this way because of industry and developers cutting and chopping their way through the rain forests of the planet. I strongly believe that our behavior is directly responsible for climate change and business plays a very important role.

According to Hawkins, business has three basic issues: what it takes, what it makes, and what it wastes. All three are connected. By what it takes means that business takes from the environment. To make what it does it requires a lot of energy. Finally, in order to produce whatever it makes it produces a lot of waste, much of it hazardous.

We cannot let business be so reckless. Actually though, if you look around, business has been making things smaller. Look at the weight of the average TV set. Many years ago they were bulky because of their tubes. Today, they are lightweight and easily carried. So, as you can see, whether by luck or because of scientific advances they are making things smaller, but they are still producing hazardous wastes.

True businesses have been making things smaller that last longer without repairs, such as TVs and cars, but yet they are making more of them. As mentioned in a previous section, we export the American way, as is exemplified in the TV show, *Dallas*.

Another aspect to consider when talking about business is the fact that we are led to believe that we have to make decisions based on the economy and not on the ecological balance. The quintessential example of this is the loggers vs. the spotted owl. Loggers want to be able to cut down the trees because they need to make a living. But they don't realize that the spotted owl needs a place to live just like the lumberjacks. How would the lumberjacks like it if someone came in with a bulldozer and chopped down their house just so they can use the wood? Not much.

Corporate business is associated with the bottom line: money. As we have seen, many businesses make their money by destroying the environment. I would strongly advise that money be spent teaching businesses to be greener and making sure that CEO's realize that they too have to breathe air and eat pesticide free food. Can this be done? See chapter 24 on solutions and find out how.

CHAPTER 8
COMMUNISM

COMMUNISM You have two cows. The government takes both, hires you to take care of them, then sells you the milk.

PURE COMMUNISM You have two cows. Your neighbors help you take care of them, and you all share the milk

COMMUNISM (reality): You share two cows with your neighbors. You and your neighbors bicker about who has the most "ability" and who has the most "need". Meanwhile, no one works, no one gets any milk, and the cows drop dead of starvation. [88]

INTRODUCTION

During the years of communism the environment in the former Soviet Union suffered innumerable insults. In the name of progress the communist countries were poisoned because environmental concerns were ignored in order to gain prosperity. The environmental damage included: air pollution, groundwater depletion and contamination, almost total elimination of the Aral Sea, pollution of Lake Baikal, soil salinization, disruption of the permafrost, depletion of subsoils, soil erosion, deforestation, acid rain and the disaster at Chernoble (high cancer rates.) [89] In order to achieve a semblance of self-sufficiency the Soviet government encouraged the ravishing of their environment to try to make ends meet financially. As we have seen it was a dismal failure. The Soviet Union succumbed to the weight of its problems. What was left was the environmental catastrophe mentioned above, as was evidenced after the Berlin Wall came tumbling down.

CONCEPT

After the fall of Communism around 1989 it was discovered that a tremendous amount of environmental destruction existed in the Eastern Block Countries. A great deal of this destruction occurred under the guise of meeting production quotas.

Proof of this devastation is shown in a chart, which shows that sulfur dioxide (SO_2) emissions ranged five to eight times that of Western Europe. Maximum tons per 1000 persons ranged from 102.4 -178.3 tons in Eastern Europe to 23.9- 61.9 tons in Western Europe. When speaking about particulates such as coal dust, differences between Eastern Europe and Western Europe are even more staggering. They range from 46.5 - 91.8 tons per 1000 persons in Eastern Europe to between 4.3-8.9 tons per 1000 persons in Western Europe.[90]

A book titled: Toxic Nightmare: Ecocide in the USSR and Eastern Europe[91] begins like this: *Not until 1989 did the Soviet Government release its first report on the national environment, a report detailing alarming pollution of the air, water degradation of soil and forest, and rapidly spreading environmental health problems. ...Only 30% of Soviet Sewage from cities is treated, 20% dumped raw, ...Almost 20% of water samples fail to meet health standards...At least 1.5 billion tons of topsoil erode annually.....Two thirds of the country's arable land has lost fertility..... Pesticide concentrations make up to 30% of the food supply dangerous to human health, etc.*

However, I would like to mention that this catastrophic damage was not only due to the Soviet's way of doing things such as their inflexible, feedback-adverse approach but partly due to the Reagan administration's obsession with the so called "Evil Empire", another name for the Soviet Union, which helped them spend themselves into oblivion by building up their military at the expense of the average Soviet citizen. So here you see how not only the Communist system helped fuel their own environmental destruction, but that of the American leadership with its misguided hatred for the Communist system. Now, don't get me wrong. I dislike their totalitarian system but if I were the President of the United States, I would have arranged to meet with their leadership and say, "Hey, let's stop this insanity of Arms buildup and work together to save the planet from environmental or nuclear destruction." Some of the environmental disasters that stand out thus far include the following:

1. **Chernobyl:** released large amounts of radioactivity from April 27-May 6 of 1986. This was detected throughout the entire world.

2. **The Aral Sea:** (in Kazakhstan, formally a part of the Soviet Union) lost 80% of its area due to the diversion of water coming from the two major rivers, (the Amu-Daria and the Syr-Daria) feeding it for the irrigation of cotton. Between 75-80% of fish species that once inhabited the lake are extinct. It should be mentioned that towns that once were on the shores of the Aral Sea (See figure 7) are now deserted.[92]

3. **Copsa Mica in Rumania:** In this town located in North-central Romania there is a company called The Karbosin Plant that produces black carbon powder.[93] In this town, soil, milk and food are contaminated by lead and cadmium. The town's people suffer high rates of respiratory infection, anemia, premature birth, malnutrition, nervous disorders and retardation. A quote by Dr. Jean Nenea who is a doctor in a factory near Copsa Mica says the following:
"Out of 3,860 employees, 3,500 are on the list of being poisoned with lead, with varying degrees of severity. In 30 years of industrial medicine I've never seen anything like this. This place is an Auschwitz".

4. **Lake Baikal:** This lake is located in the Southern part of eastern Siberia near the Republic of Buryatia and Irbutsk (Oblast province). It is a mile deep lake that contains one fifth of the worlds freshwater. Lake Baikal is polluted because on its shores are paper and pulp combines as well as dozens of factories which release chemical pollutants into the Selenga River which provides the lake with half of its water.

5. **East Germany**: One third of the rivers and forests are dead, air pollution in the cities is about 100 times the recommended safety level, and life spans are shortened by years

6. **Poland**: Perhaps one of the most polluted cities in Poland is Gdansk, the famous city where the Solidarity movement and Leck Walensa became famous. Passing through the city there is the Vistula River that makes its way throughout Poland. There are 813 Polish cities along the Vistula, which dump untreated sewage into it. The river also flushes tons of nitrogen and phosphorus, to the Baltic along with mercury, cadmium, zinc, lead, copper, phenol and chlorinated hydrocarbons. In fact one cartoonist drew a cartoon, which indicated that the Baltic as one big toilet bowl.

7. **The Black Sea:** The Black Sea borders Romania, Bulgaria, Russia, Turkey, Moldova and the Ukraine. Pollution from industry and cities has robbed the sea of its oxygen, which results in depleted fish stocks, thus

causing wholesale poverty in cities from surrounding countries such as Romania[94].

As can be seen in examples above, during the age of the Communistic regimes production took place at all costs. Environmental protection was unheard of. If one spoke up about it he or she would be locked up or executed. Now, with the downfall of Communism in Eastern Europe we see the terrible environmental damage to our sick Earth. There is no need to continue with examples. Those can be found in numerous newspaper articles and other books about Eastern Europe during the so called, "Cold War", which we (the West) may have won, but the Earth lost.

READER, PLACE YOUR OWN
PICTURE HERE OF WHAT'S LEFT
OF THE ARAL SEA. YOU WILL
BE AMAZED AT WHAT YOU SEE,
OR BETTER, WHAT YOU DON'T SEE.

Figure 7: Here should be a picture taken of the Aral Sea as it stands now. If you go to "Google" on the internet and go to images under the Aral Sea you will see fishing boats in the middle of the sand, which were once floating on water.

CHAPTER 9
CONVENIENCE

One of the many reasons for the bewildering and tragic character of human existence is the fact social organization is at once necessary and fatal. Men are forever creating such organizations for their own convenience and forever finding themselves the victims of their home-made monsters.
Aldous Huxley

Every convenience brings its own inconvenience with it.
Anonymous

INTRODUCTION

During my life on the planet Earth, I have seen many technological wonders from home appliances to instant photography which has made our lives easier and more enjoyable. I have also seen that most people especially those of us in the western world take convenience for granted. Convenience aids us in contaminating the world. Why? Because we make things for one time use and then throw them away. We now make things like plastic cups, bottles, and wrappings for small things like pens and stamps, which weigh more than the items themselves. The concept of this chapter is to show the reader how convenience is adding more pollution.

THE CONCEPT

Have any of you ever seen a breakfast food in the refrigerator of a supermarket called "Breakfast Mates"?[95] This is a food prepackaged with milk, a plastic spoon and cornflakes and costs $1.39 which is five times the price it could be purchased in a regular box. This undoubtedly seems to save people time, especially busy parents, who give the whole box of Breakfast Mates to their kids thus, eliminating personal contact between parent and child, not to mention the environmental toll this takes. Why an environmental toll because in order to produce more of these packets you need more equipment and materials. Think about it. You need milk cartons made out of wax and cardboard, you need plastic for the spoon and other things such as materials to make the ink on the carton with the name "Breakfast Mates."

If we look at other foods we see just about everything is packaged for convenience. Look at coffee now in little "tea bags," prepared waffles that you just stick in the toaster, disposable cigarette lighters, cameras that you buy with the film inside and are only used once by each purchaser, and is probably recycled, but I think that the reader gets the idea. Do we need all of these conveniences? I imagine children in Bangladesh don't even know these things exist and they are doing just fine without them. (Of course, we have to take in consideration the floods and other disasters that befall the Bangladeshi's because we are contributing to the greenhouse effect, which affects weather patterns due to our need to consume packaged convenience items.)

I would like to mention that not all things that are based on convenience are bad for the environment. Take videos for instance. Videos are rather small and are less cumbersome then old films with their cans as was used in the old days. (Remember the Old Days? When the Air was clean and Sex was Dirty!)

I really get upset when I see teachers copy tests and other documents on copy machines. Some are too lazy to use both sides of the paper. Some people don't know how to use these machines back to back. I discuss this issue when I see teachers doing it and they give me an answer such as, "I'm in a hurry" or "The students prefer one sided pages." I have even run into secretaries who don't know how to make two sided copies, so I teach them.

Another form of convenience that I notice is exemplified by people waiting to take the train at the station near my house: Every morning there is a woman who leaves her engine running while parked at the station reading her newspaper. Couldn't she shut the engine off? No. Because she has to have either heat in the winter and or cold during the summer while she is reading the paper. She probably doesn't even think about the wasted gas, the extra carbon dioxide emitted from the exhaust pipe which may cause an increase in asthma, or the wear and tear on her car. I decided to ask her why she did this and her reply was that she was cold. I figured that she could have worn something warmer. Since this episode, I have seen many people stay in their cars with their engines running while waiting for their train even though the weather was beautiful. (Go figure!) Now, let us talk about specific examples of convenience.

CARS

Many households have as many as four or more cars. This is ridiculous. In an article from USA Today during the week of Oct. 7, 1999, a comparison was made with homeowners and non-homeowners who owned cars. They pointed out that homeowners have as many as four cars whereas home renters had one or two as a rule. This probably means that there is one car for every member of the household who lives in a private home. Sure it's convenient to just get in your car and go to the market or wherever, but I think combining your trips into just one run will actually save gas and not pollute the atmosphere just for convenience sake. Because of all the cars in Los Angeles County, we should change the name of the city to "Malos Aires" (bad air), and change the county to Asthma County. (Buenos Aires, means good air in Spanish.)

In a Department of Transportation study it was discovered that traffic gridlock was on the increase with the Chicago area being the fifth worst in the nation, and Los Angeles being the number one city with the worst congestion. Now comes the clincher. Here is a statistic taken from the newspaper article from the Chicago Tribune.[96] In 1995 cars traveled 86.4 million miles per day in Cook County alone. Now realize that an astronomical unit (AU), the mean distance between the Earth and the sun, is 93 million miles. This means that if we take into consideration the mileage traveled in neighboring Kane County (6.8) million miles, with those traveled in Cook County, we already have enough mileage logged on to take Cook County residents to the sun. How's this for an exaggeration? The article pointed out that the increase in mileage traveled in the various counties since 1973 ranged from 47.6% in Cook County, to 140% in McHenry County, all within 50 driving miles from Chicago.

Think about the wasted time in thousands of hours that the commuters have to endure, the wasted money in lost productivity which is $4.40 billion and worst of all, the excess gasoline, thus putting out a tremendous amount of carbon dioxide (CO_2). This CO_2 is exhausted from 398 million gallons of wasted gasoline burned while the commuters are waiting in traffic. Perhaps this has a silver lining. Colorado drivers are so fed up that they voted for the state to borrow $2.1 billion in funds to build a new light rail system.[97] If this traffic will allow people to build mass transit systems, then it would have been worth it. There will be more on the solutions to these problems in the final chapter of this book.

I for instance, take mass transit. Do I have a car? Yes I do, but I use it only when I don't have the time to take mass transit. I also take the car to the train station where I commute to work. Let me give you an example. I teach at a college 50 miles from my house. I normally have to be at class at 9:30AM. I get up at 4:30 AM just so I can take two trains and a bus to the school. (Recently, the Pace Bus system, which is a suburban company near Chicago, discontinued all round trips to the school because they did not get the anticipated ridership from students thus, diminishing their bottom line…) Greed is more important than educating students…I had to resort to asking my students to pick me up at the station, much to the consternation of the Dean. Am I really wasting time? No. Why? Because I get a lot of work done on the train, I consider the train quality time. From talking to the conductors they tell me that there are more commuters now than before. I think that this is a trend that will still be picking up in the future because our roads are getting more congested everyday.

FAST FOOD RESTAURANTS AND BANK DRIVE INS

The word fast-food is an oxymoron. Why do people spend more time in a car line for fast food when they could just as easily go inside the fast food restaurant and buy their meal in a much shorter time than waiting for the car line in front of them? The answer is simple: People here in America and elsewhere have fallen in love with their cars and because of this they have become lazy.

I believe drive-through service actually causes more pollution because people are waiting in line at McDonalds or some other fast food restaurant while their cars are idling and thus wasting gas as well as polluting the atmosphere. These drive-through establishments probably help increase the bottom line for the owners.

PREPARED FOODS

Take for instance convenience foods. Many of the foods that we buy are already packaged. You prepare the foods even in the box by just putting them in the microwave. I am not against convenience but when I look at people eating these frozen lunches I realize the tremendous amount of packaging that goes into them. Now, I don't want to put the microwave people out of business because certainly the microwave oven is really a boon to the human race. But I want to put more sanity into the products that we put into the microwave by creating less packaging. What is the solution? Simply place foods in a plastic container that is microwaveable and used over and over again. I do it when I go and teach as far away as 50 miles from my house. I take the foods in plastic dishes and place them in the microwave at work.

FOODS IN SUPERMARKETS

When I lived in Israel during 1968-1971, I noticed that when I went to the grocery store, which in those days was a Ma and Pa shop, many foods such as bread, eggs and most other items were not prepackaged. You would bring the items to the store clerk and have him weigh them. Today most foods in the supermarket are prepackaged. Of course, some things such as fruits and vegetables are weighed before you buy them. The main problem with non-packaged items is the safety issue. Foods may become contaminated if handled by many consumers, but people have been buying their foods this way for thousands of years and they managed to survive. However, in today's world buying prepackaged foods might be dangerous due to the increase in terrorism.

Because we have to work so hard to afford the things we don't really need we don't have the time to spend on cooking at home like our ancestors many years ago. Therefore, we depend on microwaveable foods which come in throw-away plastic containers. We also depend on big gas guzzling cars even when mass transit is present. Because of our love affair with convenience and our throw-away mentality the environment continues to suffer.

CHAPTER 10
CORRUPTION

The more corrupt the state, the more numerous the laws.
Publius Cornlius Tacitus

The act of corrupting or making putrid, or state of being
corrupt or putrid; decomposition or disorganization, in the
process of putrefaction; putrefaction; deterioration[98]

INTRODUCTION

Perhaps one of humanity's greatest faults is that it resorts to corruption to get whatever it wants. Corruption is caused by greed, which allows certain individuals to accumulate wealth at the expense of other's labor and degradation of the environment. As long as certain individual humans see an opportunity to increase their own wealth they will do it no matter what the circumstances. Some people who live in countries where there is no hope for a decent paying job or even the chance to get the bare essentials, such as food and shelter, may resort to this practice because they have no choice.

Corruption occurs in virtually all the countries in the world. In China we see it in the Three Gorges Dam, which may lead to an unprecedented environmental disaster. In Indonesia and Mexico, corruption has led to deforestation and forest fires that engulfed both regions in 1997-98. In Mexico, oil spills in the Chiapas region caused pollution of the environment and destroyed local biodiversity.

The list goes on and on. The governments of their respective countries are themselves corrupt. We saw this in many countries such as Romania's Ceaucescu; Abache in Nigeria, Ferdinand Marcos in the Philippines, and Soharto of Indonesia, just to name a few.

CONCEPT

Companies feel that they can cut, chop and dig at will as long as they can make a profit. Thanks to stupid and corrupt politicians clear cutting was allowed to take place. The use of swampland for development was allowed especially along Chesapeake Bay in Maryland. This bay has abundant wildlife which is threatened with extinction because of the excessive developments there.

The best way to begin discussing the problem of corruption and how it leads to pollution is to discuss various countries in which it exists. From looking over the literature it appears that corruption and environmental degradation is rampant all over the world. Let's begin with China.

CHINA

As of this writing one of the world's greatest environmental disasters is in the making. It is the construction of the Three Gorges Dam along the Yanktze River in Southern China. It is projected to cost between $24-72 billion. The dam upon completion will generate 18,200 megawatts of power, which is a 30% greater generating capacity than the Itaipu Dam located on the border of Brazil and Paraguay. The construction of the 600 foot high dam will displace around 1.2 million people and will submerge two cities, 11 county seats, and 114 towns with its proposed 560 kilometer (350 mile) reservoir.

If the reader wants to see a simulation of what the largest town , Fengdu will look like when it gets flooded, see the September 1997 issue of National Geographic Magazine (p.17). It is apparent that corruption is running unabated. According to an article from Associated Press Online[99] Resettlement funds are being used by government officials to buy goods, and those who speak up against the project are harassed. Millions of dollars have been embezzled, and the government does not want to hear criticism of the dam.

It should be pointed out that China's projected Three Gorges Dam project is not the only project that smells of corruption.

INDONESIA

Indonesia is a country consisting of over 17,000 islands and is the world's largest archipelago. It has a landmass of 2 million square kilometers. Indonesia has the fourth largest population in the world with around 212 million inhabitants. Indonesia also had 152 million hectares of forest in 1950. In 1993 it had only 92 million hectares.Sixty million of its people depend on those forests. Yet, every year around 1.3 million hectares of forest are lost because of deforestation.[100] Much of this deforestation took place on land that was handed out to 35 players who had some political or other relations with the Suharto regime including family members and friends.

In 1997 there were many fires, which were set to clear the land. The only problem was that the rains, which normally fall in the rainforest failed to appear. Why? It is probably because of the climate change brought about by global warming. The fires, which resulted from this burning, caused a smoky haze over Singapore, Malaysia, Indonesia, and the Philippines.[101] Much of the land, when cleared, will be used for growing rice for Indonesia's increasing population.

The extent of damage to wildlife will never be known. Many animals as well as humans in this part of the world have experienced an increase in respiratory problems due to the fires. I know first hand what smoke smells like. I have been around fires when homeowners burned their leaves. Believe me it's terrible and it is difficult to breathe.

Many endemic species of plants and animals that may have had medicinal properties could have become extinct thus causing needless deaths due to lack of effective medicines. The fires at that time scared off many tourists and affected the economies of the region.

Now what is this leading to? We have an increase in human population, which must be fed. What do they do? They cut, chop, dig and burn their land to increase food production. So in the long run they will have more children thus increasing the population again so that they will have to cut, chop, dig and burn again. You figure that one out.

According to Jafar Siddiq Hamzah of the Indonesian Legal Aid Foundation Suharto has undermined the country's stability, which allowed a strong political elite to weaken a civil society. This by the way is probably indicative of much of the world's corruption

EL SALVADOR

According to the Earth Island Journal, Winter 2000 (v15, i4 p19) the government of El Salvador was held responsible for deterioration of El Spino, an aquifer, which is a major water source for residents of San Salvador.

PANAMA

Panama was cited for projects that damaged Panama Bay.

NICARAGUA

The Nicaraguan government was condemned for polluting the San Juan River and allowing the Menconic gold mine to contaminate local waters.

THE SOVIET UNION

When we see the effects of Russia's desire to increase their economy, we see a land devastated by pollution. Much of this situation is caused by corruption. In one issue of <u>National Geographic</u>[102] we see examples of the former Soviet Union devastated by environmental pollution. Much of the pollution was caused by government policies that made people do what they can to make a living even at the expense of the environment. As Al Gore points out in his book, *The Earth in the Balance,* if environmental destruction was proportional to prosperity then Eastern Europe should be economic powerhouses.[103]

BRAZIL

Chico Mendes was the organizer of the Rubber Trappers in Brazil. He fought against the greed and corruption of developers who burned and destroyed much of the rain forest. He was assassinated by one of the wealthy ranchers who was eventually caught and released. Animal smuggling is also rampant in Brazil. Brazil's environment minister [104]Jose Sarney Jr. said that "the trade in rare species was one of the biggest threats to the conservation of South America's biodiversity." The value of animals smuggled out of Brazil alone was worth around $2 billion in 2001.

PHILIPPINES

The forests in the Philippines are being decimated at an alarming rate. Ferdinand Marcos and his wife Emelda are famous for her 2000 pairs of shoes most of which were not manufactured in the Philippines.[105]

THE UNITED STATES

Perhaps one of the greatest forms of corruption takes place here in the United States under the guise of campaign financing. Is it any wonder that during presidential campaigns cries of corruption are heard regarding soft money or hard money? What do you expect if campaigns are allowed to be financed by private individuals solely for the purpose of buying votes in the donor's favor? This is a form of corruption. I remember during the Reagan presidency when environmentalists and other people wanted cars to get more miles to the gallon. The automobile companies balked at the idea so that mileages were not raised substantially. Now, over twenty years later we still see SUVs guzzling gasoline like crazy with slim hope for non fossil fuel cars in the future. Is it possible that we don't have these non-fossil fueled vehicles now because of corruption due to campaign financing? I would say definitely. Do I have facts to back me up? Not really but as of this writing there is nothing else that makes sense. What else would account for the fact that we don't have non-fossil fueled cars and have a huge reliance on fossil fueled energy sources to produce electricity? France is one of a handful of countries that gets 73% of its energy from nuclear power plants and not fossil fuels like oil and coal. But, there is a price. There is too much radioactive waste that we don't know what to do with. There are doubtless other examples of corruption in the United States.

Corruption has also contributed to forest destruction, not only in Indonesia, but in The Solomon Islands, Cameroon, Belize and Papua, New Guinea just to name a few. The forest's destruction was fostered by corrupt government policies fueled by bribery and the need to pay off foreign debts.

Many reports of this ongoing destruction stress the collateral damage, which includes damage to the surrounding forest and the building of roads, which cause further environmental damage. This also causes clashes between the local native populations and developers. Much of the responsibility was placed on the countries supporting the International money fund (IMF) such as the United States, France, and Japan. (See Table 4)

TABLE 4

The following chart lists areas around the world where the environment has been damaged due to corruption:

COUNTRY	ENVIRONMENTAL PROBLEM
Cameroon	Rain Forest destruction
Gabon	Rain Forest destruction
Congo	Rain Forest destruction
Central African Republic	Rain Forest destruction
Equatorial Guinea	Rain Forest destruction
Belize	Rain Forest destruction
Surinam	Rain Forest destruction
Guyana	Rain Forest destruction
Papua New Guinea	Rain Forest destruction
Solomon Islands	Rain Forest destruction
Brazil	Rain Forest destruction

It never ceases to amaze me how people think. Greed and corruption go hand in hand. It is obvious that I can say more about corruption but I think the point is clear. It is imperative that we in the wealthy countries help ELIMINATE CORRUPTION in poorer countries because our very lives are threatened by these practices. If corruption continues at its present rate along with the environmental consequences associated with it our very existence is imperiled. The reason for this is that the world's rainforests are the lungs of the planet by eliminating carbon dioxide and creating oxygen, which most organisms need to survive. Some organisms such as certain species of bacteria can live without oxygen. They are called anaerobic organisms.

As long as there is corruption in the world, whether from world leaders or from major corporations the environment will suffer. Corruption ensures that certain individuals remain rich while the poor remain poor, but the global environment will continue to be impoverished.

CHAPTER 11
GREED AND HUMAN VALUES

"Tax the Greedy, Not the needy"
**(A phrase located on a placard carried by
a protester in Chicago regarding higher taxes.)**

Avarice is always poor Samuel Johnson
The covetous man is ever in want
Horace, the ancient Roman poet

INTRODUCTION

Next to overpopulation perhaps the greatest threat to the environment is greed. Greed is defined in The Random House Dictionary[106] as *excessive or rapacious desire*. We see this all the time. It is obvious that there is no need to go into extreme detail here, but what I want to talk about is the relationship between greed and human values...

During the summer of 1998, there was a haze problem over the area known as Southeast Asia. This was due to fires in that part of the world set because the big conglomerates burned land to clear for use as farmland without realizing that El Nino would affect the rain patterns resulting in less rain while the fires burned out of control.[107]

I believe that the ferocity of El Nino is caused in part by anthropogenic sources (human made pollution). This is just an example of how humans interfere with our climate. Of course, greed mainly deals with human obsession over money.

Not only is greed a natural human trait, (I don't condone it), but it is amazing how our government will risk human lives because of greed. A good example of this took place at the end of the Carter Administration and the beginning of the Reagan Administration. Jimmy Carter enacted into law an "Executive Order on Federal Policy Regarding the Export of Banned or Significantly Restricted Substances" just five days before he left office.[108] A task force was set up to study the guidelines for export of hazardous goods to include pesticides, tris-treated baby clothes (found out to be carcinogenic- cancer causing) and other substances. It was obvious that the image of the United States would be tarnished if we exported products which we know are unsafe to other countries; especially those that were proven to be unsafe and caused a threat to human safety and the environment. Jimmy Carter knew that this would be a problem. But the Consumer Product Safety Commission banned sleepwear treated with tris in the United States. So, what do you think happened? Well, for one thing the American manufacturers made it available in Puerto Rico at a cut rate.[109] Why, because it was considered arrogance by the Carter Administration and the fact that American jobs would be lost not to mention that people in other less wealthy countries are not worth as much as Americans. These companies have the attitude, " Hey, lets dump on third world countries. That way we will still get our money for banned American products. What a nice move made by the Reagan Administration." This is greed without regard to global human welfare.

The idea of greed as a companion to human values is what I want to discuss in this chapter. As examples, let's discuss the following: diamonds, junk mail, car manufacturers, over-fishing, cattle ranching, the Christmas season, oil companies, developers, shark-finning, exotic pet trade, ivory, rhinoceros horns, trees.

CONCEPT

Diamonds

A good example of greed and human values is the love affair we have with diamonds. For some reason diamonds are priced very high, even though there exists an abundance of diamonds which do not justify the price. The price of diamonds are based on human values rather than the real cost which is priced artificially high when in reality they probably are worth a lot less. One thing that disturbs me is the fact that American women *must* have a diamond ring. I have mentioned to my environmental science classes that diamonds are way overpriced and when a couple gets married the money spent on diamonds could be spent on rent, food, and other life supporting necessities that married couples have to endure. There was a joke that Red Foxx told at a comedy club. He was talking about marriage and he noticed a woman in the audience wearing an engagement ring, and he asked to see the ring. Red commented on the fact that the ring looked cheap. He then asked the woman, "Did your future husband give you the *cracker jacks* that came with the ring?" [110]

There is a new term now called "conflict diamonds." These are diamonds that help fuel conflicts in Africa. These diamonds help pay for weapons which result in deaths of humans and animals and foster environmental destruction. Countries presently involved in this conflict include: Angola, The Democratic Republic of Congo, Sierra Leone and Liberia.

Junk mail

Let's take a look at some examples and how they affect our environment. Let's start with advertisers. How many of you readers out there constantly receive ads in the form of junk mail for things that you don't need? I would bet that almost 100% of you do. True there might be times when you actually buy something through those ads, but it is rare. As far as I am concerned all that paper is 100% waste. Why do we keep getting them? Simple: because the advertisers want to sell as many of the advertised items as possible. They are also betting that they will get a couple of hits every time they mail out a few hundred, for example, *Publishers Clearinghouse* from Readers Digest. They promise millions of dollars if you have the right number. Many people buy at least one of the many advertised magazines in the hope that they will have a greater chance of winning. I just send in the entry form with my number, without buying anything. Have I won? No. Do I know of other people who bought magazines in the hope that they will have a better chance of winning? Yes, but they didn't win anything either. Get the point? All those letters sent to millions of Americans just meant more death and destruction of our forests because paper is made from trees. How many trees have died just to keep the *Publishers Clearinghouse* in business?

Car manufacturers

How much money does one need? How many material things? After you ask yourself this, look around and see if you can live without an *excessive amount* of money or material goods. Let's start with a typical American symbol of wealth: the two-seater sports car. Why do we need sports cars? Well, it could be to impress girls. The trouble with sports cars is the fact that they are very expensive. What is wrong with a small car? Plenty. First it can't hold many people or a lot of luggage. It uses a large amount of gas; it takes an enormous amount of energy to produce. It is obvious that if one bought a small car like a Toyota Tercel, which uses a bit more initially in materials, but will ultimately be more energy saving because it can handle more passengers and luggage. Where does greed come in? At the beginning point: the car manufacturer. In their pursuit of more profits they will make products that they know are environmentally destructive and foolish, but in order to increase their bottom line they will build one in the hope that many wealthy people will buy them. And why will they buy them? The answer is because they were never taught to care about the environment. We have also seen that the American Way pushes people to buy and buy no matter what it does to the environment.

Overfishing

Every year the world's fishers (a term used by the U.N. to represent those that take fish from the ocean) take 90 million tons of fish out of the oceans much of which is bycatch. Bycatch is a term for organisms not wanted by fishers. Most of the bycatch is thrown back into the water either dead or dying. Our technology today allows us to use sophisticated fish tracking devices such as satellites to locate large schools of fish. We also see that in the Dutch region of the North Sea. Every square foot of sea bottom is dragged by trawlers, which destroy and deplete it of living organisms. In addition to trawling, other fishing methods are used which catch millions of tons of bycatch. These poor fish, which are trapped, usually die because their swim bladders burst during a quick ascent.[111] Humans have a similar problem when they scuba dive. They get the "bends" which means that if they ascend too quickly nitrogen in the form of bubbles will be released in their bloodstream causing embolisms (moving clots), which can prove fatal.

Why do we overfish? The answer is because we have to feed our growing population. Also, fishers want a huge profit just like most people so that they can lead a" problem-free" life, which generally means either a healthy or financially secure one, as well as being able to feed themselves and plan for their retirement.

Greed plays a major role in the overfishing of organisms. For an example: A single 750 lb bluefin tuna fish sold at a Tokyo market for $83,500. That's right, $83,500. Put another way: that is equivalent to 8.35% of $1,000,000. Not bad for one individual fish. Common sense says that if a person hears about this he will say to himself, "Hey, if the other guy can get that much for a single fish, I, too, can become a millionaire by doing it." Then guess what folks? Another gold rush! (Gold here is a metaphor for large blue fin tuna). Here we have seen how greed helps lead to environmental pollution.

Cattle ranching

One of the most destructive and unnatural endeavors that humans participate in is the raising of cattle. Many people, especially those that live in the industrialized West like to eat meat. I admit that a nice steak tastes great but, and I do mean but, it is bad for the environment. How you ask? Simple. The raising of beef requires lots of resources. 16 pounds of grain is required to produce one pound of meat or the amount of grain needed to feed 32 people. By raising cattle we are feeding them the grain, which should be intended for the millions of starving humans worldwide.[112] Consider the productivity of just an acre of fertile land. It "can produce 40,000 pounds [20 short tons] of potatoes, 30,000 lbs (15 short tons) of carrots; 50,000 pounds (25 short tons) of tomatoes or 250 pounds (a little over .1 short ton) of beef."[113] It is obvious that 250 pounds of beef is a far cry from thousands of tons of vegetables which can go further in feeding people.

Many of these cattle are raised on CAFOs (concentrated animal feeding operations). This is very bad not only for the environment, but also for humans who may contact many diseases associated with these animals such as a variant of "Mad Cow" disease (Creutzfelt-Jakob disease). The effect of tons of manure on the soil is very devastating too because of the formation of a nitrogen cloud (too much nitrogen). This nitrogen most likely has a tendency to disturb the normal microbial life in the soil.

Another aspect of raising cattle is the overuse of antibiotics, protein concentrates and even ground up cow parts as food. This means feeding ruminants (cows) to other cows. Cows are meant to eat grass and not grains because it interferes with their digestive system thus causing prolapses. Prolapses result in internal organs leaving the cow's body; a situation demanding immediate veterinary attention.

Methane gas, which accounts for 18% of all greenhouse gases get emitted from the cow's digestive systems and pollutes the air.

Greed plays a major role in cattle ranching because ranchers want to maximize their profits and in order to do this they must mistreat and raise too many animals in confined spaces which is not healthy for the cows or for the humans who will consume them.

Christmas season

One of the best examples of greed masquerades under the celebration of Christmas (the birth of Christ). Now, this may seem heretical but let's examine the facts. Right after Thanksgiving newspaper headlines state whether this will be a good shopping year or a bad shopping year. Financial experts predict whether the Christmas season can make or break a business. As a matter of fact, according to the media, the busiest day of the year is the day after Thanksgiving.

If you go shopping two months before Christmas in virtually any shopping mall in the United States, you will see that during the daytime normal business hours, 9-5, the stores and mall corridors are virtually empty. But at night they are alive with people. However, during the weeks proceeding Christmas the stores are overflowing. Try finding a parking space at one of those malls. Many malls in the United States are built out in the middle of nowhere, and the only way to get there is by car. This to me is the most absurd choice for locations for a mall because of its inaccessibility to mass transit, thus causing more gas to be consumed in getting to the mall while adding twenty pounds of carbon dioxide per gallon of gas into the atmosphere (Green house effect, maybe?) in order to buy things which in the process of their manufacturer not only add more CO_2, but more pollution. It is nice that the planet has a holiday like Christmas. But is it right that because of our traditions (see Chapter 23) we have to destroy the planet? I don't think so.

There is a radio show called, "Those Were the Days" hosted by Chuck Shaden, on Saturday afternoons in the Chicago, Illinois area. Old radio shows dating back to the thirties are rebroadcast, in their entirety. Mr. Shaden chose them to match the time of year they originally debuted. For December many of the shows had a Christmas theme. It was interesting to listen to old Ozzie and Harriet and Jack Benny episodes in which the main theme was Christmas shopping. One Jack Benny program comes to mind in particular. In this show Jack is buying a gift for his announcer Don Wilson, and due to the confusion about what Don really wants Jack gets frustrated because he has to keep returning the original gifts to find something else. This in turn frustrates the sales person. It is remarkable that these shows revolving around shopping for Christmas continue to fit into today's cultural values. Now I don't see much wrong with shopping for gifts, but I do think that something is wrong when we continue to emphasize our obsession with material goods at the price of the planet's health. Perhaps better gifts would be a hug to the hug-less, a home to the homeless, an anti-smoking system for heavy smokers, perhaps a smile to the sad, and perhaps a lifetime certificate for free healthcare. In this way gifts will have much more meaning and will have less impact on our environment.

Oil companies

If you were to look at oil companies, you will find that they are very greedy. Most people that I have talked to seem to agree that it is the oil companies that prevent research in solar and other non-polluting forms of energy. They appear to be interested in one thing only and that is money no matter what the environmental cost.

If we look at the Republican administrations over the past 50 years, we will find that solar research and alternative energy sources have been overlooked because of a greater interest in developing more oil fields no matter where they are located. A case in point is the possibility of pumping oil out of the Arctic National Wildlife Refuge (ANWR). Congress denied oil companies from drilling in ANWR a few years ago but just the idea that oil exists there lit up the eyes of the oil executives because they saw dollars and more dollars without even thinking about the environmental consequences. So in 2005 the Republican led Congress showed more interest in drilling in ANWR.

In 1973, during the Nixon administration (Republican) there were long lines in front of gasoline stations because of a perceived notion that there was a gasoline shortage. If that was the case why didn't we try to develop better energy sources at that time?

When Jimmy Carter (Democrat) was near the end of his presidency (1980) he installed solar panels to generate electricity in the White House. His successor, Ronald Reagan (Republican) tore it down when he entered the White House. When G.H.W. Bush (Republican) was president, we went to war in Kuwait because Iraq took over Kuwait's oil wells. During the Clinton years, (Democrat) there was not much talk of new energy sources but we did not go to war against oil-rich countries. In 2001 and in 2003, the new non-elected president G.W. Bush (Old Global Warming Himself...) went to war against Afghanistan and Iraq.

It is obvious that oil is destroying the world mainly because those greedy people in charge don't care about the environment or the political costs of oil. They only care about their bottom line. Yes folks, money and more money. This to them appears more important than the environment even though with our know-how we can have a better economy without depending on oil.

Developers

Let's turn next to DEVELOPERS (the dirtiest word in the environmental lexicon). As we will soon see this is not strictly an American phenomenon but one which may have been enhanced by America.

Development such as conversion of prime cropland to non-farmland uses is taking place all over the world.[114] These non-farmland conversions include residential development, industrial development, highway construction and golf courses. Only 10% of land in China is arable, compared to the United States, which has 20% arable land and one fourth of China's population. However, much of its land is marginal at best and yet developers are developing it. It is predicted that China will have around 22 million cars by 2010, compared to only 2 million in 1995. (Financial

Times, Nov. 23, 1994) This means more pavements for roads, which results in more soil drainage problems.

How many times have we seen developers cut, chop and dig up land so that they can build on it? Many times. Again, here we see greed at its peak. Money or the pursuit of money will drive anyone to destroy the environment.

We see nice expensive homes built on what was once farmland. Now it is homes and golf courses. We also see this type of scenario played out on areas with submerged aquatic vegetation (SAV) such as the Chesapeake Bay. I used to live in Annapolis, in the state of Maryland, and during my few years there, 1976-1982, I noticed huge tracts of shore land being developed for building expensive town homes. Some of them were not even pretty in my view, but because they were located on the shoreline wealthy people would buy them.[115] Not only has this land been taken away from the general public, but the non-human organisms (an organism is any living thing) such as aquatic plants, algae and fish, had their homes taken away, so that only those rich human residents who live there have access to the area not to mention… guards at the front gate of the developments to prevent unwanted humans from entering.

Shark finning

Perhaps one of the greatest atrocities being committed as I write this book is "shark-finning." What exactly is shark-finning, how is it done and why is it done? Shark-finning is the act of capturing sharks with hooks, bringing them on board a boat, cutting off their fins while they are alive and then throwing them back into the water where they are left to die. It is done so a few people can get a bowl of shark fin soup for the price of $150 or more,

Since the movie *Jaws*, sharks have been given a bad rap. Sure a few humans are bitten by sharks but attacks are few and far between. Sharks are very useful to the oceans. Since they are tertiary consumers they eat primary and secondary consumers (other fish and organisms), thus keeping them in check. When we destroy the shark populations we are interfering with the balance of nature. This type of situation is not only true in the oceans but on land as well where we hunt predators to extinction. We see that the deer population increases because humans have decimated their natural predator, the coyotes and wolves, which are tertiary consumers. The deer are primary consumers because they eat only plants.

The exotic pet trade

Another example of greed is the problem of people importing animals from other countries merely for profit without any regard for the animal's welfare. A good example of this is the trade in exotic fish. According to ABC news,[116] fantastically beautiful aquatic organisms taken from reefs around the world are being sold to aquariums, hobbyists and kids. Cyanide is used to stun the fish so they float to the surface. They are then collected and then shipped to various locations. It is estimated that 75% of the captured organisms die in transit.

Here we see greed at its worst. Human beings place values on animals and objects that probably have no materialistic value to the animals but only reproductive value which means more profits. Animals appear beautiful to us mainly because of their colored feathers such as in parrots and other birds. In nature, colors are used for many purposes such as attracting suitable mates and as warning coloration (aposematic coloring). This means that by being red or some other color they indicate to predators that they are poisonous to eat.

Outer coverings, such as the fur on mammals, which are meant to protect the animals against the harsh elements, are valued by humans for their beauty. Even in the United States, there are many people who wear fur solely as a fashion statement without any consideration for the animal's welfare. Sometimes when it gets cold in Chicago I see women wearing real mink coats and I approach them and say, "You shouldn't be wearing a mink coat because it is meant to keep the mink warm." They reply that it keeps "me" warm. The wearing of fur is yet another example of human vanity.

Other examples of this senseless exploitation of animals purely for monetary reasons include panda pelts that can sell for as much as $10,000 and a live Panda can earn his trapper $112,000 (in 1990 dollars).[117]

Other values placed on animal products are as follows:

Polar bears can sell for $6000; a saguaro cactus found in the American Southwest can bring in $15,000, and an ocelot coat can fetch about $40,000. These are just some examples of prices that people will get for these animals and their products. (These prices are in 1990 dollars).[118]

Ivory

We constantly hear about elephants being in danger. There are two basic reasons why this is occurring. The first cause is that they are in competition for the same space as the ever-expanding human population. Elephants require an enormous amount of food every day. What do they eat? Well they eat plants, which is on land increasingly used by humans for agriculture and settlements. Humans see their crops being destroyed by elephants which threatens their livelihood.

The second cause is the quest for ivory. Ivory can fetch from $72- to over $400 per kilogram. One kilogram is equal to 2.206 pounds.[119] Again, the price of ivory, which is a human value, will encourage people to poach elephants. Ivory is used for many things that humans can live without. Objects made of ivory include the following: billiard balls, handles, piano keys, decorative objects, electrical appliances and in airplanes.

Rhinorceros horns

African rhino horn is worth around $1500 per 3.5 pounds and Asian rhino horn is worth around $14,000 per 3.5 pounds. Rhino horn is used as an aphrodisiac and for dagger handles. Again, as we have always seen the pursuit of money is the driving force for Rhino horns. Humans determine the price. As we move up the ladder buyers, distributors and other middle-men make the most money out of this slaughter.

Prices are so high that just killing one rhinoceros is enough money for a whole year for the poacher. This poaching is yet another example of how greed and human values wreck havoc with endangered species.

Trees

What is the value of a tree? Notice I said value and I didn't say monetary value. Trees are very important for the stability of the planet. They of course produce the oxygen that we breathe; they act as homes for animals, plants, bacteria, fungi and other microscopic organisms. Trees take up carbon dioxide (CO_2), their roots stabilize the soil and prevent erosion; they supply water to the atmosphere by a process called transpiration (see glossary). As for human needs, trees supply the following: wood for homes, furniture products; paper and fibers, boats and other products. Without trees the environment would be in terrible shape. We can basically do without wood products but because of our human values we love and use wood.

How much money is enough

The July 2000 issue of Forbes Magazine mentioned the worth of 208 individuals.[120] The total worth of those individuals came out to be over $1,184,300,000,000. That is over one trillion dollars. Yes T is for Trillion. Yes, one trillion is a 1 followed by 12 zeros. Do these 208 people really need this amount of money? To understand this number in yet another way 1.18 trillion is close to one fifth of a light year in miles (light travels at a speed of 286,000 miles a second or 300,000,000 meters per second). Yes, a light year is the distance that light travels in one year. If this money were divided up equally worldwide then we can preserve much of our natural environment. Instead of having people chop up their environment in order to eke out a living perhaps these rich people can help the less fortunate.

Even the government gets involved with greed. According to an article in the Chicago Sun Times from Dec. 7, 2000, the Army Corps of engineers skewed numbers to get projects approved costing billions in order to expand locks on the Mississippi and Illinois rivers. It appeared that politically connected shipping and agribusiness companies were given preferential access to the process.[121]

Greed is a trait found in most people. Speaking for myself, I noticed that when the temptation is there to be greedy I have to fight it. I succeed most of the time. The trouble is that many people do not. This greed factor is instilled in society as we have seen from corporations on down to every individual. It is important to be aware of this trait and fight it, so that we don't continue to pillage and plunder the planet's bounty, which keeps us alive.

CHAPTER 12
IGNORANCE, STUPIDITY OR BOTH

Against stupidity, the gods are helpless.
Schiller [122]

Genius has limitations: stupidity is boundless
anonymous

The two most common elements in the
universe are hydrogen and stupidity.
Harlan Ellison

INTRODUCTION

This chapter deals with ignorance, *defined as a lack of knowledge or common sense.* It also deals with stupidity which is defined as *"marked by a lack of intelligence or care; foolish or careless."*[123] People are often plain ignorant or stupid about doing simple things. We see this displayed in everyday life, especially when it comes to salaries and lifestyles of celebrities. Much of the world's public is preoccupied with getting food, shelter and survival while those of the wealthy Western nations are preoccupied with totally inconsequential events such as the O.J. Simpson trial (1994). This preoccupation in its own way helped to degrade the environment by using vast amounts of energy and paper (briefs, books etc.) and distracting people from more important issues like emerging diseases caused by deforestation and global warming.

This was demonstrated at the end of the second trial of O.J. Simpson by a story on ABC's program *20/20 about* poaching of animals in Africa's

Endoke Forest. However, the main interest was most likely the victory of Fred Goldman, the father of one of the victims, which was also aired on that same program. Likewise, most of the mainstream newspapers were not concerned with the Endoke Forest while the poaching continued unabated, but with the outcome of O.J's second trial.

This single-minded focus shows that we have a skewed sense of priorities. The point that I wish to make is that OJ's trial was the sole obsession of Americans at that time. The media dwells on events that occupy people's leisure time, leaving little time for more important issues such as the environment; which is the life support system of ALL living organisms. If Americans would have spent as much time on the environment as they spent on the trial, perhaps there would not be a need for a book such as this.

Now with America being *"Bushwacked"* our environmental ignorance will continue unabated. Unless those ecologically minded speak up and force their points down the throats of the environmentally ignorant politicians, policy in this area will not change until it's too late. If we don't care about our environs then we don't have a future. For those readers who doubt this, check the media for news about newly emerging diseases, droughts, famines and continued pollution of the biosphere (the Earth's living area).

CONCEPT

Let me give you a good example of this ignorance that I have personally encountered.

I live in Skokie. Twice a week I have to teach at a college which is 50 miles from my house. I take a car, two trains and a bus to get to the campus. When I drive to the train station early in the morning, which is less than a mile from my house, I always see a woman who has a six cylinder car parked with the engine running regardless of the weather. The car continues to idle until about five minutes before the train is due to arrive. I always wondered why she kept the engine running since the temperature was not extreme in any manner. I decided to ask her. The reason she gave me was because she was cold. Nevertheless, I wonder if being cold is a good reason to keep the engine running while waiting for the train. Running engines still produce carbon dioxide and other poisons which are emitted into the atmosphere. There is a heater in the little shelter that is present at the station where this woman could be almost as comfortable waiting for the train.

The following is a list of common acts of ignorance which cause people to degrade the environment.

SECTION ONE-IGNORANCE

IGNORANCE NUMBER ONE
CFCS AND OZONE DEPLETION

One of the greatest threats presently facing all life on the planet is loss of the protective ozone layer. Ozone, symbolized as O_3, prevents ultraviolet light from penetrating the atmosphere. Ultraviolet light is responsible for skin cancers and lower plant productivity (fixation of carbon or photosynthesis). What does ultraviolet light mean? First of all let's discuss the visible spectrum of light. The visible spectrum of light that we normally see when a prism breaks it down consists of the following colors: red, orange, yellow, green, blue, indigo, and violet (indigo is similar to blue but is probably put in there because it begins with a vowel and the acronym, ROY G BIV, which is easy to pronounce and remember). Visible light consists of wave lengths between 380 nanometers which is the violet range, up to 750 nanometers which is the red range. Those wavelengths of light between 210 nanometers to roughly 400 nanometers are considered ultraviolet light.

In the last century humanity was blessed with air conditioners both in our homes and cars. Air conditioning uses a gas called CFCs or chloroflurocarbons (See appendix VI). These chemicals were once thought to be a boon for humankind because they were efficient in keeping us cool during the hot summer months in homes, workplaces and cars. However, it wasn't realized until the 1990's that CFCs were depleting the protective ozone layer, which is located in the upper stratosphere of the earth. For the discoverers of this phenomenon, Mario Molina, F. Sherwood Rowland, and Paul Crutzen, the Nobel Prize for chemistry was given in 1995. When CFCs were invented they were touted as being a miracle chemical because they worked and were considered inert (i.e. did not react). This is a prime example of ignorance since it wasn't the fact that the inventors were stupid, they just didn't know of the consequences of using CFC. Now we see that mainly because of CFCs our protective ozone layer is disintegrating and skin cancers may be on the rise along with lowered photosynthetic rates, which in the long run, means less food or no food for our burgeoning population.

IGNORANCE NUMBER TWO
EARTHQUAKES AND LACK OF COMMON SENSE

In January 1994, a 6.6 magnitude earthquake hit Los Angeles and other parts of Southern California causing dozens of deaths and billions of dollars in damage. During that earthquake many freeways collapsed causing major headaches for commuters, disrupting businesses and causing innumerable financial losses to individuals. In addition to all the smog and shootings and excessive draughts, it was the last thing Los Angeles needed.

Now whose *fault* is it that the residents of that part of the country appear to be cursed by nature and human induced misery much of which is dependent on cars, which need freeways that collapse during earthquakes. It is obvious if there weren't any freeways they would not collapse. Our car culture demands plenty of freeways for motorists to have increased mobility in order to work, shop, play, eat and enjoy other leisure activities. It is also obvious that if they didn't have many cars that run on gas there would not be the tremendous amount of smog associated with cars. Motorists probably feel that putting up with smog is just a mild inconvenience compared to not having a car. Moreover, the increase in smog is directly related to increases in asthma and other respiratory illnesses.

In May of 1994, the Santa Monica Freeway, which was damaged by the earthquake, was repaired 75 days earlier than the schedule called for. Who benefited from this? Governor Wilson, of course, who was the republican Governor of California, at the time. Is it just a coincidence that he had the highway rebuilt earlier than planned while he was running for governor for a second term? Or was he too environmentally uninformed to make people realize that a form of mass transit in addition to the highway would have been definitely better than highway construction by itself. By assuming what the environmentally challenged people want, both the environment and the health of citizens were compromised for supposed economic and political reasons. If the governor really cared about the citizens of California, he had the perfect opportunity to install a mass transit system, which would have cut road congestion, smog, car accidents, stress levels, and overt environmental damage.

IGNORANCE NUMBER THREE
WHAT'S WRONG WITH INSECTS AND WHY INSECT ZAPPERS?

Insect zappers have purple lights and electrodes. When an insect hits the electrode it is electrocuted and we hear the sizzle of a dying insect. It never ceases to amaze me that people don't understand that if you kill one insect you are not doing much to eliminate the problem. More will come and then if you kill them, still more will come .That does not solve the problem. First of all the insects were here first. People who live in homes with back yards should realize that they bought their home to live in the country to be closer to nature. They forget that the country is filled with insects. Why zap the insects? Well, it seems easy for them because stores make bug zappers readily available. Plus the zappers make an impressive display so it appears they are solving the problem. Studies of the zappers show, however, that the bugs being killed are those attracted to light. Since most people do not give off light the bugs that bother us do not get killed by the zappers so that the problem remains. Although I would like to point out that bug zappers, cruel as they may be, are probably more humane than other types of insect traps, such as fly paper and liquids. It would be advisable for everyone to take a course in ecology so that they can understand that all organisms are important even though some of them, including disease causing bacteria and mosquitoes which spread them (vectors), do not seem beneficial. Insects are part of the food chain for other organisms, and by zapping them we may be causing starvation of those that prey on insects such as bats, which have been incredibly maligned by vampire movies and the fear of getting rabies, even though they play a major role in maintaining the world's ecosystems. [124]

I am quite amazed these days at the ignorance of the human race. From the time we are born, especially those of us who are born in the "Developed Countries" we act as if nature does not matter. Case in point: We have to kill insects and mice and just about any other animal that we humans do not consider pets. When I go to home improvement stores and grocery stores I pass aisles that contain mouse traps, fly paper, traps which contain poison which when eaten causes a horrible painful death for the unlucky animal that ingests it, as well as other chemicals which are meant to kill non-human organisms. Ask yourself, who or what was here first? The animals of course! So, why do we kill them? Because we are so concerned with diseases like AIDS, insect borne encephalitis (brain inflammation) and rabies that we have demonized all animals that are not considered pets (notice that the word pets uses the same letters as pest). True, especially in restaurants, we have to be concerned with mice mainly because of their droppings but as a rule, a few mice in the house will not cause much damage and besides, it's nice just to have company.

Figure 8 Here we see an insect zapper. This one
contains a lure to attract and kill insects.

IGNORANCE NUMBER FOUR
THE LOW PRICE OF GASOLINE IN THE UNITED STATES

During the spring of 2000, gas prices in the Illinois-Wisconsin area reached almost $2.50 per gallon (WOW!) People all over the area were complaining and the Illinois governor and President Clinton joined the chorus. I, myself, was telling people just the opposite, that gasoline prices should be double that price, and perhaps even more. Why? Because we are wasteful with our natural resources and most people don't realize it. By us driving our SUVs, instead of walking we are using energy at a rapid rate, thus destroying our environment. An example, is the demand by oil interests to drill in the Arctic National Wildlife Refuge (ANWR). It was unfortunate for the planet that oil was found there. It was more unfortunate that we let who was then Congressman Frank Murkowski (now Governor of Alaska) know about it because he was willing to cut, chop and dig it up just so he could appease his Republican constituents. Once again, the familiar pattern of appeasing political and business interests takes precedent over concern for the environment and common sense. The public gets fooled with politicians advocating low oil prices. Low prices encourage more fuel consumption, larger vehicles, traffic problems and, of course, more air pollution.

If gasoline were cheaper, what would we do? Would we help other countries such as Haiti have a higher standard of living as we do? Would we even help our poorer American citizens? No, we would probably run to the malls and buy other things which took lots of oil energy to make, and then throw them out when we get tired of them. Nothing like a little cynicism, huh? It's as if the oil embargo of 1973 never happened, or that we hadn't even gone to war in Kuwait in 1991. These historical events never seemed to have happened because we were blinded by our love affair with oil. We learn very little from past experiences especially when we deal with oil and big companies that have essentially acted as if they were independent countries. Almost every talk show lately is talking about the price of gasoline with very little talk going towards alternative resources such as the most promising and pollution-free source of energy: the sun (solar). You know readers; it makes me think that most people don't pay any attention to the sun. It is just there for their amusement. They don't realize that the sun supplies the planet with food and life and that, maybe, just maybe, we should use it to power our economy.

IGNORANCE NUMBER FIVE
SUV'S AND CHEAP GASOLINE

Where is common sense? As we all hear in the media, SUVs are growing in popularity while their gas mileage is declining. We are fighting a war in Iraq because of oil. If we didn't have these gas guzzlers then we would not have to be in Iraq. Just look at the gasoline mileage from an SUV sticker that I photographed in a new car lot. (See figure 9)

Figure 9. Here we see a picture of a sticker from an SUV. Notice that the mileage is 15 miles per gallon in the city and only 20 mpg on the highway. That is pretty low mileage compared to other available cars. (Photo by author)

On the other hand many of you are probably asking if gasoline were $5 per gallon how would the poor afford to get to work? The answers are the following: take mass transit if available: if they have to drive to work, convince their bosses to give them an increase in salary to cover gasoline increase; tell them to buy gas efficient cars instead of 6-8 cylinder cars which are gas guzzlers. Will these solutions work? Probably not. So what do we do? Well, we must spend time and money going full force to invest in alternative energy immediately, and I mean immediately. Will we do it? Probably not. For possible solutions to this problem see the last chapter on solutions (chapter 24) on eliminating fossil fuels.

SECTION TWO-STUPIDITY

At the time of this writing I am three months past my 54th birthday. During my 54 years, I have seen lots of stupidity. After beginning work on this book, I realized that many things that we take for granted are really stupid things that result in pollution. Let me give you some examples. Let's call each of these stupidities.

STUPIDITY NUMBER ONE
THE PERCEIVED PRESIDENT WHO IS AGAINST FAMILY PLANNING

In January of 2001, George Bush was inaugurated as the 43rd president of the United States. (Many pundits believed that he really lost, but our Supreme Court by a 5-4 vote ruled otherwise). One of the first things that

Bush did was to restrict funds for family planning in developing nations. Now, as was mentioned in the introduction, perhaps the biggest problem on the planet is that of human overpopulation. In fact, most of the environmental problems are caused by humanity and their overwhelming numbers. Do we really need more children who may eventually die of hunger before the age of six as we have seen in Ethiopia? Do we need passersby to find unwanted newborn infants in dumpsters? Unfortunately the plight of unwanted children is a persistent social problem in both the developing world as well as in richer countries. George W. Bush appears to be interested in appeasing the far right constituency of the United States rather than the majority of U.S. citizens. We will wind up paying the price for these extra unwanted mouths-to-feed by having to ship grain and soldiers overseas as we did in Somalia in the late1980s. World overpopulation in many developing countries is contributing to depletion of fish stocks, elimination of arable land and forests, deterioration of groundwater, the melting of polar ice caps, and global warming. All these environmental insults may just lead to the Earth being uninhabitable for all of its citizens. The Bush administration just doesn't get it.

STUPIDITY NUMBER TWO
FLOATING GAMBLING CASINOS

I teach at Waubonsee College, which is located in Sugar Grove, Illinois. In traveling from my house to Waubonsee Community College, (I take the train by the way) I pass the Hollywood Casino,in Aurora, a town close to Chicago (around 50 miles away or 80 kilometers). What is ridiculously stupid about this situation is the fact that casinos in Illinois, and probably in other states, have to be offshore. This means that gamblers lose their money while on a cruise to nowhere. Yes, that's right! The boat has to move a mile or so, and then come back to shore because of the geography of the area. This means that fuel has to be burned while polluting the air with carbon dioxide and other organic chemicals, while the gamblers are losing their money. In addition to this, we fought a war with Iraq because they attacked Kuwait because of its oil, the stuff that makes these boats run. Did soldiers, (possibly relatives of these very gamblers) animals and civilians die just so we can have oil powering these boats?

How could presumably intelligent legislators in Springfield, the capital of Illinois, allow gambling ONLY on moving riverboats, hence the term offshore? Stupid and ridiculous. The politicians who instituted this rule are evidently catalysts for proliferating the bastions of environmental ignorance nation wide. In all fairness, the riverboats now, in 2004, at least in Aurora, are permanently docked and do not leave the shore. Maybe the politicians lost their bottles of stupidity pills.

STUPIDITY NUMBER THREE
OVER-FISHING

Trying to catch as much fish as possible even though it means depleting fish stocks is a form of stupidity. You may consider over-fishing a form of poaching. The reason why people are over fishing is probably due to economic reasons. The need to make a living, as well as industry demands have encouraged this activity. It is obvious that if people don't earn enough they will do anything to get money. This of course is not only true with fishers but with many other endeavors that involve over harvesting the world's resources. What amazes me is that technology allows countries to over-fish with impunity. New satellites and other sensing devices allow ships to hunt schools of fish and thus encourage over fishing. Satellite fishing may be a boon for the fishing industry but it is detrimental to the marine ecosystems because it interferes with the food chain by killing unwanted organisms (bycatch). Here we see that technology helps humans to destroy our planet.[125]

Let's look at the anchovy catch between the years 1964 and 1971. Between these years Peruvian anchovies accounted for 20% of the total fish catch. Biologists from the Food and Agricultural Organization (FAO) warned that this harvest was exceeding the estimated sustainable yield. Disaster struck in 1972 when an El Nino event struck. This destroyed the anchovy industry because the anchovy population was already decimated by over fishing. Since 1983 the industry has recovered slightly.

STUPIDITY NUMBER FOUR
THREE HUNDRED YEARS OF AIR POLLUTION
BEFORE ADDRESSING IT AS A SERIOUS PROBLEM

It's been over 300 years since John Evelyn wrote a book on air pollution and we still have this problem in today's world. He lived in England between 1620-1706 and wrote a book about air pollution in London entitled *Fumifugium or The Inconvenience of the Aer and Smoak of London* (1661) (This is old English). He mentioned the fact at that time that coal was brought in which contained high sulfur content and was used in breweries, salt and sope-boylers, lime burners and in other industries. According to Evelyn, churches looked old, clothes and furnishing were fouled, paintings were yellowed, bees were killed and human health and well being were ruined because of air (aer) pollution.[126]

As in Evelyn's time we continue to be complacent about air pollution. Meanwhile, asthma and other respiratory problems are increasing at a great rate in cities such as Los Angeles, Bangkok, Thailand and Mexico City (some environmental books suggest that we change the name to Make-Sicko City). How come we waited so long to even address the problem? In my opinion, we were not interested in cleaning up the air because business interests are a priority instead of the environment. Cough! Cough!

STUPIDITY NUMBER FIVE
THE FAILURE OF THE UNITED STATES CONGRESS
TO RATIFY THE NUCLEAR TEST BAN TREATY.

One of the most horrifying events in human history occurred in 1945 with the invention of the atomic bomb. You would think that killing with bullets and conventional bombs would be enough. However, bombs of incredible mass destructive power such as the atomic bombs dropped on Hiroshima and Nagasaki became weapons of mass destruction not only for humans but also for the environment. Of course in order to produce these abominable weapons they had to be tested.

It wasn't so bad that the United States with its intelligent and reliable personnel was the first to build and test these weapons, but the clincher came when other countries started building them because we had them- namely the Soviet Union. We outspent the Soviet Union into oblivion during the Cold War. Now that the Cold War is over why are atomic weapons still being tested? Because the military industrial complex is still a thriving business. It is no coincidence that when congressional bills are proposed that would limit or eliminate a certain class of weapon, they are usually defeated.

During the week of October 14, 1999 in a purely partisan vote, Congress failed to ratify the Comprehensive Nuclear Test Ban Treaty (CTBT) by a vote of 51-48.[127] This treaty was previously negotiated by the United States and its NATO allies. A total of 67 votes are needed for passage. Most republicans voted against the treaty while the majority of democrats voted in favor of the treaty. The republicans' reason for voting against the treaty was politically motivated and directed against President Bill Clinton. It was obvious that with Clinton in the White House for seven years, the republicans wanted to embarrass him in front of the world.

Once again insignificant human interests interfere with common sense when dealing with the world's environment. The importance of this treaty was that it would have prevented environmental damage by radiation exposure to plants, animals, bacteria, fungi and all other biota and non-biota (Biota is a term meaning living organisms).

STUPIDITY NUMBER SIX
KILLING LIVE TREES TO BURY DEAD PEOPLE

Perhaps one of the greatest injustices to befall nature is the human custom of burying people in caskets, formerly called coffins, generally made out of wood. Here, a live tree is cut down to house a dead person. Silly isn't it? Did you know that trees supply us with oxygen, and they also take away carbon dioxide (CO_2) from the air and serve as homes to animals, fungi and bacteria?

Another thing to be aware of is the fact that many people on this planet sleep on hard floors made of mud while dead middle class or rich people in America have a nice soft bed to rest on permanently until they decompose. you know the word for that? It is called "dirt nap". Only on this planet do rich dead people sleep better than live poor people. Maybe the planet Mars has the same problem. Think about it.

Figure 10. Here we see two typical caskets made out of trees that once were alive. (Photo by author. Courtesy of the Weinstein Funeral Home, Wilmette, Illinois)

As can be seen by Figure 10, there are two caskets: one is totally finished and one is unfinished. Maybe the unfinished casket will remain unfinished even with a body in it because the person who ordered it for their loved one feels that he has an environmental responsibility by not allowing the chemicals of the finished casket to destroy the decomposition process by killing the microorganisms involved.

Nature replenishes the soil by decomposing the dead animals and plants. The organisms involved are bacteria and fungi (there is an old saying, "Old *composers* never die, they just *decompose*).

STUPIDITY NUMBER SEVEN
TALES OF THREE OF THE WORLD'S MOST STUPIDEST WOMEN
(The third being called *"Of mice and one woman"*)

I am going to recount three stories that show the stupidity of people when it comes to the environment. These three stories that I intend to relate to you involve three of the most stupid women that I have ever met (men are stupid also, but in this case these three stories involve women).

TALE #1

Let's start with stupid woman number one. I teach at various colleges in the Chicago area. One day I was taking the commuter train called Metra from the Edgebrook Station to Union Station in downtown Chicago. It is only about a 22 minute trip. During the normal work week there are many people on the train coming from the North suburbs of Chicago. Many people read the two major newspapers, the Chicago Tribune and the Chicago Sun Times and others such as USA Today, the New York Times and The Wall Street Journal. When almost everyone left the train, I found a copy of the Sun Times left on the overhead rack which is usually the case at Union Station. I saw a woman behind me and told her that I was taking the paper to read and that it was a form of recycling. She suggested that I buy my own newspaper. I told her that this is really a form of recycling and asked her if she reads newspapers that were left on the train. She says that she buys them. OK, you figure. Needless to say I mentioned this incident to my Environmental Science Class, and they got a kick out of this.

TALE #2

The second story takes place in Miami, Florida. It was Christmas break time at all of the colleges that I teach at. I decided to take five days off during Christmas to see my aunt and uncle who spend the winter in Lake Worth, which is a town about 65 miles north of Miami Beach. One day while I was there I took a local commuter train called the Tri –Rail which was a fantastic bargain, at $9.25 round trip which included buses from the Miami Station to Miami Beach. I went to downtown Miami and was looking at the tourist stores. I entered one of them and noticed among the souvenirs which included plates, mugs, and key chains etc. depicting Florida, and a shelf that had alligator heads. (See photo below-fig 11). Yes, real alligator heads that were shining because they had shellac. I mentioned to the sales clerk, a woman, that I didn't think that it was nice selling actual heads of once-alive alligators. I also mentioned that it was wrong to kill them just so they can be turned into souvenirs. OK, now hear it comes. She said that "Alligators kill people too, you know." (I must admit that this incident reminds me of a story about a man who was on a bus in Chicago. He was sitting next to a woman who was tearing up the local newspaper and throwing the pieces out the window. The man asked the woman, "Why are you throwing the newspaper pieces out the window"? The woman replied, "To keep the alligators away". The man replied," I don't see any alligators". The woman replied, "You see, it must be working"). Needless to say I almost hit the floor with shock and felt like throwing her to the alligators because of her attitude. Yes, it may be true that alligators kill people but I doubt that they kill with weapons and actually hunt people down as we do with alligators. I must admit that I didn't see any alligators walking the Miami Beach streets.

Figure 11: Souvenir Shop located in Miami Beach, Florida
with alligator heads for sale. (Photo by author)

TALE #3

This third tale is perhaps one of the most interesting of the three and I have thus named it "Of mice and one woman" after John Steinbeck's famous novel "Of Mice and Men." The true story goes like this. When I first began teaching at Waubonsee College in 1991, Tuesdays were divided up with a one hour class in the morning and a lab later on in the afternoon. In between class and lab I would rest, read and have lunch. I was resting in the teachers lounge, lying on the couch when I overheard a secretary saying "Hey, did you hear what so and so did (name I don't remember) with two mice that she found on a glue trap? She took them and threw them in the garbage alive." Immediately, my ears perked up and I asked the secretary to show me which garbage pale she threw them in. She took me there and fortunately for the mice, they were in a clean bag. The two mice were squeaking, although one of which had his eye poked out. I immediately took out the glue trap and brought the mice down to the prep lab and tried freeing them. I had to do it gently because I was afraid to break their fragile legs. About 45 minutes later after using acetone to free the glue from one of the mice a lab assistant came over and told me that he will finish because I had to go to lab. After class I asked the lab assistant if he was successful and he said that he had to sacrifice the mouse that had his eye poked out (sacrifice is the polite term used by biologists which means "killed") but he saved the other one. He showed me the saved mouse and it was placed in a small fish tank minus the water. I then put leaves, nuts for food and some water there. About two days later I saw the mouse jumping and trying to escape. I mentioned what happened with the mice to a nice student of mine and she said that she would take the mouse and free him in a field far from the school which she did.

By the way it appears that God was with me on this one. A day or two after saving the mouse's life I got two teaching jobs at Columbia College in downtown Chicago. The course names were "Human Involvement in the Environment" an environmental class and the other one, "Animal Ecology and Behavior". I am still there today, twelve years later. Interesting isn't it?

STUPIDITY NUMBER EIGHT
SHOPPING CENTERS THAT ARE ABANDONED
WHILE NEW ONES ARE BUILT NEARBY.

One day on my way to one of the schools that I teach at I passed a shopping center that has been turned into a ghost down. There is only one store operating, Carson, Pierre Scott. The rest of the stores are closed and covered with overgrown plants (See figure 12). The area is quite big encompassing many hectares of land (each hectare is equivalent to 2.47 acres). How could a once-thriving area like this go to ruin? Probably because people who used to buy there were distracted by prettier shopping centers with more things to buy a few miles away or maybe it became out of the way for people. Just a few miles away from this mall developers are building another one from scratch.This reminds me of the question once posed to someone: "You've seen one shopping center, then you've seen them all (themall). Get it?

Figure 12 Here we see part of a shopping center that was turned
into a ghost town near the city of Chicago. (Photo by author)

Figure 13- Here we see what's left of the parking lot of the same mall
as pictured in figure 12. Notice the grass growing from the cracks..
This shows that nature is very resilient. (Photo by author)

By the way according to the book, *How Much is Enough* there are more shopping centers in America than there are high schools.[128] This shows that our priorities are for business and not for educating our young people.

STUPIDITY NUMBER NINE
SPENDING MONEY ON DRUGS LIKE VIAGRA (A SEX ENHANCING DRUG) WHILE MUCH OF THE WORLD STRUGGLES WITH OVERPOPULATION AND DISEASE

Isn't it interesting to note that the world is overpopulated in many areas, while the developed world is obsessed with sex? Hence, the proliferation of sexual enhancing drugs such as *Viagra* while much of the world's people suffer from lack of drugs for such diseases as AIDS, malaria and *Schistosomiasis*.[129] While the West supplies new drugs to increase sexual performance, poor countries continue cutting, chopping and digging up their lands in order to get money for their survival. These lands are their life support systems. So here you see the countries with the most needs are destroying their life support systems while we in the developed countries seek pleasure no matter what the cost.

Stupidity and ignorance are prevalent in our human society. What is the sense of having an educated public if priorities, many financial, take precedence over common sense? We saw this when I wrote about the California earthquake and the building of freeways instead of building a decent mass transit system consisting of a light rail system. A light rail system would help decrease carbon dioxide and smog. We also see that Americans who are in love with their cars insist on cheap gasoline which just adds to the nation's pollution burden or we see the funeral industry cutting down beautiful and stately trees just to build coffins. But the ultimate insult to the planet is the marketing of *Viagra* as the wonder drug. We know we have a population problem. The last thing that the planet needs is a drug that enhances the male's sex life so that he can help increase the already overpopulated Earth with more humans. With all the education out there on the planet we know the ecological effects of these activities but we fail to act in a responsible manner.

CHAPTER 13
IMPRESSIONISM

You never get a second chance to make first impressions-Anonymous

INTRODUCTION

In order to make their point many people will go to great lengths to impress their audience, even if it involves environmental damage. In figure 14, we see the Chicago River dyed green for St Patrick's Day. This was solely done to make an impression on the public by politicians and business leaders. Even if this dye was a food coloring, I'm sure that the local residents (fish, bacteria, algae and zooplankton) could care less. In this chapter, I want to give a few examples of this phenomenon. We will start with politicians (what else is new?) and go on to Oliver North and his lawyers, followed by sports cars, then large homes, guns for votes, almost empty pages in books, and trophy hunters.

Figure 14 . The Chicago River dyed green for St Patrick's day. (Photo by author)

THE CONCEPT

POLITICIANS

During the last six months of the Clinton administration, the media had a field day detailing the president's extramarital affairs. In order to make an impression, Republican Congressman Henry Hyde of Illinois presented 33,000 pages of depositions and papers associated with the affair of Bill Clinton and his extramarital women accomplices. The 33,000 pages of paper are what concern me. Anyone who is alive and well and eats and breathes knows that there is something inherently wrong with this scenario. What's wrong with it? The paper of course! Who in his or her right mind will read 33,000 pages of nonsense unless he/she is a fanatic who wants to dig up dirt on President Clinton. How many trees have been destroyed because of this stupidity? I think, you, as the reader understand where I am coming from.

Due to the idea of making an impression, thousands of pieces of paper are being copied and subsequently wasted in order to keep the agenda of certain misguided individuals such as Hyde and other Republicans. Their goal was to discredit Clinton and attempt his resignation. How many copies of those 33,000 pieces of paper are being made with total disregard of the environmental costs? I would hate to find out.

OLIVER NORTH AND IMPRESSIONISM

Another case in point were the lawyers of Oliver North. Remember the Iran-Contra affair during Ronald Reagan's so called "watch" on the country? Brendan Sullivan, North's lawyer, appeared not to care about the environmental damage that his office was causing as long as he could make a great impression on the public. There was one aspect of North's trial that I will never forget. In a statement made by one of North's lawyers it was argued that there were so many documents in this case that if they were piled next to Oliver North they would be taller than him. Well, guess what? According to a picture in the local newspaper that is exactly what we saw. Brendan Sullivan and his environmentally illiterate friends photocopied thousands of sheets and stacked them in a pile next to Mr. North. It was funny seeing Oliver standing next to so many documents just to make an impression. But, you have to realize that lawyers are out to win a case no matter what it takes whether it is good for the environment or not.

SPORTS CARS

Let's not dwell only on lawyers. Let's talk about guys who want to impress some girl. I have seen this many times. Guys will drive a two-seater sports car, which in my opinion is useless except for picking up girls and running from the police in a holdup. Why, because you can't fit much in the trunk and only two people can ride in comfort. Although sports cars are generally small they often have large engines that burn too much fuel. Here is impressionism at its worst. Sure, buy a sports car and go out with the girl. Will you marry her? Probably not!

Figure 15 Here we see a two-seater sports car. It is quite expensive and can't carry more than two people comfortably. It can't even carry the usual amount of luggage. It may only be good for picking up girls. However, here we see a girl driving it. Maybe she wants to pick up a guy. (Photo by author)

LARGE HOMES

Let's consider large homes. How many of you have big homes because you want to impress someone? I have been living around the Chicago area now for almost 14 years. Because of my teaching and doing asbestos air monitoring, I had the opportunity to travel to all parts of the city. The city of Chicago is incredibly diverse. There are some fabulously wealthy people living here as well as incredibly poor individuals. The west side of Chicago is loaded with abandoned and boarded up homes, stores, bars, and just about everything else that can be run down. It's amazing that we here in the United States tolerate these two extremes.

Over the last 20 years, I have noticed that homes are getting physically bigger while poverty is increasing and family size is decreasing. I personally know of an individual who wanted to make an impression on her friends and coworkers. She convinced her reluctant husband to buy a bigger house even though the house they lived in was perfect. So the husband caved in and they bought the wife's dream home. A few years later the wife's company that she worked for was downsized so she lost her job. Needless to say the house still had a high mortgage. Because of the bigger home and lower cash flow for the family they have exacerbated their problems.

Let's look at the environmental consequences. The bigger house initially required more resources to build, which were taken from the earth. Factors such as low mortgage interest rates and availability of building materials encourage more building of large homes even in a depressed economy. (see figure 16)

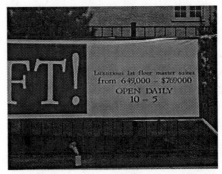

Figure 16. Large homes in suburb of Chicago. Note the exorbitant prices. (Photo by author)

GUNS FOR VOTES

Let's look at George W. Bush. When he was running for governor of Texas for the first time he shot a bird on the endangered species list. Of course, he didn't realize the bird was listed as endangered, but I believe he was out shooting because he wanted to get the votes of the NRA (National Rifle Association) .The gun lobby here in America has lots of clout, especially with republicans.

It's amazing to what lengths politicians will go to make impressions on people to get their votes even if it means pain and suffering on poor innocent animals. They do it because they regard animals as disposable. This case was a photo op just by chance. If the bird (killdeer) was not endangered this would not have made the news. However, since the bird was on the endangered species list and was shot by Bush, the press had a field day.

Whether the bird was or was not on the endangered species list is not the point. The main point as is obviously shown was to make an impression on the Texan voters who are in love with their guns. A life was taken for the sake of votes. Now ask yourselves, who weeps for birds killed by politicians hunting for votes?[130]

How much wildlife needs to be destroyed for the pleasure of special interest groups such as the NRA?

ALMOST EMPTY PAGES IN BOOKS

Now let's take a look at a totally different way in which impressions are made. In 1994 Richard Preston wrote a book which brought to light the problem of the *Ebola* virus˜ The name of the book is the "*The Hot Zone.*" It recounts the events which happened in the Reston, Virginia primate holding facility just 30 miles from the White House. The book is an excellent book. However, there is something not environmentally correct with the book. The problem is as follows: After the first few pages there are eight pages with just one or two sentences describing the different areas of USAMARID; The United States Army Medical Research Institute of Infectious Diseases ; an example of which is as follows on page xiiii- **Processing ...You are cleared to enter ....**

That's right. That is all there is. Now what's wrong with this? To answer that question lets go to the front jacket. Reading from the inside jacket cover we find this part of a paragraph:

"As the tropical wildernesses of the world are destroyed, previously unknown viruses that have lived undetected in the rain forest for eons are entering human populations."[131]

Now, let's examine the error of the publisher's ways. Here goes. Ask yourself, why are there eight pages with very few sentences? Obviously the publisher wanted to make an impression on the reader. OK, but let's ask ourselves how many pages are in the book. The answer is around 310. For every 40 books printed the publisher could make another full book if he didn't place these eight pages with just one sentence. Put another way, for every million books printed that would leave 8 million pages with one sentence. The publisher could have printed another 25,806 books with just those extra pages. Lots of paper you say? Now, I am for good books myself, but if a book such as "The Hot Zone" which is about a deadly virus that has about a 90% fatality rate on humans and possibly on animals, why are there so many wasted pages? Is it possible that by cutting down the trees in Africa we humans are somehow causing the virus to be spread? Ironic, isn't it? The point that I am trying to make here is that impressionism is rampant in our society. Now, it is good to make something respectable, especially a book, but do we have to waste so much paper on empty pages?

TROPHY HUNTERS

When hunters kill dear with big antlers they don't realize that they are weakening the populations of deer. Females want to mate with those deer with the biggest antlers. If hunters kill these animals then there will only be deer with less vigorous genes. Predators of deer, other than humans help strengthen their populations by weeding out the weak and sick deer. By killing weak and sick animals the predators help the populations survive and retain their vigor. When human hunters kill these animals with the good genes just to show off their trophies in their living rooms, they are harming the natural environment. Of course, many of them, if not most have never taken an environmental class discussing the importance of all organisms on the planet. All animals, whether charismatic or not have an ecological function. The only organisms on the planet that have no conceivable ecological functions are human beings (*Homo sapiens*) because all they appear to do is cut, chop, dig, burn, and destroy. I am still waiting for someone to tell me the ecological function of humans.

I once went to a home of an appraiser who happened to be a big game hunter. An insurance company told me to get a personal item appraised in order to have it insured, so they gave me the name of an individual who does appraisals in his home. I went to the address given and when I was let into the house I was in deep shock. The house was loaded with stuffed mammals. It looked more like the Field Museum in Chicago than a home. I asked the appraiser if there were many of those animals left in the wild and he assured me that that was the case. I still doubt it.

Figure 17. These antlers are on a ceiling and made into chandeliers. They are also on a wall. These antlers were from once-alive deer. (Photo by author)

Sometimes people want to impress other people for many reasons. However, when it damages the environment it is not worth doing. If only one person does something small in order to impress another that is fine but if many people want the same things such as buying a bigger home or car then it can be devastating to the environment.

CHAPTER 14
LAZINESS

There was this contest offered in a state many years ago. A group of men got together and wanted to have a contest to determine the world's laziest man. They finally found a candidate and went to see him. He was lying on the grass a few miles from the nearest city. The men went up to him and said". Mr. Jones, you just won $500, the award for being the world's laziest man. Mr. Jones then said" Roll me over and place it in my pocket"

INTRODUCTION

It is evident that many people would like to do things on behalf of the environment but for some reason they don't do it. One reason may be due to laziness. That's right laziness. Here in America it is easier to be lazy than in many other countries because we have things too easy and we don't like to be inconvenienced.

CONCEPT

Have you ever seen a lazy person? Some are incredibly lazy similar to the joke at the beginning of this chapter. What does laziness have to do with pollution? Plenty!

Let me tell you a story. Once, when I was living in Maryland, I lived on the second floor of a garden apartment building. In the apartment below lived an elderly married couple. At night it would be amusing to look in their bedroom, inadvertently of course, because their bedroom was on the first floor and facing the parking lot. They would leave their shades up.

What was so amusing was the fact that they had a dresser, which contained two TV sets. They would each watch their TV at the same time while in bed. Anyway, about a mile from the apartment complex was a recycling bin for glass and newspapers. I would normally make an effort to recycle the newspapers at the recycling place. So, one day, I saw the man come out of his house with a large stack of newspapers to be thrown away. I then asked him, "Why don't you recycle them?" His reply was, "Eh!" and then he threw away the papers. Unfortunately, this is the response of many people throughout the world. This building should have had its own recycling bin!

PAPER AND MORE PAPER

NEWSPAPERS

It takes 500,000 trees to make one Sunday edition of the New York Times. Despite the increased use of computers, computer faxes, and other "non-paper" machinery, our society is still buried with paper products. Imagine if everybody behaved like that gentleman in the introduction. An indication of the number of trees consumed on an annual basis is located in Table 5.

TABLE 5

FACT	NUMBER OF TREES
Sunday N.Y. Times	500,000
Recycling a single run of the N.Y Times would save	75,000
If every American recycled 10% of the N.Y.Times, there would be	250,000,000 trees saved annually
Average number of paper bags used in one year in a supermarket: 60.5 million	700 bags per tree
Annual tree consumption per person in US	Seven trees or 2 billion per year
Junk mail per year per American=13,000 pieces	Many trees

132

PAPER FOR TESTS

Laziness is a fact of life. I see this all the time. Being a teacher I see laziness from other professors as well, especially, at the local copy machine. I once saw a teacher making an 11 page test. I asked her," Why don't you do it back to back?" Her response was" I'm too lazy, and I don't have enough time." I told her that I would offer to help her copy this material back to back but she refused.

Another instance really shocked me. At the time of this writing, I teach at five colleges in the Chicago vicinity. At another college where I teach, I was upstairs on my way to a class, when I noticed that a student-aid was making copies of a test. It had 150 questions all multiple -choice. The student was making 20 copies of the test in which each test came out to 30 pages. I asked him, "Why don't you copy them back to back?" he answered, "The copy machine can't do it!" Even with the machine not operating properly, double sided printing is still possible by manually inserting each sheet of paper in the drawer. Simple math tells you that 30 pages times 20 equals 600 pages, Yes, that's right more than a ream. Here's the irony of the situation; the test was for an environmental science class. When I asked the teacher why he didn't give instructions for double printing his reply was that he did instruct the aid to print back to back.

PAPER PLATES AND UTENSILS

Let's take one case of laziness, which really bugs me. When I go to certain people's homes for family affairs or parties, the hosts almost always use paper plates, cups and plastic silverware. I ask the hosts why they don't use real plates considering that there are not that many guests. The usual answer is "I don't have to wash the paper plates." I tell them, "Look I will wash the dishes." I enjoy doing it if I know that the environment won't suffer, but nobody listens to me. All this wasted paper and plastic from utensils winds up in landfills, and much of it is not biodegradable. Consider the following figure of landfill composition as indicated in Table 6.

TABLE 6
COMPONENTS OF A TYPICAL LANDFILL
IN THE UNITED STATES

Garbage Component	Percentage (%)
Paper	37
Yard waste	18
Metal	10

Garbage Component	Percentage (%)
Glass	10
Food	8
Plastics	7
Other	10

The United State's landfills are filling up at an alarming rate. This material does not easily decompose. The garbage business is a wonderful business because business is always picking up.

CAR OIL

Another example of laziness is when people dispose of their car oil down sewers instead of taking it to a recycling center. This needless to say is very bad for the organisms that live in the sewer. Yes, that's right, residents of the sewer. These residents include bacteria, protists (single celled organisms bigger than bacteria –see glossary for definition and descriptions) and other organisms. Hey, they got a right to live also!! Right?

Why Drive When You Can Walk

Other examples of laziness include driving two or three blocks to go to the store. In fact, I noticed this while I was outside working on my lawn. I saw my neighbor, a middle aged woman, going to her car. After about ten minutes, she returned with a box of Dunkin Donuts. It occurred to me that the donut shop was only two blocks away, and she could have walked. Being a little chubby, the exercise would have done her good. Eating those donuts would have been counterproductive due to the fact that donuts contain excessive amounts of fats even if she did walk.

The Sheila Jackson Lee Story (Even democrats waver sometimes)

Lazy people come in all shapes and sizes. Representative Sheila Jackson Lee, is from Houston, Texas. [133] Sheila is a member of Congress, who is reported to live close to the Capitol. One block to work, Sheila has chosen to be chauffeured in a government car by a member of her staff. Yes, chauffeured. Now, the fact that she is a Democrat doesn't help because they are seen as more environmentally aware. This is the kind of behavior one would expect from our environmentally misinformed representatives, but human is human, I guess. I myself, go out of my way to walk to any place nearby. In fact, at one of the colleges where I teach, I walk because it is only a 15-20 minute walk.

What amazes me is the fact that Sheila acts like a queen. According to an article in The Weekly Standard, she is quoted as having said, "I am a queen, and I demand to be treated like a queen." My addition: *Even if it means adding more carbon dioxide to the atmosphere*! You know Congress people should set an example. If Sheila can drive one block to work in Washington, what will stop other environmentally unaware people from doing it? I should point out that I still respect Sheila for her beliefs about the political climate in Washington.

Why Drive, When You Can Take the Train

Another case of environmentally unaware individuals includes John Sununu. Sununu had to resign as Chief of Staff, under *the elected*, George Bush Senior (1992). Evidently he is another member of Washington's political group who like to drive at taxpayer's expense when he could take the train. He is famous for taking a limousine from Washington to New York to attend a stamp show. Now I used to live in Arnold, Maryland, a suburb of Baltimore and Washington, and when I would go to New York, which was quite often, I would take the train. I felt that it was unnecessary to drive because the distance is about 200 miles. Even though Sununu was Chief of Staff at the White House he could have taken the train, but because he felt that he was too important he took a limousine. I bet he didn't even think about the environmental consequences of his trip. True, many people drive the distance everyday from Washington D.C to New York City, but maybe they, too, should use mass transit. It would certainly keep the air a little cleaner. You readers out there can criticize me for making a big stink about this episode, but things like this are endemic in this country especially with the low price of gasoline, yes that's the low price of gasoline.

Of course if a person is an invalid or a senior then they have a good excuse to drive. BUT, we all know of lazy people who, for whatever reason, refuse to exert a little effort to help save the environment even in a minor way.

I SET AN EXAMPLE

Let me give you an example about myself. I teach at a college, which is 50 miles from my house. It would take one hour and fifteen minutes to drive there by car, and about two hours by train. I get up on Tuesday and Thursday mornings at 4:30AM (0430 hrs.) just so I don't have to drive the 100 miles round trip. The way that I get to the school is to drive one mile to the Edgebrook train station, where I catch the train to downtown Chicago. Then, I take another train to Aurora. A student, whom I pay, then picks me up at the station and takes me to the college. I should mention that there used to be eight round trips by the Pace Bus Company to the school, but in the infinite wisdom of the management they were cut down to zero roundtrips. This loss of service I must add is bad for the students who have no other way to get to the college.

This is another example of how our institutions such as schools and shopping centers are built around the car without consideration for the environment.

Laziness is a trait just like greed or temptation that has to be overcome. It is worth a little extra effort to save the environment by doing something as simple as saving an empty soda can on your way to work for the recycling bin. Ultimately, environmental laziness means: The excessive use of products and services for your convenience, such as using a car instead of walking, or using fresh paper when used blank paper is available.

CHAPTER 15
LOW STATUS OF WOMEN
(FEMALE GENDER BIAS)

"Women are nothing but machines for producing children."
Napolean Bonaparte.

"What would men be without women? Scarce, sir, mighty scarce."
Mark Twain.

INTRODUCTION

When women are relegated to low status the situation is not good for their quality of life and ultimately, the environment. This is especially true of women in developing countries, who have little control over their bodies and sex. Many would be killed if they deny their husband's sexual advances or rebel against marrying the father's choice. This sorry state of affairs greatly contributes to overpopulation because many women have no access to contraception or prenatal care. This chapter addresses how women's low status can be devastating to the world's environment.

CONCEPT

To emphasize the low status of women here are two stories out of Egypt which should be told. In 1997, a man beheaded his daughter because she eloped. He displayed her head to the local villagers in order to regain his honor. In a village north of Cairo, a man set his nineteen year old daughter on fire by throwing gasoline on her and lighting the match in front of his community. [134] Terrible!

There are many problems associated with being a woman in today's world. These problems have devastating effects not only on the women themselves but also on the environment. In her wonderful monograph, "Correcting Gender Myopia"[135] Danielle Nierenberg states eloquently the plight of women in developing countries. One is horrified upon reading the fact that the Bush administration (G.W.) took away money for family planning in the developing world. This imposed even more appalling conditions on many women such as being forced to give birth under unsanitary conditions, lack of adequate obstetrical care, and a high mortality rate during childbirth. In addition to the 800,000 abortions there are still millions of unwanted children which place a tremendous strain on the environment.[136]   Not only are women subjected to those conditions mentioned in the previous paragraph but now they have to deal with AIDS in which 41% of all adult cases are women. This, too, will place a strain on the environment. As we have seen in many countries the people, who are aged between 15 and 50, are subjected to AIDS and it is this age group that is the most productive. These are the people who build the buildings, who plant and harvest the crops, who take care of both the young and elderly. If they die because of AIDS then who is left to tend to the chores that have to be done? No one is left. What happens to the environment?

Now, we have another problem. Not only are women at the bottom of the barrel when it comes to fair and equal treatment like that of men, but girl babies are not wanted either. In many countries the male child is desired and not aborted. Female babies on the other hand are aborted after the parents find out through ultrasound that their babies are girls. Now imagine this. Suppose you are a father and you want your wife to have a baby boy. Ok, the first child is a girl. Well, let's try again. The second child is a girl. Well let's try again. The third child is a girl. So on and so on. Many people will keep on trying until they get a boy, so meanwhile they are increasing the population not only of unwanted girls but of people in general. Do you see how this can be catastrophic to the environment?

Women are the ones who manufacture the global population. They give birth to babies, which eventually consume, consume and consume the resources of the planet. If a woman can't say no to sexual advances and then she gets pregnant, in many cases the baby will come, thus adding to the planet's burden. If education is a priority for women within their cultures, then they will realize that too many children are not a good choice for themselves or for the environment. If you look at chapter 17 dealing with overpopulation we can see what too many people can do to the planet, especially if they are impoverished. Each baby (above the allotted two that I think people should have) needs to be fed, housed and clothed. This means less cropland for each individual. It also means more resources being used including less clean water for domestic use and more trees being felled for wood, essentially, more environmental degradation.

CHAPTER 16
THE PERCEPTION
THAT NATURE *DOESN'T EXIST!!!!*

*What we call man's power over nature turns out to be power
exercised over other men with nature as its instrument.*
C.S. Lewis

INTRODUCTION

Does nature exist? Well, to city dwellers probably not. What is "Nature"? Well, according to me, nature is everything in the physical world not touched by humans. City dwellers don't see much of it because everything is concrete. Even trees planted on sidewalks are planted in a mound of dirt surrounded by concrete. (See figure 22) Now, if kids grow up in this environment as I did many years ago in New York City, they would think that the whole world looked like one mass of tall buildings. Boy was I glad that my parents took me to Peekskill, New York for a visit. I actually saw trees, grass and some wild animals. Wow, the whole world was not composed of tall buildings as I had previously thought.

From the way we see the planet being run by world "misleaders"[137] it is obvious that they too don't know that nature exists. They act as if they own everything and that they can destroy it if they wish.[138] Many examples include Saddam Hussein to our own George W. Bush, our first unelected "resident of the White House".[139]

CONCEPT

AIR

How many people do you know who really care about nature or for that matter know that it exists? Not many. They all take for granted that the air they breathe is just there like magic. Well, let's see how clean and pure the air is in Mexico City, Bangkok, Calcutta, or Houston[140]. The air in those cities is atrocious much of the time, and it is a wonder to me, how people survive. Cities like Mexico City hardly have a day when the ozone level is below the standard. It is generally way above the maximum standard we allow, yet people still manage to survive-- if you call that surviving. Air is nature and nature DOES EXIST.

Figure 18. This is a picture of the sky. Clouds are made up of water. The air in the sky contains 78.09% Nitrogen (N_2), 20.94% oxygen (O_2), .93% Argon,(Ar) an inert gas and .0370% carbon dioxide (CO2), plus many other gases but in extremely small percentages. The air that you don't see should be clean and free from pollutants. (Photo by author)

WATER

What about water? Is it in infinite supply? No, yet people treat it so.

What gives us the impression that it is in limitless supply? Simply stated the fact is that every time we take a bath or shower water comes out of the faucet nonstop, continuously. To be more explicit let me tell you a story. At one of the Chicago colleges that I teach at there is a swimming pool. During a six-week period, I noticed that the shower was on nonstop because the faucet got stuck in the 'on' position. I was not able to shut it off. I mentioned this to the lifeguard and he told me that he was aware of the situation but that the water is shut off at night. Here again, we see that most people including the lifeguard have a callous attitude toward wasted water. However, during the last week of class, I noticed that the shower had stopped.

I never forgot the value of water since I saw the movie, *The Flight of the Phoenix* (1965) with James Stewart. The story concerned a flight that crashed in the Sahara Desert leaving only a couple of gallons of water for the entire group of survivors. The story details how they improvised building a makeshift plane from the wreckage and eventually survived. Ever since watching this movie, I became obsessed with the value of water. This also brings to mind a famous episode from the TV series, *The Twilight Zone*, entitled the "Rip Van Winkle Caper" in which the protagonists at first traded gold for water and then killed for water. Water is obviously more important than material items because our lives depend on it.

Simply stated water is nature in its purest form and we should realize it and protect it at all costs. It should be pointed out that many predictions indicate that future wars will not only be fought over oil but more importantly over water resources. [141] Water is nature and nature DOES EXIST.

LAND

It is obvious that we need land for almost everything we do. If we treat it just like any object that has no value it will be destroyed. We build our homes, plant our crops, and do virtually everything else on it, including the destruction of it by warfare without any regard for the biodiversity within it. We use mass tracks of land for human recreational activities on golf courses, which is the quintessential example of wanton waste. It is estimated that there are around 15,000 golf courses in the United States alone with more being built every day throughout the world, including China. In the Chicago area alone, there are over 218 golf courses. All golf courses regardless of where they are located require vast amounts of water and pesticides.

The point that I am trying to make is that we have to think about what we are doing to the land strictly for the benefit of humans without regard for the natural residents such as bacteria, fungi, plants, protists and animals. All this is part of nature whereas golf courses are not nature, and in fact destroy the very land that they are situated upon.

One of the things that we humans have been destroying is wilderness which is defined as: *An area where the earth and its community of life are untrammeled by man, where man himself is a visitor who does not remain. An area of wilderness is further defined to mean an area of undeveloped Federal land retaining its primeval character and influence, without permanent improvements or human habitation, which is protected and managed so as to preserve its natural conditions and which (1) generally appears to have been affected primarily by the forces of nature, with the imprint of man's work substantially unnoticeable; (2) has outstanding opportunities for solitude or a primitive and unconfined type of recreation; (3) has at least five thousand acres of land or is of sufficient size as to make practicable its preservation and use in an unimpaired condition; and (4) may also contain ecological, geological, or other features of scientific, educational, scenic, or historical value.*[142]

It's amazing that we consider pristine areas in the United States not as objects of beauty but something that we can exploit for financial gains. God, Mother Nature or the Almighty gave us these wonderful lands. Let's enjoy them as they are without cutting, chopping and digging. Land is nature and nature DOES EXIST.

FOOD

Ask anyone where the food that fills the supermarkets' shelves comes from. They will say food factories. Yes, but where does the food really come from? It comes from the soil and sunshine of nature, to put it a better way. It grows. So where do pigs and cows come from? Well, they are part of nature. They have to eat the crops that humans grow from the dirt. Then they are brought to the slaughterhouses where they are processed into meat. They come from nature.

WOOD

Ask people, where does the wood come from? They might think that it comes from the lumberyard. Yes, it does, but where does the lumberyard get the wood? Trees of course!!! Where are the trees? Trees are in the forest. Why do forests exist? To stabilize the soil, absorb carbon dioxide (CO_2), produce food, act as homes for other organisms including humans and control climate. Yet the world continues to use wood at an unprecedented rate ignoring the fact that TREES ARE NATURE.

Figure 19. This is a tree. Trees are plants which act as homes to animals, insects, plants, fungi, bacteria and protists. They help stabilize the soil by preventing erosion and also act as a food source for us humans as well as supply oxygen to the world.

FOSSIL FUELS

People don't think about where their oil, coal and gas come from. They know that it comes from the ground. Yes, but originally where did it come from? It came from dead plants and dinosaurs. If we keep using it at current rates we too will become extinct (See consequences of global warming in the introduction).

MEDICINAL DRUGS

Here is one for you. Where do aspirin and many other drugs that are really miracle drugs come from? Yes, you guessed it! Nature. Many of our antibiotics that treat infections are treated with penicillin that comes from a fungus related to the fungus that makes blue cheese blue (also known as Roquefort).

Do you get the point? WE GET EVERYTHING WE HAVE FROM NATURE ONE WAY OR ANOTHER, BUT THIS IS NOT DRILLED INTO THE HEADS OF STUDENTS, POLITICIANS, BUSINESSMEN, OR MEMBERS OF ANY OTHER PROFESSION WORLDWIDE!!

Ask your common businessman who is reading the Wall Street Journal. What is he reading? He is reading the paper. Yes, the paper: A former home to plants, animals and bacteria and possibly many fungi.

WHO OWNS THE PLANET AND WHAT IS NATURE?

Do you remember the 1991 Gulf War, better known as "Gulf Wars, Episode 1?" It took place in January of 1991, during Papa Bush's reign as president of the United States. Saddam Hussein, whom I must add never took an environmental class with me, dumped the equivalent of three supertankers of oil into the Persian Gulf killing trillions of algae (figure 20), copepods (figure 21), which are the world's most abundant animal, birds, fish and countless other marine organisms. Why did he do it? Well, for one thing, he probably thought that it had some military significance. It had none, that's right, zero, nunca and efis (in Hebrew). He didn't realize that the Gulf and its aquatic life are part of nature. He probably said to himself, "What the hell. I will pollute the Gulf!"

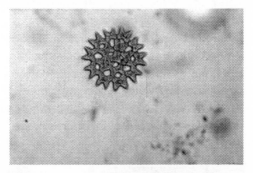

Figure 20. This is member of the green algae called *Pediastrum*. They are members of the phytoplankton or plant-like organisms. They are very pretty and are the base of the food chain. They produce oxygen and act as a food source for copepods and other types of zooplankton. (Photo by author)

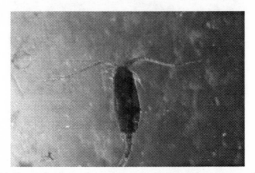

Figure 21. This is a picture of a copepod. Copepods are members of small animal-like organisms called zooplankton. These are found in both freshwater and saltwater all over the planet. They are part of the food chain. They eat little plantlike organisms called alga. (Photo by Author and Moshe Gophen)

George Bush Sr. had much of Iraq carpet-bombed. What about the poor animals, plants, bacteria, and people who were killed and incinerated? Well, that's the way it goes. We destroyed countless animals, plants, bacteria and fungi for selfish reasons which in this case, was for oil. If Iraq was a wheat exporting nation none of this destruction would have occurred. Do you really think that Papa Bush really gave a_____ (put your own explicative here)? No. Nature doesn't appear to be a priority in his brain, mind, psyche or whatever you call it for if he did he wouldn't have started that war. Bomb! Bomb! Bomb! Now, if he purposely did that he must have realized that the bombing would boost his popularity. Where? Here in America because the American people (perhaps better known as "Sheeple") would believe almost anything in the name of patriotism that is shoved down their throats by the so called liberal-media-which-"ain't"-so liberal. And I thought that Americans were intelligent.

Here we see a good case why people have to get educated about the environment and in the study of ecology. It's amazing to me to see the lack of common sense that has permeated our culture. This is indicative of the paradox that exists worldwide. The poor must exploit the land and resources just to survive while the rich exploit these same things for pleasure and profit. ***Just because something is there doesn't mean that we have to take it and exploit it until nothing is left.***[143]

Figure 22 Here we see a tree in the middle of a sidewalk in Chicago. Its scenes like these that make city dwellers wonder "is this nature?"! (Photo by author)

Fig.23

What is wrong with this picture?

This is a piece of coral. Coral belongs to the same group of organisms as the jellyfish (The phylum Cnidaria). They are 100% aquatic organisms so why are they are on a bookshelf in someone's home? Is this nature?

CHAPTER 17
OVERPOPULATION

When a teacher asked in what part of the world the most ignorant people were to be found, a small boy volunteered quickly, "In New York City." The teacher was amazed and questioned the lad as to where he had obtained his information. "Well" he replied, the geography book says that's where the population is most dense."
Unknown

This reminds me of another story. There were these two boys talking. Sam says to the other, Hey Joe, I understand that your mother gave birth to her twentieth child. Joe replied, "Yes, that's right, Sam." "What did you name Him?" Joe said," at first, we named him John, but then we found out we already had a John in the Family."
Unknown

INTRODUCTION

Throughout this book I have listed many causes of environmental pollution but all of the real causes can be attributed to one *main* cause and that is human overpopulation. When we look at agriculture, greed, defense, energy etc., as causes of pollution, we realize that all of these factors involve the misuse of nature's bounty by human beings.

If we look at the group of equations below we find the following:
EQUATION: MORE PEOPLE = MORE POLLUTION
MORE PEOPLE= MORE LAND DEGRADATION FOR FOOD
MORE PEOPLE=CONTINNUED LOSS OF LIVING ORGANISMS
SUCH AS TREES, ANIMALS, BACTERIA and FUNGI

MORE PEOPLE=MORE WATER POLLUTION
MORE PEOPLE=MORE AIR POLLUTION
MORE PEOPLE=MORE LAND POLLUTION
MORE PEOPLE=MORE UNEMPLOYMENT
MORE PEOPLE=MORE WARS

If we look at the long list of environmental degradation listed in the first chapter of this book, we notice that virtually ALL, and I stress almost ALL of the environmental problems listed is a direct result of human overpopulation. As of the year 2004, there are approximately 6.4 billion people on the planet, one third of which live in China and India. The first billion was reached around 1870. The second billion was reached around 1930. In the mid 1950s there were around 2.5 billion. The average growth rate is around 1.3% worldwide. Every second five people are born and two people die, thus, a net gain of three people, [144] with approximately 10,000 being born per hour. At this current rate, the world's population will double in about forty years. [145]

CONCEPT

Added to the burgeoning human population there are approximately 16.1 billion domesticated animals. This fact is significant because such animals require a great deal of food that instead could be used to feed humans. Cash crops such as coffee, bananas and cotton also take their toll on land by utilizing tremendous amounts of water, ala the Aral Sea in the former Soviet Union (See figure 7 which takes you to the internet). These crops do not add food value to the local residents, but instead, profit multinational food corporations.

What do humans have to do with pollution? Plenty!!! We have to feed, house, clothe, educate and take care of all humans as well as the domesticated animals on the planet. In order to do this we need food which comes from farmland.

A few years ago troops from the United States entered Somalia, a country in East Africa, in order to save millions of starving people who had much of their food looted by bandits. The devastation in Somalia was caused for the most part by greed, under the misleadership of the misleader, Said Barre. It became clear that Somalia was a nightmare, which may have been the precursor to other similar catastrophic events, such as, the genocide in Rwanda, and the Gulf Wars (caused by the presidents named Bush). If we keep producing more humans, the whole world may look like Somalia.

We are already witnessing another catastrophe taking place right now in the former Yugoslavia. Like Somalia, we see plenty of guns, but not much food. It never ceases to amaze me that there always appears to be a shortage of food, but plenty and plenty of guns. It sure makes you wish that guns were edible.

Here in America the average number of children per family is a little over two. In Somalia it is around 6.6. We must first realize that in order to curb environmental degradation we must limit the human population in order to maintain the ability of the planet to support them. There is a special word for this ability and it is called ***The Carrying Capacity.*** Simply put, The Carrying Capacity is defined as the maximum population that an area can sustain without bringing in outside resources. If we exceed the carrying capacity of an area, that area will eventually stop supporting its life. Perhaps the best way to describe this is the analogy about a small house. Think of the planet as a small house. Let's say you normally have three people living in the house with only a $50,000 yearly salary. Now think! How would it be if you had ten people living in it, still with the same $50,000 salary? You couldn't even buy enough food unless you went to stores like Aldi, located here in the Chicagoland area. You can buy a few bags of Ramon noodle soup for only 89 cents. You might be able to feed those ten people with only that, but what about clothing, medical care, education, special needs, etc? It would be tough!

Now, what about space or lack of space? Pretend that this house is the planet earth. We need this space to grow our crops, maintain our institutions, clean up waste, and provide places for recreation. If we continue in our present ways the quality of life would be undoubtedly compromised, making life miserable for everyone. We would no longer be able to sustain ourselves. This is exactly what would happen to the earth if population growth were not halted. Sure we talk about human life mainly, but what about animal and plant life (non-domesticated of course)?

Can one imagine a planet without the lovely song of birds, or the tapping and pitter-patter of animal feet? If people keep having children, which will result in overpopulation of this small planet, we will only hear the pitter-patter of children's feet. We will not hear the pitter-patter of other animals.

One of the reasons why we have overpopulation is the influence of the far right, here in America, as well as beliefs of various religions. Under Ronald Reagan, who was president in the 80's, the world's population increased due in part, to his paying attention to the far right by not aiding countries in family planning programs.[146] This is discussed more in the chapter dealing with politicians and their friends. I myself know of families in Israel and in America where there are over ten children per family from the same parents. Sure it's nice to have many children, but the world cannot tolerate or afford that many per family. The world seems gigantic in scope, but too many people, having too many children slowly adds to the depletion of the planet's life support systems.

There is a proverb, one I actually thought about myself. It goes like this: The more people you have the more pollution (brilliant, isn't it?). This is especially true in the United States because we tend to destroy the environment at a greater rate than other countries because we have the every-thing-we-see-now attitude. See chapter 4 on The American Way. According to Paul Erlich, each child born in the United States does about 200 times the damage that a child born in Bangladesh does. The reason for this is because we need more of everything or so we perceive. Actually, our society makes us believe we need more things.

Because of the media we are being brainwashed into believing that the more you consume the better off you are. The condition of our planet has proved the old saying, *"The one who dies with the most toys wins."*[147]

Somehow when we watch the evening news on TV in the comfort of our own home here in America, it is as if we are watching a science fiction movie taking place on a faraway planet. The media packages significant stories in 30 second sound bites while more frivolous stories such as the affairs of sports and entertainment celebrities such as Michael Jordan and Michael Jackson are deemed more important and thus given more air time. Events taking place in Somalia, Ethiopia, Rwanda, and in other turbulent places around the globe are mentioned in the media. These images show us that devastation like death, disease, and turmoil are everyday realities in these places. I don't want to be a pessimist but we here in the Western world may suffer the same fate if we don't face reality.

What is the best way to determine the amount of damage a person over 65 years does? Well, let's just count the number of grandchildren. If they have more than four grandchildren they have helped to do some environmental damage. Why four? Because we have just replaced the grandparents with their children. Once, while watching one of the daily, morning TV shows the host was discussing a baseball team made up of players over 80 years old. The host mentioned that one of the players was a grandfather with 63 grandchildren (or 59 too many). I almost went through the roof when I heard this. But the host's reaction indicated that this was something to aspire to. However, you don't need to be a great mathematician to realize that if everybody had 63 grandchildren we (all of the world's citizens) would really be in trouble, assuming that we all survive.

THE JEWISH DILEMMA

I have a dilemma because I'm Jewish, and I am trying to curb the world's human population growth. We know that during WWII, six million Jews were killed by Hitler in the concentration camps. In 1948, the State of Israel was established as the only Jewish state in the world. As a Jew, how do I reconcile the fact that we need more Jews on this planet with the fact that there are too many people in general? Does the fact that there are too few Jews allow us to break environmental laws and produce more Jews? Religious Jews in Israel probably don't even consider this by the fact that many of their families consist of five or more children. They probably don't even consider the environmental aspect from a family planning viewpoint. From an environmental point of view we must carefully consider this dilemma. As we have seen overpopulation in any group wreaks havoc in the environment. However, from a historical and cultural perspective it's important for the Jewish people to survive.

In the book *Beyond Malthus,* [148] (a Worldwatch Institute Publication) many issues related to human overpopulation are discussed. These include the effects that overpopulation has on the fate of the earth's life support systems; not only for humans but also for other organisms which are included in the all inclusive category of *Biodiversity.* Other issues discussed include over-fishing, grain and energy consumption, all of which can have a huge effect on the earth's environment and climate. All of these are greatly dependent upon human overpopulation.

JULIAN SIMON'S LOGIC

The other reason why we accept overpopulation is because of the misguided people who don't really know a lot about ecology, as environmentalists do. Anti-environmentalists, such as the late Julian Simon, an economist at the University of Maryland, advocated producing more humans because he believed that people will solve all the world's problems. Simon is the author of several books, one of which is called *The Ultimate Resource* in which he writes about how people can solve problems caused by their own presence on the planet, and that overpopulation is not a serious threat. He further states that as a whole, bigger populations make sense. To state it simply, he assumes that technological improvement depends on the number of people available. He says that data prove this. The larger the number of people available, the larger number of scientists and the larger amount of scientific knowledge produced.[149]

Simon fails to realize that high human populations mean increased competition between people and animals. At present, there are approximately 16.1 billion domesticated animals. Most of these animals are vegetarians (herbivores) and thus need food in the form of grain. We need the same grain that they eat. According to the energy transfer rule, cows need roughly ten pounds of food to gain one pound of flesh.[150] In other words, if you eat meat you are eating ten times the amount of grain that you need because you are eating the grain that the animals eat, albeit not directly but through the animal. This simply stated means that if we were all vegetarians we would need 90% less grain grown thus, being able to feed the human population better and more efficiently.

URBAN SPRAWL

Another worrisome aspect of population growth is urban sprawl, which is the tremendous use of land used for human consumption. One of the best examples of this is the picture of a suburb of Las Vegas, which can be described as an asphalt jungle. The picture shows private homes for many square miles.[151]

According to the transportation research conference sprawl is defined as follows: [152]

1. Unlimited outward extension
2. Low-density residential and commercial settlements
3. Leapfrog development
4. Fragmentation of powers over land use among many small localities
5. Dominance of transportation by private automotive vehicles
6. No centralized planning or control of land-uses
7. Widespread strip commercial development
8. Great fiscal disparities among localities
9. Segregation of types of land uses in different zones
10. Reliance mainly on the trickle-down or filtering process to provide housing to low-income households

Another aspect of urban sprawl is described by Jane Jacobs below.

FROM JANE JACOBS:[153]

Jane Jacobs is the author of the book , *The Death and Life of the Great American Cities.* In the front jacket of the book there is a statement that I would like to quote now. "But look what we have built with the

first several billions: Low income projects that become worse centers of delinquency, vandalism and general social hopelessness than the slums they were supposed to replace; middle-income housing projects which are truly marvels of dullness and regimentation, sealed against any buoyancy or vitality of city life; luxury housing projects that mitigate their inanity, or try to, with a vapid vulgarity; cultural centers that are unable to support a good bookstore; civic centers that are avoided by everyone but bums who have fewer choices of a loitering place than others; commercial centers that are lack luster imitations of standardized suburban chain store shopping; promenades that go from no place to nowhere and expressways that eviscerate great cities. This is not rebuilding of cities. This is the sacking of cities.
The above quote speaks for itself!

CAR POPULATION

There are over 510 million cars in the world today of which 125 million are located in the United States.[154] In the United States there are approximately 0.6 cars per person. A lot, huh? You bet! This means that due to our affluent way of life, we can have cars, too many cars, and the destruction that comes with them. Just think of all the CO_2 being emitted from the exhaust pipes. Now, roughly all over the world car populations are on the increase, as is the human population. It is obvious that as poor countries become more affluent, more people can afford cars, which leads to increased land degradation in order to build car based infra-structure such as roads, gas stations, and malls.

Figure24 Here we see a huge gathering of people at the beach during an air show in Chicago, the summer of 2003. (Photo by author)

Figure 25 Here, we see two SUVs on a busy Chicago street. (Photo by author)

It is obvious that the world's biggest problem is overpopulation and the inequities between the rich and poor countries. Overpopulation causes widespread environmental destruction because every single person needs food and shelter. If we compare a rich family who has two children and lives in the United States with that of a poor family with six children in a country like Nepal, does that mean that the six children family does more damage to the environment than the two children household? No, because the rich family uses more environmental resources living higher on the hog, even though they have a smaller family size to support their higher standard of living. The poor family may not use as many environmental resources, but in order to eke out a living, they may have to poach animals or cut down trees for wood.

CHAPTER 18
PARADIGMS

Our paradigm now seems to be: Something terrible happened to us on September 11, and that gives us the right to interpret all future events in a way that everyone else in the world must be with us. And if they don't they can go straight to hell.
Bill Clinton

INTRODUCTION

What exactly is a paradigm? A paradigm, according to The Random House Dictionary is a sample or pattern.[155] For those of us who are accustomed to doing things in certain ways it can be said that we are trapped by paradigms. Let me give you an example. Many years ago when watches just had hands a Swiss citizen came up with the idea to take away the hands and use numbers instead. Boy, did people rebel. How can you have a watch without hands? Now, of course, most clocks and watches, at least the ones that I see, are digital, including the one that I am wearing now. But I think you, the readers, already understand the idea. Most people get bogged down in a fixed pattern. This chapter deals with simple things that we take for granted, such as the need for a large military, using farm land for private homes, pesticide use, and low fossil fuel costs. Although there are literally thousands of other paradigms worldwide, I am just concentrating on these few to make my point.

THE CONCEPT

Paradigms are prevalent in our society because of tradition. As a child growing up in New York City, I would constantly hear about the threat of communism and why we should devote all our energies to defeating it and that we needed a big military (paradigm number one) because we had many enemies. We did not realize that we had more severe problems on our hands such as the creeping threat of air, land and water pollution. We also didn't realize the hidden threat to our genes by radiation from above ground nuclear tests, which were meant to develop nuclear bombs and protect us in time of war. But just the opposite occurred by risking most inhabitants of the planet to diseases associated with fallout from radiation such as cancer and genetic mutations. We had to do something about them by preparing militarily. We also had to increase our dependence on oil even though we knew that it was very polluting and damaging to our environment. Yet, because of tradition and lack of foresight Americans as well as citizens of other countries are dying because of oil and for other obscure reasons.

In addition to our obsession with the military and the nuclear bomb, we find ourselves leaving the cities and moving to the suburbs formally called farmland (paradigm number two). For those of you who didn't know, farmland is used to grow crops on. If we keep expanding our population on arable land (land which is good for growing crops), we may not be able to feed our growing population.

In order to grow these crops, we were told that we had to use pesticides (paradigm number three) even though in this day and age we have found ways to circumvent these substances (see chapter 24 on solutions). Cheap gasoline (paradigm number four) especially, in the United States is believed to be a right that we all take for granted. However, as we are finding out, it is too damaging to the environment. This chapter deals with the above paradigms.

PARADGM ONE
THE MILITARY

Here we see especially how deadly the military is. In March of 2003, the United States has been an occupying power in Iraq for ambiguous reasons. We see how deadly the military can be by the fact that we have killed over 100 thousand civilians and countless Iraqi soldiers. In addition to Iraq, there are wars all over the planet such as the ongoing conflict between the Israelis and the Palestinians, the civil war in the Sudan, the war in Chechnya, and numerous conflicts on the African continent. Why are there so many wars? Perhaps, because we have armies which have to justify their existence. Well, let's examine this. Perhaps the largest expenditure next to social spending is on the military. Do we really need such a gigantic military that eats tremendous amounts of our budget? I think not. However, when you speak to the average citizen, and, of course, politicians who are running for reelection, that is the first stand that they take. Yes, let us spend and spend on our military as if that is the way to actually defend ourselves from some enemy that is far away. It is obvious that since September 11, 2001, we need a bigger military because in trying to retaliate on poor countries such as Afghanistan, who can't defend themselves, WE HAVE CREATED MORE ENEMIES, which will justify a bigger military. This is also true in Iraq and Afghanistan with the killing of innocent civilians by mistake. WE ARE CREATING EVEN MORE enemies. (See Appendix V)

We have plenty of enemies within, and now, from without. But perhaps the main enemy is fear and arrogance. Our arrogance fosters fear and hatred, thus, perpetuating the need for guns in our homes, and ultimately a large intransigent military force. The proof of the fear factor was emphasized in the movie, *Bowling for Columbine*, by Michael Moore.

By utilizing our military in such a way that prevents it from actually defending us is an obscenity. While watching a movie called "*And the Band Played On*" which was about the AIDS outbreak here in the United States it showed a TV newscast in which the then present Ronald Reagan pledged to cut all budgets except that of the military. This was real footage. When I saw this part I almost flipped out. To me the only real budget cuts should have been made from the military and basically nothing else. But as you can see politicians and myself are diametrically opposite in our ways of thinking. Don't you think that we have enough military weapons to include submarines, guns, bullets, missiles etc.? I would think so. But those 'smart' generals got to have their way.

The military continues unabated to produce lots of pollution from their endeavors such as making plutonium for nuclear bombs and producing a myriad of other military materials. The underlying reason for this buildup of weapons is due to the fear factor. This is the fear of being attacked by an enemy, yet paradoxically the very "protection" that the military provides is also endangering every species on the earth's surface. How? By developing weapons of mass destruction (WMD) we are increasing our risks of certain types of diseases such as cancer and immune system disorders by poisoning our planet with effluent (waste) from the testing processes. The major concern that comes to mind is the testing of nuclear weapons in the oceans, and testing above or below ground. We are still exposed to minute particles of radiation from leaks . Many of these tests are done in the Pacific Ocean by the French on atolls (coral islands). Because of this we may be exposed to radiation by eating contaminated fish.

We can think of at least two ways concerning this issue: Let us assume that we have real enemies including those manufactured by our arrogance towards both democratic and non-democratic countries. If this is the case then we are doomed by the idea that we have to test our weapon systems which may endanger our very lives and the ecosystems by adding radiation and other substances. These substances may be mutagenic (causes changes in chromosomes) in the cells of our bodies. If, on the other hand, we really don't have real enemies then we could spare the environment of weapons development and devote our energies to making the whole world safe for everybody. I never understood the "cold war" mentality where the former Soviet Union and the United States had nuclear missiles facing each other. If there was a nuclear exchange the whole world would have been doomed and not just our two countries. A solution to this conundrum is developed in the last chapter.

PARADIGM TWO
SINGLE FAMILY HOMES ON FARMLAND

One of the things that really bugs me is building homes on what once was prime farmland. It is true that people need homes but why cut, chop and dig good farmland when there are plenty of other, albeit, non-excellent locations to build homes? The answer is easy to figure. Developers need to make a living. What better way then to pay a farmer for his land and make a financial killing by building expensive homes that no minimum wage earner (currently the minimum wage here in the United States is $5.15 per hour) can hope to afford. I am speaking specifically about a group of homes on my way to one of the colleges that I taught at on Tuesdays and Thursdays, from 1991 to 2003. I had been going to this school for twelve years now and I remember a few years ago there was a farmhouse with many acres of land. A developer bought the land and demolished the farmhouse and there are now close to 100 single family and town homes.[156] The range in price is from $140, 000 to over $200,000. Obviously these are for people who can afford that much money. But my gripe is that these homes could have been made at a lower cost and house more people comfortably if they were built as garden apartments. Yeah, I know that many people want their own home. But, you know something? If you come home every night from a hard day at work all you need is a nice roof over your head. It is true that I live in a single family home as of this writing, but for many years I lived in an apartment. I felt lucky that I had a roof over my head after seeing how other people both in the United States with our homeless and in other countries where we see whole families living in a one room home such as in Haiti or in Nepal..

If more people would be happy with a roof over their head in a dwelling as part of an apartment complex, less land would be needed. As mentioned above garden apartments are very comfortable and adequate. I lived in one and was very happy. I had all the amenities that I needed including enough space for my belongings. I also realized that I did not take up a lot of land as those of single homes do. In America there are over 70,000,000 private homes. It is obvious from these numbers that if many of these people lived in garden apartments there would have been less destruction of farmland. Is a private home in the suburbs really a part of the American Dream or were Americans sold a bill of goods through our newspapers and politicians running for office?

PARADIGM THREE
PESTICIDE USE

We are taught that without pesticides we would not get crops. Well that is partly true. It is also suggested by many scientists that if we got rid of pesticides like DDT then malaria would return. In our quest for pesticides we are destroying non-target organisms with the paradoxical effect of increasing the numbers of the target organisms. Non-target organisms are those which we hope to save such as food crops and other beneficial soil organisms. Target organisms are those such as insects which attack our crops. Millions of pounds of pesticides are being produced worldwide every year. Many of these pesticides accumulate in individual organisms including humans.[157] Ask your local farmer how he has been bombarded by salesmen convincing him to buy their pesticides. They convince him that the crops will be destroyed by pests without these chemical pesticides. We see this demonstrated in the increase in mutated animals such as six legged frogs and various cancers in humans. Well, it just so happens that now there are ways to prevent crop damage by pests without the use of pesticides. These include biological and genetic controls.

PARADIGM FOUR
THE LOW PRICE OF GASOLINE IN THE UNITED STATES

During the early summer of 2000 and 2004 gasoline prices in the Chicago area were over $2.00 per gallon, a very low price. Politicians were beside themselves about the situation because consumers which are their constituents got upset about the higher price of gasoline. From listening to talk shows I got the impression that the callers did not care about the environmental consequences of excessive gasoline usage, only about driving more miles (kilometers) for less money. I myself believe that gasoline under $10.00 is ridiculously low contrary to what most Americans think. Why, because we are selfish and drive large gas guzzling automobiles because people want them. Many of these people buy these large cars because they are there. (See chapter 6) Consider the paradigm here? We are made to believe that low gasoline prices are a right and not a luxury. Yet, ask yourselves why we went to Iraq in 1991 and again in 2003. If Iraq had wheat instead of oil as an export, we would not have been there. We are destroying our environment for the sake of low gasoline prices and bigger cars, specifically large vans and Hummers (Hummers get between 8 and 10 miles per gallon, while the newer hybrid models get over 60 miles per gallon). When prices are high it's as if the sky is falling and only politicians could lower them. People were complaining because they were not used to gasoline prices in the $2.00 range even though Europeans and Israelis were paying the equivalent of $5.79 or more per gallon (as of June 2004). In 2000, politicians were having meetings about the topic and even went so far as to cut the state and local taxes on gasoline.

The federal government as well as the Illinois government gave us reasons why gasoline was higher. Some of their explanations were that gasoline needed to be reformulated to cut back on pollution. This would add to the cost of gasoline. Another theory was the possibility that there was a shortage of gasoline in the Midwest region of the United States. Anyway, what it all boiled down to was the fact that consumers complained and prices were lowered about one week after they peaked. This to me was absurd because people would hop in their cars and drive excessively, and of course, the politicians only thought about being reelected because the summer of 2000 was when the national nominating conventions were to take place. Politicians would do anything to get votes; even if it meant degrading the environment because none of them ever took an environmental class with me to understand the consequences.

Figure 26. A price list of gasoline at a local gas station in the
United States. Notice that the price is only around $2.45 which is
very low compared to European prices. (Photo by author)

We must not let ourselves be controlled by paradigms. Things change all the time. It is imperative that we humans change our opinions as the needs dictate. Just because we are locked into certain patterns doesn't mean that we don't have the will to change them for the benefit of the planet.

CHAPTER 19
RESPECTED, DISRESPECTED AND PIOUS INDIVIDUALS WITH IDIOTIC IDEAS INCLUDING...POLITICIANS, TALK SHOW HOSTS, MISGUIDED ENVIRONMENTALISTS, ETC., ETC.

"Man's relationship to nature is no longer determined by nature but is subject to the rule of political management on a scale beyond normal comprehension " [158]

"They see no value in the environment for itself. A mountain, a stream, a forest have value only for human use, and the importance of that use can always be expressed in dollar terms."
A statement made by a member of the Colorado Water Quality Control Commission when talking about two Republican legislators.[159]

INTRODUCTION

Perhaps one of the greatest causes of environmental pollution is the attitude that politicians do not even consider the environment when making policy decisions which are perceived to benefit their environmentally unaware constituents. These are the people whom we elect (at least in free countries and prior to the year 2000) to carry out our policies. Unfortunately many of the politicians love to submit to the will of the people whether it makes sense or not. If most people want it and it is morally wrong they will do it anyway. A good example of international politics, when the environment is not considered, is the following:

Because of international politics we constantly see actions which are unwarranted. An example: El Al, Israeli Airlines has routes to the Far East. They were not allowed to fly over Saudi Arabia thus increasing the flight time by four extra hours not to mention the excess amount of carbon dioxide (CO_2), which will add to the greenhouse effect. Again we see human nature interfering with proper environmental practices.

Another issue of politics: Despite having large oil fields, Mexico is a country that is relatively poor. Why couldn't the United States buy its oil from Mexico thus sparing a large supertanker trip across the Persian Gulf and the Atlantic Ocean? The answer is easy...because Saudi Arabia will be upset with us due to their close ties with the Bush administration. If we did get our oil from Mexico, we would be accomplishing things that we should have done in the first place. Number one would be to increase the wealth of Mexico thus preventing an inflow of unwanted immigrants. Two, we will be preventing aquatic pollution by preventing the prospect of oil spills caused by super tankers in transit. But, human nature and politics being what it is prevents common sense approaches like this.

We also have to clump together politicians as a primal cause of global pollution. Another example which is perhaps the most blatant act of environmental terrorism in the history of humankind occurred in 1991, during the Gulf War between Saddam Hussein and the coalition forces led by George H. W. Bush, then President of the United States. Hussein had his army destroy about 742 oil wells thus setting them on fire, which no doubt devastated the air and the surrounding environs.

The list goes on and on about our *wonderful politicians*. A few words about the Bush administration (1988-92) are in order. When Bush was running for president the second time he vowed that he wanted to get oil from the Artic National Wildlife Refuge (ANWR). This was a bad idea. There are many reasons why it is bad. The first one is due to the fact that if we had a leak or an explosion we would contaminate part of the refuge. The second one is that if we built more fuel efficient cars and developed solar powered cars we wouldn't need that oil anyway. Three, if we knew that there is oil available, what would be the incentive to develop alternative energy sources knowing the environmental ignorance of the American population.

CONCEPT

POLITICIANS, DICTATORS, ETC.,

DAN QUAYLE

In his wonderful book, *The Paradox of American Democracy* [160] John B. Judis talks a lot about America and how big interests are betraying the public trust. There are lots of facts about the republican administration's attacks on the environment. One in particular sticks out. When Dan Quayle was Vice President, the Bush administration set up a council on competitiveness, in which Vice President Quayle was the head. The council was merely a way that businesses could fight environmental or safety regulations. There is a quote from Alan Magazine, Director of the Council on Competitiveness, a council set up prior to the Bush administration's council on Competitiveness which goes like this: "We brought in a Who's Who of top corporate leaders who.... kept regaining Quayle with the recommendations we had. Every now and then he (Quayle) would look up from his food and he'd ask a question, just to get it going. He didn't make one declarative sentence the entire time we were there. It was as though he didn't understand these issues and couldn't care less."

GEORGE W. BUSH

Perhaps the best way to begin discussion of G.W. Bush is to mention some recent headlines. Like the old saying goes, "One picture is worth 1000 words" I believe headlines convey the same message.

HEADLINE-Tuesday Jan 23, 2001-Bush restricts abortion money- Chicago Sun Times (see figure 4)

HEADLINE- March 13, 2001- Bush won't regulate carbon dioxide- Excite on Internet

HEADLINE- March 22, 2001- Bush opposition to clean air accord, risky, Activists say- Chicago Tribune

HEADLINE—March 22, 2001 Bush suspends Clinton mining restrictions on US land- Chicago Tribune

HEADLINE- March 31, 2001 Bush defends rejection of climate treaty - Chicago Tribune

HEADLINE- March 30, 2001 Bush shuns climate treaty
-Chicago Sun Times

HEADLINE- Bush withdraws New Arsenic standard as high arsenic levels close parks- March 22, 2001
-Beyond Pesticdes.org/news.html-V 23, 2001

HEADLINE-Climate change debate has US in minority
-March 31, 2001-Chicago Tribune p.3

HEADLINE- Senate OKs Alaska drilling-March 17, 2005
-Chicago Tribune

If I repeated every headline in every newspaper where Bush's environmental attitude was displayed I would need hundreds of pages to do so. Here is just a sample.

Now that we have been bushwhacked thrice in the last 15 years, it appears evident that we (all of the Planet Earth and its inhabitants) are in serious trouble. From the first day since George W. Bush's inauguration our environment seemed to be in danger if not in deadly peril. Since day one we have read in newspapers about his lack of environmental awareness and his enthusiasm in eliminating environmental regulations on the grounds that it will cost too much money.

It is precisely because of the GOP's stance about humanity: their obsession with the misguided idea that money and its unending pursuit is the ultimate Holy Grail of the American Constitution. For example, Bush's reasoning for lowering standards on global warming and arsenic in water supplies is that he believes that it will cost his rich campaign contributors too much money. We know that many of the polluting industries especially those of the coal and oil are big contributors to his campaign and the campaigns of the Republican Party.

Bush is also incurring the wrath of European countries because they think, rightly so, that he is interested in generating wealth without regard for the future. Belgian energy minister, Oliver Delieuze, has said that Bush's position was a "political scandal and catastrophe for the environment"[161]. French President Jacques Chirac, said that Bush's stand on global warming was "at a time of global warming and of a disturbing and an unacceptable challenge to the Kyoto protocol...of spreading deserts, and impending freshwater crisis of major proportions, how can we affirm the right to a protected and preserved environment? The right of future generations."

I think that by now, the reader gets the picture. When we elect politicians (G.W. was selected by the U.S. Supreme Court and not elected, or so it appears) to high office, we should be sure that they are educated especially in subjects that affect the planet like the environment. Without this education we get people like Bush who consistently gives the impression that the environment doesn't even exist. (See chapter 16). Bush and his advisers have adopted the stance that reducing emissions through costly short term measures is unjustified, and that scientific forecasting of climate change is too imprecise to agree to long-term, international, mandatory cuts in greenhouse gas emissions. Well, wait until mosquitoes start giving out their calling cards in the form of disease.

RONALD REAGAN

Ronald Reagan just passed away while I was reviewing this chapter. I know that most Americans praise and admire Reagan but I am not one of them. There are many reasons for this of which three come to mind.

Number One: Reagan won the election to the presidency under a cloud but different than that of G.W. Bush. I am not much of an historian but in 1980, when the election occurred there were 52 American hostages being held in the United States Embassy in Teheran, the capital of Iran. It appears from various documents that the Republicans made a deal with the Iranians that they would hold the hostages until the American election, trying to insure a loss for the then president, Jimmy Carter.[162] Unfortunately for the world's environment and the future of the planet they succeeded. Jimmy Carter lost the election. Now I am not a history professor or politician so I am not here to either praise or condemn Reagan's political legacy, but only to condemn his environmental stance. Based on other documents his political legacy probably would not be much better than his environmental legacy.

Number two: It has always been my opinion that Reagan was one of the most environmentally uninformed presidents ever. I say this not with hate, but belief. The evidence for this was demonstrated by the people he appointed to his cabinet. The two main figures which come to mind are Anne Gorsuch (Burford), head of the EPA, (Environmental Protection Agency) and that of James Watt, Secretary of the Interior. In fact, there was even a book written about his assault on the environment, which is quoted in this section. It is called" "A Season of Spoils: The Reagan administration's attack on the environment" by Jonathan Lash, published by Pantheon Books.

Number three: When Reagan entered the White House after Jimmy Carter left he tore down the solar water heater from the White House roof that Carter placed in order to encourage alternative sources of energy.

Needless to say the solar energy industry plummeted after this event thus having propelled the world back into the gauntlet of the dinosaur age of gas guzzling autos, wars fought for oil and increased asthma, just to name a few. [163] Ask yourself how many people have died worldwide because of this environmentally ignorant and stupid policy. Because of the continuum of war and air pollution caused by using fossil fuels thousands and maybe millions of precious animals, plants, bacteria, fungi, and humans have been and will be annihilated. I always believed that President Jimmy Carter had the foresight and vision that U.S. presidents should possess. Presidents are symbols of national and international progress and they set the tone for the benefit of their citizens. By Reagan's act of removing the solar water heater, his true corporate-colors were revealed.

Whenever you ask people about his presidency they say that Reagan was great because the economy was in better shape than that of the Carter administration and helped eliminate the Soviet Style of Communism.

Now here is an example of pure stupidity. When Reagan was president he "proved that he was macho" by standing up to the Russians. We always had to be ahead of them especially in the nuclear arms business. It seemed to me that whenever the Russians would advance a nuclear system we had to one-up-manship them.

We had to build more nuclear bombs, which were more powerful. We built up, they built up and we would build up even further until the Soviet Union virtually went bankrupt because they couldn't keep up and they collapsed. During the Reagan presidency the world had the greatest number of nuclear weapons ever (see Table 7). Now Americans are praising that action by Reagan, who actually imperiled the world more. First, the economy of the former Soviet Union is in shambles. Soldiers and others have not been paid for months. Why? Because there appears to be no money. Why no money? Because they spent it all trying to keep up with us here in America. Now, who's minding the nuclear store? Maybe unpaid soldiers? Reagan's legacy is a disaster. Has anyone noticed that during his presidency the AIDS epidemic began as well as the noticed decline in the ozone layer? Coincidence you say. Well, maybe.

If you would look at the number of nuclear missiles, we notice that during the Reagan -Bush years, 1980-1992, the number of nuclear warheads worldwide was 69,478 in 1986. In 1997, the count was down to only 36,110.[164] This number is totally ridiculous and scary as well. It's a nuclear *A-bombination*. See Table 7 for numbers of bombs. (There is a slight discrepancy between Table 7 and that of M.Renner in Vital Signs, see endnote 164)

TABLE 7
Global Nuclear Stockpiles, 1945-2000

Year	U.S.	Russia	U.K.	France	China	Total
1945	2	0	0	0	0	2
1946	9	0	0	0	0	9
1947	13	0	0	0	0	13
1948	56	0	0	0	0	56
1949	169	1	0	0	0	170
1950	298	5	0	0	0	303
1951	438	25	0	0	0	463
1952	832	50	0	0	0	882
1953	1,161	120	1	0	0	1,282
1954	1,630	150	5	0	0	1,785
1955	2,280	200	10	0	0	2,490
1956	3,620	400	15	0	0	4,035
1957	5,828	650	20	0	0	6,498
1958	7,402	900	22	0	0	8,324
1959	12,305	1,050	25	0	0	13,380
1960	18,638	1,700	30	0	0	20,368
1961	22,249	2,450	50	0	0	24,729
1962	27,100	3,100	205	0	0	30,405
1963	29,800	4,000	280	0	0	34,080
1964	31,600	5,100	310	4	1	37,015
1965	32,400	6,300	310	32	5	39,047
1966	32,450	7,550	270	36	20	40,326
1967	32,500	8,850	270	36	25	41,681
1968	30,700	10,000	280	36	35	41,051
1969	28,200	11,000	308	36	50	39,594
1970	26,600	12,700	280	36	75	39,691
1971	26,500	14,500	220	45	100	41,365
1972	27,000	16,600	220	70	130	44,020
1973	28,400	18,800	275	116	150	47,741

Year	U.S.	Russia	U.K.	France	China	Total
1974	29,100	21,100	325	145	170	50,840
1975	28,100	23,500	350	188	185	52,323
1976	26,700	25,800	350	212	190	53,252
1977	25,800	28,400	350	228	200	54,978
1978	24,600	31,400	350	235	220	56,805
1979	24,300	34,000	350	235	235	59,120
1980	24,300	36,300	350	250	280	61,480
1981	23,400	38,700	350	274	330	63,054
1982	23,000	40,800	335	274	360	64,769
1983	23,400	42,600	320	279	380	66,979
1984	23,600	43,300	270	280	414	67,864
1985	23,500	44,000	300	359	426	68,585
1986*	23,400	45,000	300	355	423	69,478
1987*	23,700	44,000	300	420	415	68,835
1988*	23,400	42,500	300	411	430	67,041
1989*	22,500	40,000	300	412	433	63,645
1990*	21,000	38,000	300	504	432	60,236
1991*	19,500	35,000	300	538	434	55,772
1992*	18,200	33,500	300	538	434	52,972
1993*	16,750	32,000	300	524	434	50,008
1994*	15,380	30,000	250	512	400	46,542
1995*	14,000	28,000	300	500	400	43,200
1996*	12,900	26,000	300	500	400	40,000
1997*	12,425	24,000	260	450	400	37,525
1998*	11,425	22,000	260	450	400	34,535
1999*	10,925	20,000	185	450	400	31,960
2000*	10,500	20,000	185	450	400	31,535

*U.S. (from 1988) and Soviet/Russian (from 1986) warheads include those in active, operational forces; retired, non-deployed warheads awaiting dismantlement; and weapons in reserve. For recent years, the estimate for the former Soviet Union/Russia is 50 percent active, 50 percent retired/reserve/

If we look at the chart we notice that during the Reagan years 1980-88, the total number of nuclear weapons stockpiled was the highest ever recorded, with the year 1986 having the most with 65,057 nuclear weapons ready worldwide to be used against an enemy? [165] If all of these weapons were used I doubt that the world's environment would support anything but the lowly cockroach. (In defense of the lowly cockroach, I feel that they deserve more respect then they get because of their ability to survive radiation exposure. Most people like to destroy them, but they must have an ecological function or else they would not have been put here by God or other heavenly beings).

Look at the Soviet Union, today with crime, violence and poverty lurking in the streets and the high incidence of incurable Tuberculosis in Russian prisons. [166] That is partly due to Reagan's idiotic idea that we have to defeat communism at all costs without regards for the consequences of a nuclear exchange. Environmental damage of an exchange like this would include the extinction of most of the world's organisms as well as genetic mutations. Do the movies *Rhodan*, *The Omega Man*, and *Five*, mean anything to you? These movies dealt with the consequences of mutations after nuclear wars. Instead of us trying to out maneuver the Russians, we should have invested money in helping them overcome their difficulties as well as helping them to solidify a lasting peace. The ridiculous cold war was partly to blame for our poverty here in America as well as the poverty in the Soviet Union.

In a wonderful book entitled, *The Season of Spoils: The Story of the Reagan's Administration Attack on the Environment*, by Jonathan Lash, Katherine Gillman and David Sheridan, the Reagan administration's attack on the environment is detailed. In the book it is pointed out that household names of the 80's such as Anne Gorsuch (Burford), the former EPA administrator and James Watt (Secretary of the Interior) proved their unwillingness to support the environmental laws that they were appointed to protect.

In a reference to Anne Gorsuch and her friends, a member of the Colorado Water quality Commission, Myrna Poticha said, "They see no value in the environment for itself. A mountain, a stream, a forest have value only for human use and the importance of that use can always be expressed in dollar terms. This means, of course that, only uses need to be protected and use for development has the highest value of all."[167] Statements like these are still hallmarks of Republicanism as well as those dreaded developers.

As a matter of fact, after Jimmy Carter left office, the Reagan administration was looking for conservatives to fill EPA positions, but there weren't enough republicans with an environmental background.

An example of an incorrect stance includes not making known the hazardous effects of pesticides because of economic considerations. Permission to use pesticides such as EDB, Ethylene dibromide, used to kill nematodes (unsegmented roundworms), which cause plant diseases was issued despite the fact that it is a known carcinogen of animals. The use of DBCP, dibromochloropropane, also a nematocide, especially on pineapples in Hawaii, was approved even after it was suspected of causing sterility in factory workers producing it. In 1977 when the EPA put restrictions on some uses of DBCP, Robert R. Phillips, the executive secretary of The National Peach Council made a suggestion regarding factory workers who make DBCP. "If possible, sterility is the main effect. Couldn't workers who were old enough that they no longer wanted children accept such positions voluntarily? Or could workers be advised of the situation, and some might volunteer for such work posts as an alternative to planned surgery for a vasectomy or tubal ligation, or as a means of getting around religious bans on birth control when they want no more children?"[168]

Another example of republican insensitivity towards the environment during the Reagan administration is explained in the following statement. The use of Heptachlor to get rid of termites was allowed for some uses despite its toxicity. But perhaps one of the biggest insults of the Reagan administration came when he tried to dismantle a badly needed regulatory impediment towards unchecked pesticide dumping in foreign countries. This is the story: Many pesticides were manufactured in the United States. They were banned or restricted for use in the U.S. because of their toxicity as well as low tolerances on food products. Many of the companies felt that it was OK to send them to other countries so that they will recoup some of the money invested in the pesticides manufactured. This law would have allowed notification to the importers of these chemicals that they were banned in the United States. But due to the fact that some of Reagan's supporters might be hurt financially, they tried to rescind the law.[169] According to them it was OK to help their friends remain financially solvent, even though it meant death and environmental contamination to the recipients of the banned pesticides.

In 1979, during the last year of the presidency of Jimmy Carter, an interagency task force was formed to prepare guidelines governing the export of hazardous substances including pesticides, drugs and other goods.[170] Five days before he left office Jimmy Carter enacted into law, "The Executive order on Federal Policy regarding the Export of Banned or Significantly Restricted Substances"; however, Ronald Reagan rescinded the order several weeks after taking office.[171] He essentially allowed our pesticide conglomerates to continue dumping their poisons in developing nations. Wonderful! Just wonderful!

James Watt was the Secretary of the Interior under Reagan. He wanted to sell off some of the national lands as well as work to destroy many environmental gains that environmentalists had fought for. Because of this, thousands of concerned citizens, myself included, signed petitions to get rid of him. Tip O'Neil, who was then Speaker of the House, showed newsmen the thousands of petitions that environmentally minded Americans signed. Yet, Congress allowed him to remain until he, Watt, made some very insensitive remarks about who he had on a coal board. It is interesting how "God" intervened in this case. By placing racist and insensitive words in his mouth, He ("God") accomplished what thousands of Americans wanted: Watt's resignation or retirement from the Interior Department. [172] Reagan also vetoed the Clean Water Bill, in the 80's. For the life of me, I can't figure out why.

JESSE HELMS - *Republican*

Here, again, we see another politician doesn't appear to care about the environment or the health of most Americans. It appeared to me Jesse only cared about the health of the tobacco industry and perhaps other merchants of substances that cause misery in humans. There was a battle going on in the senate about weather to prevent cigarette smoking on domestic airline flights. He was against the ban despite evidence that it made stewardesses (flight attendants) sick, passengers sick and smelled up the planes. But, because he is from a top tobacco growing state (North Carolina), he had to fight for tobacco interests despite the fact that over 400,000 Americans die each year because of tobacco related illnesses. He just wanted to get reelected, which he did to my dismay, and probably to the delight of the pulmonary specialists.

It should be noted here as well that Jesse Helms was the Chairman of the Arms services Committee and he did not want to ratify the START (Strategic Arms Reduction Treaty) to eliminate nuclear weapons because of reasons that do not hold water, thus threatening nuclear destruction worldwide.

RUSH LIMBAUGH - *Republican*

As many of you know by now there is a radio personality on the air. His name is Rush Limbaugh. He is an extreme right winger as is evidenced by his views. He is also partly intelligent, egoistic, unaware and environmentally challenged. What does Mr. Limbaugh have to do with pollution? Too much! So pay attention and here goes.

A man of his intelligence should be able to use his gift in a more useful manner than just bashing liberals, the environment and women who want equal rights as men have. He has a tremendous audience (20,000,000) most of which are right wingers like him. His views and values are totally different than mine. He says that there is no global warming based on listening to people like the late Dixie Lee Ray, the former governor of the state of Washington and former head of the Atomic Energy Commission. (now called The Nuclear Regulatory Commission) and to other people..

Limbaugh likes to poo poo many environmental dangers. He also is against animals. He doesn't realize that animals play an ecological function. He criticizes mosquitoes, the red squirrel and other animal species. He should take a course in environmental science and he may learn that every organism has an ecological function whether we know what it is or not.

Let's see why he is so bad. He may be bad for the environment because many people believe what he is saying. Limbaugh has convinced many of his listeners that the stability of the economy outweighs the longevity of ecological stability. People who like Limbaugh believe jobs will be lost if we worry about the environment thus we cannot **AFFORD** to save the environment. Again, Mr. Limbaugh loves to get callers that agree with him. Naturally, we all need allies who agree with our viewpoints. I know that there are people who agree with me. Fine! There are also those who don't agree with me. That is fine, too.

Mr. Limbough is a showman. He makes lots of money espousing his views. As Limbough has said himself, in his book, *The Way Things Ought to Be.*(Pocket Books, 1992) "My views on the environment are rooted in my belief in Creation...I refuse to believe that people, who are themselves the result of Creation, can destroy the most magnificent creation in the entire universe." Okay. But it seems to me that he would be better off saying some good things about the environment. After all, he lives in the environment as well. I think that he forgets that his money literally comes from trees. Hence, the paper. The coins, whether they are silver, gold or platinum, come from the earth. The New York City apartment house he used to live in is located on land that is in the environment. It is made from material found on the planet. These include sand, which is used in windows, and the plastic items which come from oil, which are found in his kitchen and elsewhere. The wood for his furniture and other fixtures come from trees. True, I have never been in his kitchen, let alone his house, but I have never seen a kitchen without some plastic items. I assume that he has to breathe clean air also, albeit, in New York at least at ground level, the air is not so good. At present, he lives in a mansion in Florida, which I assume contains glass, plastic and wood. So you see, Mr. Limbaugh is a product of the environment. He happens to be lucky that he lives in America and not in Bangladesh, where poverty, flooding and homelessness are rampant.

I do think eventually he will come around to our way of thinking. He also does not realize that the things we do locally to the environment have global consequences. Take a look at deforestation, for instance. Have you ever asked yourself, what are the effects of cutting down trees at the pace that we are doing on the environment? Well, take a look at Hurricane Andrew (1992). It was a massive hurricane as was evidenced by the speed of its winds and property damage (billions of dollars). For every degree that the earth heats up hurricanes get stronger because they derive their energy from the oceans and with the heat they get more powerful. Deforestation contributes to climate destabilization. Also, with tree cutting, the atmospheric oxygen supply will decrease. I have yet to see this, but ecological common sense says that it is so, but we are not really sure if the bulk of the oxygen comes from the oceans or Tropical Rain Forests.

There is a theory that I think we should all pay attention to, especially those Rush Limbaugh fans. We are all glad that whaling has basically been eliminated. Not 100% as of yet, but we are heading that way. There is a theory that if we hunted all the great whales to extinction we could deplete the oxygen supply of the planet. How is this possible? Simply put, it goes like this. *Euphausia superba* is the name of the krill, the organisms that whales eat. These are shrimp-like organisms that make up the bulk of the diet of many whales. They exist in patches by the tons. These in turn eat the algae, small plant-like organisms that serve as the base of the food chain

(See figure 20). Not only do algae serve as a food source, **BUT** they produce the oxygen. If you kill off the whales the krill will proliferate, thus multiplying and eating the algae which produce the oxygen. If you have tons and tons and tons of krill eating the diminished tons of algae, there won't be any algae left to produce the oxygen, thus depleting the world's supply of oxygen; assuming most of the oxygen comes from the oceans. So my friends, be careful when it comes to the environment. Do not believe everything you hear from guys like Rush Limbaugh and his ilk. He needs a course in environmental science.

JOHN SINUNU- *Republican*

Here we have another perceived anti-environmentalist. Not to mention the fact that Mr. Sinunu has eight children which according to environmentalists may appear to be six children too many. He was the Governor of New Hampshire, who eventually became Chief of Staff (1982-1992) to George H. W. Bush [173] (remember him, the environmental president?) It is amazing how fate works. Get a load of this. Mr. Sinunu was Chief of Staff at the

White House. He was able to go anywhere he wanted by any means, at least he thought so. First, he said that Americans must have their cars, thus encouraging more gasoline consumption. Okay, so much for mass transit. Anyway, as fate would have it he took a limousine to New York City to attend a Stamp Show. New York is approximately a four hour drive from Washington D.C. That, in itself, is not bad, but, and here I emphasize BUT, there is train service called Amtrak from Washington D.C. to New York City. But being Chief of Staff and a former governor, he feels that he can do whatever he wants. He undoubtedly sets a bad example because as of this writing we are in the midst of a second war in Iraq, mainly because of oil. Maybe if he were less arrogant and more environmentally aware he would have taken Amtrak. The cost of two secret service agents and Sinunu himself would have been less than the limousine trip.

He just represents the "Hey, I am rich and live in America, therefore, I can do what I want with total disregard for common sense and a sense of well-being for the planet, and the hell with mass transit!"

THE POPE *formerly John Paul II (1920-2005)*

If there ever was a politician or human being, who can literally determine the fate of the planet, by his/her decision, it is the Pope. At present, John Paul II is Pope, but his views regarding population control are outdated and outmoded. He is against birth control and abortion without REAL alternatives for stopping the escalating birth rate in the world. As I write these sentences, there is a conference on Development and Population happening in Cairo, Egypt. As can be expected, there is a lot of bickering and dissension regarding these issues by countries accusing each other of interference.

In October of 1998 an organization in Italy called" *Domus Galilaeana*" was sponsoring a conference honoring my father, Dr. Silvano Arieti and his work in psychiatry at the University of Pisa in northern Italy (Tuscany). I took it upon myself to write a letter to Pope John Paul II telling him that I will be in Italy because I have a stopover in Rome for about three hours. And that if possible, I might meet with him or one of his representatives regarding the Catholic Church's stance on birth control and contraception. The letter is the following:

Office of the Pope
The Vatican
Rome, Italy

David F. Arieti

Dear Your Holiness,

I am an environmental scientist and college instructor in the Chicago, Illinois vicinity. I will be coming to Italy on October 3, and leave the 5th of October in order to attend a conference honoring my father, Dr. Silvano Arieti, who was a world famous psychiatrist. The conference is being held at the University of Pisa, located in the town where my beloved father was born.

The reason I am writing you this letter is because as an environmental science instructor and scientist, I am very concerned about the state of the world's environment which appears to be deteriorating at an impressive rate due mainly to human overpopulation. You are the one person on this planet who can make a difference for the health of the planet by allowing your followers to use contraception and other birth control methods other than the rhythm method. Because if we keep overpopulating the planet at the present rate, I foresee more hunger, warfare and total collapse of humanity as we know it.

I want to be able to present either you or your associates with the facts regarding human overpopulation on the planet. I will be arriving in Rome at around 10AM, on the 3rd of October, and go on to Pisa, later on in the afternoon. I was wondering if I could meet with one of your associates or even yourself at the airport, to discuss this matter in person. I hope that you will take my request seriously or just give me a reply as soon as possible before I leave on October 3, 1998.

Enclosed, please find a copy of my resume, a list of the major environmental problems on the planet and a poem entitled,
"Prayer for Children"

Thank you for your attention.

Sincerely,

David F. Arieti

The following is the prayer for the children that I sent the Pope, which I found at one of the schools where I was involved in asbestos removal. The author is unknown, but it is very appropriate in today's world of the rising gap between affluence and poverty.

PRAYER FOR CHILDREN

We pray for children
>who sneak popsicles before supper,
>who erase holes in math workbooks
>who can never find their shoes.

And we pray for those
>who stare at photographers from behind barbed wire,
>who can't bound down the street in a new pair of sneakers,
>who never "counted potatoes",
>who are born in places we wouldn't be caught dead,
>who never go to the circus,
>who live in an X-rated world.

We pray for children
>who bring us sticky kisses and fistfuls of dandelions,
>who hug us in a hurry and forget their lunch money.

And we pray for those
>who never get dessert,
>who don't have a safety blanket to drag behind them,
>who watch their parents watch them die,
>who can't find any bread to steal,
>who don't have any rooms to clean up,
>whose pictures aren't on any body's dresser,
>whose monsters are real.

We pray for children
>who spend all their allowance before Tuesday,
>who throw tantrums in the grocery store and pick at their food,
>who like ghost stories,
>who shove dirty clothes under the bed and never rinse out the tub,
>who gets visits from the tooth fairy,
>who don't like to be kissed in front of the carpool,
>who squirm in church or temple and scream in the phone,
>whose tears we sometimes laugh at and
>whose smiles can make us cry.

And we pray for those
>whose nightmares come in the daytime,
>who will eat anything,
>who have never seen a dentist,
>who aren't spoiled by anybody,
>who go to bed hungry and cry themselves to sleep,
>who live and move but have no being.

David F. Arieti

We pray for children who want to be carried and
    for those who must,
    for those who we never give up on and
    for those who don't get a second chance.
Take care of all these, Your children, O Loving God and
    and guide us to reaching out to them. AMEN!

                          Author Unknown

After returning back to the United States, I received a reply from the Apostolic Nunciature in Washington D.C., the equivalent of the Vatican Embassy. It is shown below.

SECRETARIAT OF STATE

FIRST SECTION · GENERAL AFFAIRS

From the Vatican, October 12, 1998

Dear Mr. Arieti,

I am directed to acknowledge the letter which you sent to His Holiness Pope John Paul II and I would assure you that the contents have been noted. I regret that the late delivery of the letter made it impossible to send an earlier reply.

With good wishes, I remain

Sincerely yours,

LEONEOD BREZHNEV *(The former Soviet leader in office 1964-1982)*

You may ask yourself why Russia is in such a mess economically and environmentally. Maybe because of its misleadership under Brezhnev this was a leadership of corruption. Why did the Soviets destroy their environment in the name of development? It was because the leaders wanted to stay in power. The environmental degradation associated with the Soviet Union is a story of abominations. In order to increase their economy the people had to cut, chop and dig so as to utilize their resources and try to prosper. Under Brezhnev's leadership, all that cutting, chopping and digging was to no avail. The former Soviet Union was left in a state of shambles as we have seen after its fall. The environmental damage continues to be catastrophic. The Soviet Union spent a lot of its financial resources on the military in order to keep up with the United States, which in turn caused neglect of their environment. **(See the book *Ecocide in the USSR*)**

A good example of this neglect was the aftermath of the Chernobyl incident (1986) after Brezhnev died in which an explosion caused release of radiation which killed many people years later and damaged 125,000 km² of territory. The fact that the explosion was kept secret did not help and delayed proper responses. Much of Europe was contaminated with radioactive fall out, which eventually found its way to the food chain resulting in the possibility of continued deaths in both humans and animals.

GOVERNOR PETE WILSON OF CALIFORNIA- *Republican*

In January of 1997 California had an earthquake which registered 6.6 on the Richter scale. [174] Pete Wilson was the governor of California at the time. An incredible amount of damage was inflicted on the residents in the Los Angeles area due to the quake.. Damage included freeways falling, homes flooded, fires raging and lots of misery. Is God to blame or are the very people who live there to blame? Let's face it. Los Angeles appears to be cursed with riots, fires, earthquakes, droughts, smog, mud slides and bullets flying all over the place. To make matters worse, the cost of living in many parts of Los Angeles is very high. It seems funny that people will pay astronomical prices just so that they can live in a cursed city. Wilson spent a lot of time and energy encouraging rapid rebuilding of the freeways which were damaged during the earthquake. He missed an historic opportunity in redeveloping mass transit specifically for the Los Angeles area. It was shown that after the earthquake people took what little mass transit there was for around four days until road detours were set up. Once the detours were set up car loving *Homo sapiens* got back into their cars thus missing an historic opportunity to be weaned from their automobiles. It is true that by taking mass transit (trains) the travel time undoubtedly increased. However, if the transit system of the 1930s and 1940s were left in tact then travel times would have been significantly less. In the 1930's and 1940's Los Angeles had perhaps the best mass transit system in the world known as the Red Line. It was dismantled so that the automobile moguls could make cars thus giving many individuals their own means of personal transportation (supposedly enriching themselves), thus causing one of the greatest concentrations of urban sprawl in the whole world.

There would have already been a network of above ground commuter trains if they hadn't gone towards the "car culture". In 1968, Los Angeles had a referendum towards building a light rail system for commuters similar to the one in Chicago. Corporate culture was staunchly against it and placed anti-transit signs on billboards all over the area. Needless to say it was voted down by the ecologically apathetic, smog-breathing residents of California whose children are now suffering increased rates of asthma. Not to mention the increased cost of cars because of the feeble emissions controls. The short sighted Californians cared more about a slight increase in taxes than their physical and fiscal wellbeing.

FRANK MURKOWSK - *Republican*

The present governor of Alaska Frank Murkowski was also a senator and Chairman of the Senate Energy and Natural Resources Committee. On April 8, 2000 he gave a radio address as a rebuttal to the then President Clinton's Saturday radio address. In his address he scolded the Clinton Administration's dependence on foreign oil. The emphasis on his speech was to convince the public that Clinton should open up the Arctic National Wildlife Refuge (ANWR) for oil exploration. He complained that oil prices were too high and that Americans did not want to pay these high prices. He also said that we lost 147 Americans in the 1991 Gulf War (In mid 2005 we lost over 1,600 American soldiers and there is no end in sight). If we look closely at his address we see the following: Republicans do not want to upset the oil barrens with alternative energy sources. Murkowski criticized Clinton's policy of not finding alternative sources such as hydroelectric power, pollution-free nuclear power, etc. Does he know what the term refuge means? According to the *Collegiate Dictionary*, refuge means the following: 1. *Protection or shelter, as from danger or hardship. 2. A place providing protection or shelter: haven or sanctuary.* I'm sure Murkowski's house is a refuge after a hard day's work of being governor. I don't think he would appreciate an oil rig in his living room, even if there were billions of barrels of oil under his living room couch.

Why can't we leave well enough alone? Has Murkowski ever heard of the 1973 oil embargo, which caused havoc with motorists and gas stations? Probably not. To refresh your memory let me give you a synopsis because I was in graduate school at the time and I remember it well. After the Arab Israeli War of 1973, the Arabs imposed an oil embargo on the West. This caused long lines and prevented gas stations from being open all night. Tempers flared and some deaths from outraged motorists took place. All this because we depended on foreign oil sources without the appearance of performing research into solar power. It is now 30 years later and not much in the way of solar energy has been offered to the public other than solar panels to generate electricity. In fact, the average fuel efficiency of American cars has gone down. Don't forget the 100,000 Iraqi deaths, more than 1600 deaths of American soldiers, 40,000 wounded soldiers and the countless number of dead bacteria, fungi, plants, protists and other animals.

How come we spent billions on the military in 1991 to defend an oil supply that we would not have needed if we developed non-oil energy sources? I'll tell you why. Because I sincerely believe that it was not in the best interest of the politicians to insist on solar energy development because the oil barrens would not be too pleased. Solar energy would take away from their profits despite the fact that Americans are giving their lives to protect "Our Way of Life". This is a quote from George Bush[175], in a documentary about advertising narrated by Sut Jhally, a college professor.

THE UNITED STATES CONGRESS

On Feb. 6, 1999 I was listening to National Public Radio and the newscaster mentioned that our Congress will not sign bills that will allow abortion in Third World countries despite the fact that those Third World country people need birth control. However, with a republican Congress what do you expect? Also at the time of this writing, the Congress was debating whether to impeach President Clinton because of his lying despite the fact that King Hussein of Jordan was on his deathbed. This fact may have had severe consequences not only in the Middle East, but throughout the world because of the explosive situation there.

Yet, Congress was still intent on impeaching Clinton despite the fact that perhaps thousands or perhaps millions of sheets of paper were being used to write down the proceedings of the trial. This paper represents homes to millions of organisms including worms, birds, bacteria, fungi and countless other organisms. Don't forget that paper is made out of wood from trees. I can honestly say that millions of people are probably turned off 100% with Congress because of this impeachment nonsense. With this Congress you can kiss common sense goodbye. Perhaps the best definition of congress came from the populist Jim Hightower who asked the question, "What's the opposite of progress?" The answer: Congress.

CONGRESS AND THE NUCLEAR A-*BOMB*INATION

One of the greatest fears that I have as well as many other people is the fact that we are living in a world with nuclear bombs. For 59 years the world has been faced with the prospect of total annihilation from these monstrosities. Finally some country's leaders have come to their senses and decided that it was high time to end the nuclear arms race. The US and the Soviet Union were the main players in the nuclear club but other countries such as Iran, Pakistan and India were also working on developing the bomb. Here we are in the year 2001 and we are still making these dangerous toys because we have to keep up with our neighbors in the nuclear arena (India and Pakistan). In October of 1999 Congress had the opportunity to ratify the Nuclear Test Ban Treaty and sure enough they vetoed the treaty on party lines of which 51 were Republicans, one was an independent and 44 were democratic. *What a bunch of highly intelligent nitwits, the Republicans of course!*

I should point out that in those days the Senate had 54 Republicans so there were in fact four which voted for ratification as well as all of the Democratic senators. According to the Republican senators they did not want to sign it because they feared for their grandchildren, or so said the newscasters. In this case it was mainly the Republicans who decided not to ratify it. Could it be that the republicans feel that they are free from being vaporized if we are attacked by a nuclear bomb? Perhaps they don't realize that if they don't sign it, there may not be any grandchildren to worry about because their sons and daughters will have become part of the atmosphere. They continuously come up with excuses with a total disregard for the consequences. Many countries will take their cue and learn from us but if you look you can see that Congress could care less about these issues because they are more concerned with image.

Congress has to project the idea that they are for a strong defense even if it means weakening our stance with the rest of the world and possibly causing its demise due to contamination from producing and testing these bombs. You know readers, the atmosphere is already polluted. Do we need to pollute the atmosphere more than it is with vaporized Republicans in an accidental nuclear explosion?

DIXIE LEE RAY *(1914-1994)*

In her book, *Trashing the Planet*[176] the late Dixie Lee Ray (former head of the Atomic Energy Commission now called the Nuclear Regulatory Commission, and the former Governor of the State of Washington) tried to convince the reader that the world was not being polluted and destroyed by human kind's activities. She poo pooed the idea that global warming was caused by humankind's CO_2 emissions, that acid rain is not bad, that pesticides are good for us because without them the demands for food would not be met (p.17 of her book). Perhaps the most idiotic statement is found on page 153 in which she suggests that nuclear waste, after removing useful isotopes, should be disposed of in proper containers in the ocean.

How would she like to be a fish or crab swimming over a container of nuclear waste? More insidious is the possibility that the fish swimming over these containers may wind up on someone's dinner plate. [177]

Ray's reasoning for deep-ocean disposal is the fact that there are about 323 million cubic miles of seawater in the ocean and that should be enough to dilute the waste (p.153). This may sound like a lot of water to dilute the waste but I don't think that anybody would like to eat fish from an area knowing that there may be small or infinitesimal amounts of nuclear waste in its tissues.

In addition, Ray (p.154) states that Jackson Davis, a biologist from the University of California, at Santa Cruz found that if we add radioactivity to the oceans, the algae, which are microscopic plants, may not be able to photosynthesize. Photosynthesis is the production of oxygen while taking in carbon dioxide (CO_2). Most of the oxygen that is in the atmosphere comes from photosynthesis whether from land plants such as trees or aquatic plants such as algae.

According to Ray, even if the sea gets contaminated with radioactivity natural processes will remove it from the water. However, waste products like Plutonium, yes, Plutonium, the stuff that nuclear bombs are made of has a half life of thousands of years which means that every so many thousand years its radioactivity is cut in half.

Ray has ideas about global warming like those of the present Bush administration. She states (p. 42) that if we try to reduce carbon dioxide emissions it will seriously impede our standard of living and our economy. Here again, we see that maintaining our standard of living is more important than saving the planet for its inhabitants of the future. Whatever the case, Dixie Lee Ray is no longer with us. She passed away in 1994. I should point out that if she were embalmed she would not become part of the food chain for many more years because the chemicals used in embalming would inhibit normal decomposition by bacteria and fungus.

TRENT LOTT - *Republican*

Trent Lott was the Senate Majority leader until he put his foot in his mouth during the celebration of Strom Thurmond's hundredth birthday party in Congress. While listening to Lott during a newscast he made a statement regarding the high price of oil now in America (March 2000). Gasoline was near $2.00 per gallon. He said that maybe we should drill in the Arctic National Wildlife Refuge. George H. W. Bush (the ex-president) said the same thing when he was running for president the second time. He lost by the way. Instead of suggesting that we use oil in the ANWR maybe he should have said, "Hey, now is a good time to conserve gasoline." But coming from a Republican, who evidently lost touch with reality, what do you expect? He is evidently trying to please his constituents who only care about how much money they have without regard for the environment which sustains them. He is good at making non ideal statements. He also made the statement that homosexuality is like kleptomania. I can't believe that people of his supposed intelligence can make such idiotic statements.

JULIAN SIMON *(1932-1998)*

Here we have a famous economist who believes that humans can solve virtually any problem.[178] In the book by Daniel Chiras, Simon argues that more people mean more scientists and larger amounts of scientific knowledge. In addition, he says that bigger populations make more profitable social investments such as railroads, irrigation systems, and ports. He ends his essay with the following "The more people there are, the better off the world would be."[179] You know, ever since I can remember we have education. What is the use of learning things if we can't put them to use. For example, I learned all my life from living and reading newspapers and books that we have lots of problems because of too many people. And here we see Julian Simon, who is the only "intelligent" human that I know of who advocates the fact that we need more people to help solve our problems. How many geniuses like Einstein or Isaac Newton are produced every decade? Evidently, not many because I believe it is a folly to produce millions of humans just to create one or two geniuses. Every second five people are born and two people die with a net gain of three. In the minute and ten seconds it took you to read this paragraph the world had a net gain of 210 people.

HARRY HARLOW

Harlow served for many years as editor of the Journal of Comparative and Physiological Psychology. In 1960, he received the Distinguished Scientific Contributions Award from the American Psychological Association, and in 1967, he was awarded the National Medal of Science. He was also the psychologist who did Nazi-like experiments on monkeys. In the experiments he used equipment and methods which inspired names such as "the tunnel of terror" and "the well of despair."[180] When I was taking psychology in college, I remember the teacher showing us movies with Harlow and monkeys cowering when he took away their cloth diaper which was their security blanket and their only source of affection. They had no real mother such as one who would care for them. At first I thought, 'hey, this is a good psychological researcher" but now, I realize that he was like the infamous Dr. Mengele, the Nazi war criminal who did horrendous experiments on Jews in the concentration camps. When I was taking psychology in the 60's, I respected Harlow but now I despise him because of his horrendous experiments on monkeys. I wonder how many people in the field of psychology respect him now.

The reason I am adding Harlow's experiments to this section is due to the fact that researchers who are like Harlow, and I assume there are many, have little regard for the organisms they are experimenting upon. These organisms include monkeys, rabbits, mice, rats, and even single celled organisms. I feel that these poor organisms were subjected to torture chambers much like those that we hear about throughout history. The name of the chapter in the book where I got the information from is called "Monkey Hell". No organism should be subjected to this type of cruelty just to come up with conclusions about human babies. Eventually Harlow himself felt that these experiments were not too helpful in our understanding of healthy behavior. This type of attitude where organisms are considered to be humankind's chattel is not only prevalent in the scientific community but in others as well. I asked a psychology professor at one of the colleges I teach at about Harlow's experiments and he told me that performing these types of horrible experiments was accepted practice at the time. As an aside, I am sorry to say that my father who was a world famous psychoanalyst told me that he had lunch with Harlow at one time.

As we have seen, people who are the cultural leaders in the various fields of human endeavor have immense influence over the environment in their time and beyond. As we have seen it works both ways. One little idea, such as placing a solar water heater on top of a building, has a symbolic worth of trillions of dollars towards saving the planet by encouraging development in solar power. By removing it can have the opposite effect of leading us to the abyss of environmental destruction.

CHAPTER 20
POVERTY AND AFFLUENCE

The answer is: Affluenza
Question: What is the major disease that we in the West suffer from?

Remember the poor-it costs nothing
-Mark Twin

INTRODUCTION

When we listen to the news lately (1998) we hear of the disaster taking place in both Indonesia and in the Brazilian Amazon; the fires which are burning because landless peasants are trying to eke out a living by cutting, chopping, digging and burning up the rainforest so that they can grow crops to survive. The reason for this is because of the shear poverty of the people, not only economic poverty but poverty of common sense and the spirit. The governments of those countries are ignorant when it comes to environmental matters. People will destroy their land in order to try to make money for survival purposes. We see this all the time. But poor people are more apt to do this when there are many of them as is the case in Brazil.

We in the Western and more affluent countries seem never to be satisfied with more and more. In fact it appears that the more we have the less healthy we are. We in the West suffer from effects of Affluenza such as high debt, with an average debt of $7500 owed in credit cards, increasing work stress and declining physical health such as is demonstrated in the increase in obesity and other diseases.[181]

Of the world's 6.4 billion people, 4.7 billion people live in the impoverished countries. Of those 3 billion live on less than $2.00 per day while 1.3 billion live on less than $1.00 per day. [182] Of this number 40,000 die of preventable diseases per day, 1.3 billion don't have access to clean drinking water, and 130 million children don't go to school.

It should be pointed out that the majority of the poor nations on the planet are in Africa,[183] while a few are in Asia, the Middle East and in South America. Can an American imagine living on less than $2.00 per day? Well the following countries do: Mozambique has an annual GDP (Gross Domestic Product) of $80 per year; Ethiopia has a GDP of $100 per year; Niger has a GNP of $270 per year, based on 1993 dollars. Now it appears to me that if people live on the edge of just existing while other countries such as those of Western Europe and the United States have a very high standard of living, that something is dreadfully wrong with humanity. It is no wonder that the citizens of those impoverished countries resort to professions such as poaching, forest destruction and crime. In addition we see an increase of diseases like Kwashiorkor, Marasmus, and vitamin A deficiency, all three being related to poor diets.

CONCEPT

It is unfortunate that the countries with the most ecological diversity such as Brazil and Indonesia are the countries with the greediest, corrupt and incompetent governments. The United States, on the other hand, has one of the world's most stable governments but we lack the morality in our Congress when it comes to poverty. We also don't have the shear biodiversity as does Brazil and the rest of the tropical countries.

If one would look at a map he or she would find that the majority of poverty is found in specific regions of the world that in those countries, which we consider poor, have an ecological problem. That's right, they are victims of ecology. How, you ask? Well, according to an article by a top academic economist, Jeffrey Sachs, 93% of the 30 highest income countries live within the temperate and snow zones of the world while the majority of the poor live in the tropical countries. There are 39 tropical or desert countries, which live in poverty. Sachs calls those, the HIPC's (high indebted poor countries [184]). He points out that life expectancy is 51 years of age in the HIPCs vs 76 years of age in temperate zones, and the GNP is $1,187 in HIPC vs $18,800 in the temperate zones.

Many of these Third World governments don't seem to encourage family planning, which in turn will lead to increased environmental degradation.

As was mentioned in Chapter 4 on the American Way, most people want to emulate America in the hope that they can be like us financially, believing that having lots of money will foster happiness and endless prosperity. When I see how we live, and how our politicians want us to keep our way of life, i.e. lower gasoline prices, I get quite upset. Ever since I can remember I have seen movies of starving children, especially in Africa. I feel guilty that here in America we are far away from this horror. I then realize from teaching environmental science that Africa not only has to deal with poverty but a whole Pandora's box of diseases such as AIDS, the Ebola Virus, River Blindness also known as Onchocerciasis, Trypanosomiasis (sleeping sickness), Schistosomiasis (bilharzia), malaria and Chagas disease just to name a few.[185] The main reason why these countries are subjected to the above diseases is because they have warm climates. These climates help produce large populations of mosquitoes and ticks, which are vectors. (See Appendix III).

Often I read about Third World countries and see children with Kwashiorkor and Marasmus. Both diseases are caused by lack of protein in their diet because their mothers are no longer able to breast feed them properly.

We are continuously immersed with pictures of starving Africans. In May of 1998 we read about the starving people in the Sudan in Northern Africa. If you look at the type of Biome in which the Sudan is located, we see that the area is mainly desert. The biggest problem facing most of the Third World is poverty, which makes people do whatever they have to even if it means for lack of a cleaner word, "Fouling their own nest!"

We also see that the search for gold in the Brazilian Amazon also leads to degradation. Common sense will tell anyone that in our efforts to make poorer people reach a livable standard it is important that we in the industrial and affluent world help them reach a form of sustainability. The wealthy countries have billions of dollars and the poor countries are kept in poverty to their detriment and to the detriment of the environments of the world. More degradation means more poverty. Perhaps the people who live in these places will acquire the insight of the Costa Rican's by allowing their natural resources to be used as tourist destinations instead of fuel for cooking.

POACHING

Perhaps one of the reasons why we are losing diversity is due to poaching. Poaching is due to the fact that the people are impoverished and they have no other means to eke out a living. Now we are running into social issues here, but as the reader can probably guess these two issues, environmentalism and social issues, are intimately related to one another. If poachers were able to earn a decent living then perhaps poaching would stop. One of the greatest threats to both plant and animal diversity is poaching.

Isn't it ironic that here we risk losing our natural wealth because some people don't have any material wealth to speak of. I should point out that of course, there are incredible inequities as far as wealth distribution go. Money is a human made tool, which is defined as a medium of exchange. It is amazing how far some people will go even to get the bare minimum of wealth. I will discuss more of this in the final chapter, which is on solutions, but I would like to mention this: Forbes Magazine said a while ago that the richest 400 people in America have more than 1 trillion dollars in wealth. A trillion by the way is equal to $1,000,000,000,000.

TREE HARVESTING

We keep hearing almost on a daily basis about tree cutting in the Amazon. Why are people cutting down the trees? Money! They have to get money to keep their economies from collapsing even if it involves the collapse of the environment. Not only is money the driving force but many North Africans are cutting down trees for fuel wood for their stoves.

WORKING FOR LOW WAGES

When people work in sweatshops their lives are basically ruined for life. They sweat and toil all day for little wages and virtually have no life outside of the factory. Nowhere was this better demonstrated than with Jim Keedy, an activist, who went to Indonesia and saw how workers lived on $1.25 per day. From a radio interview (Sept. 5, 2000) on NPR he mentioned how he lived on $1.25 per day like the workers in Nike's shoe plant. His story was summarized in this interview and more could be had on his webpage which is: www.nikewages.org.[186],

Mr. Keedy makes the point that Mia Ham, an athlete, earns $2,842 vs. $1.25 per day for the average Nike worker. Tiger Woods earns the equivalent of $55,555 per day for endorsing Nike. There are around 8600 rupia per dollar, so that means that Tiger Woods earns 470,000,000 rupia a day compared to 10,700 rupia per day, for the average Indonesian worker. Every day Tiger Woods is paid the equivalent of the daily salary of 45,000 Indonesian workers.

Now you may ask what do low wage earners have to do with environmental pollution? The answer is simple: Low wage earners can't afford adequate housing. How can they even attempt to have a decent pollution-free life if they have no money for proper plumbing and waste removal, for both humans and animals?

Now let's take this issue to other countries and other low wage earners. Chances are that this situation will be the same. With people working extremely hard under abominable conditions, what do you expect? These people work hard and have no ability to better themselves let alone their environment. As we have seen, their environment will suffer and the individual humans who live in those environments will suffer, also. What about the children? It is horrifying to think about the plight of the kids. There is one story, which broke my heart. It was about a Belgian worker who was a volunteer in Zaire. She recanted the story of a little girl who was eating grass and another one eating the waste from a brewery.[187]

It should be pointed out that Zaire's national debt is $12 billion, which amounts to $236 per person.[188] This is pretty bad considering that the annual income for the average citizen is $110 per capita, per year. That is why it is insane to expect these countries to pay off their debt to rich countries like the United States, whose citizens live in paradise compared to countries like Zaire.

THE TOTAL ENVIRONMENTAL TOLL OF POVERTY

(See affluence)

When a large percentage of the world's population live in ecologically sensitive areas the environmental toll is great. It includes the loss of soil fertility, desertification, soil erosion, deforestation, depleted game and fish stocks due to over hunting and fishing; loss of natural habitats, species and ecosystems; depletion of groundwater resources and pollution. Then to top it off the degradation just mentioned just places the people in a more precarious situation by exacerbating their poverty, which places their health in jeopardy.[189]

TABLE 8

POVERTY	AFFLUENCE
LOSS OF SOIL FERTILITY	LOSS OF SOIL FERTILITY
SOIL EROSION	SOIL EROSION
LOSS OF NATURAL HABITATS SPECIES AND ECOSYSTEMS	LOSS OF NATURAL HABITATS SPECIES AND ECOSYSTEMS
DEPLETION OF GROUNDWATER	DEPLETION OF GROUNDWATER
DEPLETION of GAME AND FISH STOCKS	DEPLETION of GAME AND FISH STOCKS
POLLUTION	POLLUTION

Notice that in each category of Poverty and Affluence, the destruction of the environment is the same.

Let us discuss each one separately:

POVERTY – LOSS OF SOIL FERTILITY

Why do we have loss of soil fertility? Let us first look at poverty. We lose soil fertility because we have too many people getting plots of land on soil that is not good for raising crops. A good example is the soil of the tropical rainforest. The soil, called oxisol, is soil of the warm, moist tropical regions of the planet. It is thin and acidic with poor fertility. When impoverished people try to till the soil and grow crops on it the nutrients get depleted rather rapidly and then the people have to move on. A process called laterization (the production of laterite) occurs: Laterite is the soil left behind after the nutrients have been depleted. It appears reddish-yellow and becomes hard. Also, impoverished people want to grow cash crops which are very water-intensive but don't really feed the people. Good examples of cash crops are coffee, sugar and cotton.

AFFLUENCE – LOSS OF SOIL FERTILITY

How does affluence cause loss of soil fertility? Simple. We in the rich countries, especially in the United States, want more and more. We over pave cities and when it rains water floods the pavement and leaches out the nutrients. We also produce acid rains with our industry. When chemicals like sulfur dioxide (SO_2) and Nitric oxides (NO_2) mix with water they form acids such as sulfuric and nitric acid which causes metals and other substances to be taken out of the soil. This loss of metals and other nutrients is called leaching. The water containing these substances is called *leachate.* Thus, with the nutrients being depleted soil fertility gets degraded.

POVERTY – SOIL EROSION

Why does soil erode? Simple. It is because we humans seem to think that we know better than nature. Poor people will do whatever it takes to eat. Take China for example- Once China had many forests in its Northern Plain, but they were cut down and converted to cropland.

Plants have two major functions: the absorption of water and stabilizing the soil. Stabilizing the soil means holding the soil together so that it doesn't erode. We see erosion take place when trees and other plants are cut at their roots. Poor people tend to destroy the trees so that they can build and pave over them for the improvement of their living conditions. If they build factories and roads then they will become more prosperous, or so they seem to believe.[190] In China it is estimated that the amount of topsoil lost is 480 metric tons per acre.

Those people in Northern Africa and in other places also depend on plants and trees for their fuel to cook with. Thus they will denude the forests in order to get firewood for cooking. (Common sense says that a good solution to this problem will be to get cheap solar cookers to these people. See Chapter 24)

AFFLUENCE – EROSION OF SOIL

Here in the United States we have a huge soil erosion problem. We have intensive farming practices which help deplete soils. We use lots of fertilizers and pesticides which help kill weeds. We also grow crops like corn and soybeans in rows which help leave the soil exposed to wind and rain for most of the growing season. We in the rich countries like to eat lots of meat. Production of this meat means having cows. Sheep graze on the land which helps to increase soil erosion. We are also destroying cropland in order to build more homes. We see this occurring a lot in Illinois. It seems development is very important here and in other rich countries at the expense of the environment.

POVERTY – LOSS OF NATURAL HABITATS

Perhaps one of the greatest examples of destruction of natural habitats is the loss of the Tropical Rainforests. Poor people need to sell the trees for as much as $10,000 per tree. They will mine for gold if found in that area. In fact they will do whatever it takes to make a living. As mentioned above with soil erosion, desperately poor people will cut down the trees in order to make tree plantations, wood for fuel, or for agricultural land without realizing that this destruction will destroy the very land that feeds them food and oxygen that they breathe. In fact with the slash and burn methods today they are of course contributing to the increase in carbon dioxide which will result in global warming. It should be pointed out that by doing this the ecosystems get degraded.

Poor people will also destroy ecosystems by permanently poisoning them with pesticides. Some poor people who can't read know that pesticides kill animals as well as fish. They say to themselves "Hey, maybe we can fish by using pesticides." So these people throw in some pesticides and get some fish and eat them without realizing that they may poison themselves.

Poor countries like China are destroying their natural habitats by building golf courses. This is a game of the West, but the Chinese see dollar signs dangling in front of their eyes. Sure Westerners will come to China to play golf when they can literally play in their own backyards. Golf brings in money ; preserving natural habitats does not bring in money.

In addition, many of these people live in countries which have numerous mineral resources that are needed by the West or rich countries. We, in the

West, encourage this degradation because we need the products in order to maintain our high style of living without regard for the environment. I'm sure that the reader can also name some other examples of destruction.

AFFLUENCE – LOSS OF NATURAL HABITATS

Let's take a good example, here in Illinois, where I am writing this book. There is a city about 50 miles from Skokie called Aurora which is located near good farmland. This farmland is being replaced by expensive homes that only those with means can afford. Greedy developers, who care more about their bottom line than nature's bottom line, are eating up this precious land. Not only are these homes being built on good land, these homes are being built together with golf courses. In fact, if all the lawns in the United States, which include golf courses and front yards were assembled together, they would cover an area equivalent to 25 million acres or 10 million hectares (one hectare (Ha) is equal to exactly 10,000 square meters). This area is equivalent to the combined areas of Vermont, New Hampshire, Massachusetts, Connecticut, Rhode Island and Delaware.[191] Not only is land being used, but golf courses are very water and pesticide intensive. According to a 1993 study by the University of Iowa Medical School, there were 618 golf course superintendents who had high frequencies of cancers of the lungs, intestines, brain and other body parts.

We, in the West, build colleges, homes, roads etc. on land that was once free of humans. We call this urban sprawl. In fact a good example of sprawl was in the Los Angeles area. A family bought a home near the canyons, and tragically their baby was eaten by a coyote. The coyote's natural food sources were destroyed due to urban sprawl perpetrated by developers. Developers line their pockets with more money by building on wherever land is available and with the attitude: ***The hell with the environment! My bank environment is more important!!!!!!!!!***

POVERTY – DEPLETION OF GROUNDWATER[192]

One of the problems of countries that are poor is the lack of availability of water supplies. It is estimated that about 1.5 billion people in the world lack adequate supplies of good quality freshwater. Roughly half of the world's six billion people lack good sanitation as well. It's possible that people without good sewage facilities can contaminate their groundwater supplies.

It should be pointed out also that people in poor countries have to spend up to two hours per day fetching a meager supply of water from wells and other sources. Good examples of this are the countries of Mali and Ethiopia, both of which are in Africa. In many countries water has to be bought. In addition, in some countries water has to be boiled thus polluting the atmosphere with smoke from fires used to boil the water. The poor spend much of their time just trying to get the basic necessities that we in the rich West take for granted.

AFFLUENCE – DEPLETION OF GROUNDWATER

As we have seen in poor countries the populations spend hours getting water. We in the affluent countries just go the kitchen or bathroom sink and just turn the faucet on without realizing how lucky we are compared to the world's poor. I'm sure some of you have known people who also take long showers without any thought of how much water is wasted. I take a less-than-two-minute-shower. [193]

When a country is affluent it takes for granted what it has and this is especially true of water supplies. In the United States I pass many farms where crops are being irrigated with water that seems to have an endless supply (much of which just evaporates immediately). Much of this water comes from the Ogallala Aquifer which underlies eight states. Aquifers have slow recharge rates and may take thousands of years to recharge once they are empty.[194]

POVERTY – DEPLETION OF GAME AND FISH STOCKS

Countries in Africa are suffering from too many poor people which in order to stay alive, have to poach. Poaching was mentioned earlier in this chapter.

Many animals, called "Bushmeat", (no relation to the occupant of the Whitehouse) are hunted to the verge of extinction. Bushmeat includes gorillas, monkeys, deer and other large mammals which are sold in the local markets. Since the people are so poor they have no other means to make a living. Simply put, they do it for survival.

In addition fishing fleets from many of these countries are virtually depleting the world's oceans by using trawler nets. They scoop up virtually everything they find.

AFFLUENCE – DEPLETION OF GAME AND FISH STOCKS

Hunters in both the United States and in other countries go hunting every year and hunt animals for sport. Many of these hunters are relatively wealthy. In fact, a hall in the Smithsonian Institute in Washington was named after one of these hunters who donated $100 million to it. Those of us in the wealthy countries hunt just for the shear fun and "sport" of it. I myself can't see killing an animal as a sport considering they have no way of defending themselves. The best definition of "hunting" is described in a book by Gene Brewer, called, "On a Beam of Light"[195] which is the same author who wrote "K-Pax" made famous by the movie. In the book the protagonist and hero, Prot, defines hunting as follows: "Hunting is no sport, it is cold blooded murder. If you can outwrestle a bear or chase down a rabbit, then you can consider yourself a true sportsman".

Wealthy countries also have modern fishing fleets which use satellite technology to locate and hunt down schools of fish. Since they have lots of money they can deplete the oceans with little effort.

POVERTY – POLLUTION

Have any of you ever seen a slum in a Third World country? I have. Not only in pictures, but in actuality. Sewage is literally flowing in the streets. Water from industry is going directly into rivers and oceans. The air, try breathing in Mexico City, is so pungent your eyes water, your lungs hurt and you wish you were somewhere else. This is basically true in other cities as well such as Bangkok, Thailand. Not only is the air polluted but the land and groundwater are polluted as well. This is because poor countries can't afford the technology to clean their countries up.

AFFLUENCE – POLLUTION

I have a rule. Those who have more, pollute more. It is simple. Those who have more things pollute more simply because they are involved with the manufacture of more things. Who can afford to buy bigger and more expensive things than they need? The rich of course. Those readers who are wealthy, look around your homes. How much junk do you have that you spent a small fortune on and don't really need or use? Speaking for myself, some, if not, a lot. But other people have lots.

Big cars like Hummers can only get around 8-10 miles a gallon. What a waste of gasoline. The wealthy can live farther from their workplaces and drive to work. Poor people may have to live close to work but may have to breathe and eat contaminated air and food. Some poor workers may live far away from work and depend on mass transit such as trains and busses. In order to live an affluent lifestyle we must pollute more.

WASTE

One of the greatest aspects of an affluent society like ours is waste. That's right, garbage and more garbage! We place our garbage in landfills, the largest being in Fresh Kills, Staten Island, New York. They receive 26 million pounds or 13,000 tons of garbage per day. When looked at another way, Fresh Kills, (what a name) takes only .018% of the total amount of garbage produced each day in the United States.[196] This amounts to 47 pounds of fuel, 46 pounds of construction materials, 21 pounds of forest and farm products, 6 pounds of industrial minerals and 3 pounds of metals, which consists mostly of iron and steel for each and every American. It should be pointed out that the debris from the World Trade Center disaster also wound up in Fresh Kills. To make matters worse, again, according to Hawken every year Americans are responsible for 3.3 trillion pounds of carbon dioxide (CO_2) as well as billions of pounds of food, styrene and chemicals both organic and inorganic as waste. Again, to sum it all up, America dumps 50 trillion pounds of waste a year. [197]

Most of us don't realize that we produce this amount. You know the old saying, "Out of sight, out of mind." Here, it fits well.

POVERTY AND AIDS

Perhaps one of the saddest stories to come out of the newspapers after the turn of the present century (2000) is the fact that millions of people in Africa are dying of AIDS, leaving around 11 million orphans. All this was highlighted in an article from the Chicago Tribune from August of 2002.[198] In the article there was one woman by the name of Busiswe Nhleko who was taking care of 24 children by herself, ten of which are her own, and the rest are orphans from some of her relatives who died of AIDS. Ask yourself what will happen if only the very young and very old are the only ones left alive? Remember it is the people between 15 and 60 which do most of the work. It will be up to the rest of the surviving world to take care of them. Think of the collapse of ecosystems if these people are left to fend for themselves.

It is ironic that whether a country is rich or poor the environmental damage is astronomical. Historically, the indigenous cultures of the world knew how to live in the environment without destroying it. A rich country exploits the resources to build more and more, while the poor country through political corruption plunders its resources and sells its soul while its poor eke out a living. Either way, precious resources including living organisms such as plants and animals as well as non-living resources such as fresh water supplies are being systematically destroyed because of the convoluted human ethos (moral nature).

CHAPTER 21
SEARCH FOR THE PERFECT PEAR, APPLE, PEACH etc.

The true perfection in man lies with not what he has but what he is.
Oscar Wilde

INTRODUCTION

What do we mean by the "perfect peach?" This is a symbol which simply means perfection of any kind. We, in the United States, and perhaps elsewhere will not buy any fruits or vegetables that have blemishes on them. This attitude originates from the misguided belief that blemished fruits or vegetables, besides being harmful, have less taste, flavor and nutrition. In reality, there is only one disease that I know of that can be spread from vegetable to human and that is a fungal infection found on celery. [199](See Fig. 27.)

Figure 27 Here we see some apples from a farmers market. Notice that they are not perfect. Why? Because they have blemishes. What's wrong with a blemished fruit? In most cases nothing. We are just used to seeing them that way in markets all over the United States and elsewhere. (Photo by author)

CONCEPT

I once worked for an industrial hygienist who was a perfectionist. Everyday I would have to send out letters to various plants such as electroplating or other industries that had toxic discharges. I would try to set up appointments between the industrial hygienist, myself, and industrial representatives. The purpose of these meetings was to discuss ways of eliminating toxic waste. Every time I would have a letter typed or printed the industrial hygienist would check it for mistakes. If there was even one typo, whether it could be corrected with whiteout or not, would have to be reprinted again using another clean sheet of paper. The hygienist felt that all the letters must be perfect without any blemishes. I must admit that I was annoyed at this because I was wasting paper for no good reason. But he wanted perfection. Now multiply this same episode a million times over at the various offices around the world and just imagine how many sheets of paper we are using and just wasting- millions and millions of sheets everyday. Every person in the United States uses around 335 kilograms of paper per year. The average in the world per capita is around 51 kilograms. (One kilogram is equal to 2.206 pounds).[200]

You know, if I was reading the letter and saw a blemish or whiteout I would accept the letter and perhaps his business. Why? Because I am a realist. Anyway, a sheet of paper to me represents the past home of an animal, plant or fungus as well as part of the world's life support system. Yeah I know that most people don't think like me and perhaps I may be thought of as a fanatic. But, you know, who cares. I am me and think the way that I think. I am proud of that.

What is it with our obsession with perfection? I don't know. My father wanted me to be perfect. I told him that I could only do the best that I can. I realized that perfection is an impossible task. If you come close enough that is good enough. Hey, don't get me wrong. It's nice if you can get perfection but you shouldn't destroy the environment trying to achieve it. Let me give you some examples…

PERFECT FRUIT

Let's go back for a moment and discuss the perfect peach, perfect apple or perfect fruit of any kind. What's wrong with the perfect fruit? Plenty. First of all in order to make them "perfect" they have to be coated with pesticides or some other chemical. As mentioned before, there is nothing wrong with slightly blemished fruits and vegetables. What is wrong are people's attitude about perfection; a misguided attitude shaped by the media, advertising, and the food industry. In many countries the "perfect" fruit is exported while the local residents eat the remaining "imperfect" fruit.

There are many pests which cause plant diseases. The organisms responsible for plant diseases are mainly fungus. Other organisms which cause plant diseases are bacteria (only six genera and 190 species), parasitic higher plants, viruses, nematodes (unsegmented round worms) and some environmental conditions such as being too cold or too hot.[201]

When we go to the supermarket we see very shiny apples that are so shiny they can reflect an image of the person holding it. The same is true with cucumbers. They, too, contain a waxy substance to keep them fresh longer. Now what's wrong with eating fruit that is not shiny? Most of the time nothing. We here in America like perfect fruit or perfect anything for that matter. However, it should be realized that by adding more chemicals to fruit they place our lives at risk. The chemicals may not be healthy for those of us who ingest them.

At one school where I teach there are plenty of apples and pears growing on trees. Most of the apples and pears are slightly blemished. I went and picked some and ate them. Boy, were they delicious. I brought some to my students and asked them if they would eat them. Most were afraid to eat them. I ate the apples in front of the students and told them that they were good. Not only good, but delicious.

PERFECTION IN OTHER WAYS

Now I am not familiar with all manufacturing processes but I would imagine that every industry throws defective products away instead of finding some other use for them. I know that clothes and sheets and other items are called irregular. These are sold as irregular at discount prices.

The most important thing is that people are fed. It makes no difference that the food is aesthetically pleasing. This is also true for almost every item made in a market economy. If a refrigerator is new but has a dent it could be sold at a lower price and still perform in the expected way. This could be true for anything.

CHAPTER 22
THE NEED FOR A MONSTROUS DEFENSE BUDGET AND WARFARE

A country cannot simultaneously prepare and prevent war.
Albert Einstein

Never think that war no matter how necessary
nor how justified is not a crime
Ernest Hemingway

What difference does it make to the dead, orphans, and the homeless?
Whether the mad destruction is wrought under the name of
totalitarianism or the holy name of liberty and democracy.
Ghandi

Only the dead have seen the end of war
Plato

INTRODUCTION

What is the function of the military? Most people will tell you that it is for our defense. But ask yourself what are they defending? We, in the United States are actually situated far away from enemies, yet we are determined to attack any country no matter where they are in the world due to our ability to get there. Wherever there are aircraft carriers in the world there is potential for major conflict, especially between the United States and other countries as we've seen in episode two of The Gulf Wars: the latest war in Iraq instigated by Bush II.

179

It is important to note that in trying to protect us the military is actually destroying us because of the pollution that they create such as too much nuclear waste in making plutonium (Pu) for nuclear bombs. Not only is there too much nuclear waste but there is too much conventional waste, as well. When we bomb countries we kill people by the thousands, but who weeps for the trillions of bacteria, animals, plants, fungi, and protozoa that are killed?

Figure 28 Here is the front page of The New York Daily News, dated December 24, 2002. Does December 24th of any given year mean something? Yes, By *George, it does. This is Christmas Eve. How about that? Now look at the headline showing Secretary of Defense, Donald Rumsfeld. Look at his eyes and notice his enthusiasm. It is guys like him that make war look glorious even though it destroys plant life, bacterial life, fungal life, viral life and of course human life.*
(New York Daily News. L.P. Reprinted with permission and "Copyright 2004, Knight Ridder/Tribune Media Services. Reprinted with permission.)

CONCEPT

In most countries, the defense budget is the largest segment of the entire annual budget which outweighs other necessary needs such as healthcare, education, mass transit, agriculture and scientific research. The military budget takes up needed billions of dollars for human and other earthly causes such as protection for the environment. Excluding the cost of war in Iraq, the 2004 military budget is $399 billion, almost $100 billion more than during the Clinton administration's military budget. The US budget is shown below:

TABLE 9

LOCATION	DOLLAR AMOUNT IN BILLIONS OF $
MILITARY	399
EDUCATION	55
HEALTH	49
JUSTICE	36
HOUSING ASSISTANCE	30
INTERNATIONALAFFAIRS	29
NATURAL RESOURCES AND ENVIRONMENT	28
VETERANS BENEFITS	28
SCIENCE AND SPACE	24
TRANSPORTATION	22
TRAINING, EMPLOYMENT AND SOCIAL SERVICES	20
GENERAL GOVERNMENT	18
OTHER INCOME SECURITY	16
ECONOMIC DEVELOPMENT	14
SOCIAL SECURITY AND MEDICARE	8
AGRICULTURE	5
ENERGY	4

Source: a flyer distributed during the 2003 air and water show at North Ave. beach, Chicago, IL

CHART #1

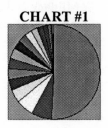

If you view chart #1 you will see that the thinnest part is the $4 billion spent on energy where it should be one of the largest sectors. Take a look at the distribution in the chart and ask yourself, why did we go to Iraq in 1991 and again in 2003 both under a Bush, one elected and one selected by the Supreme Court? BECAUSE OF OIL, FOLKS! YES, OIL! Now look at the energy budget. There is just $4 billion for energy. Why did we go to Iraq? The answer is, of course, because of energy. How many people died? Thousands died, including Iraqi civilians and our US soldiers. Why did anyone have to die? The answer: Because the world has a failed energy policy. We in the United States must have our cheaper gasoline when other countries must pay four times as much for gasoline. The budget, when totaled, is $785 Billion with the bulk at 51% going toward the military so that we can pollute the world with fossil fuels, increase the carbon dioxide concentration, encourage climate change and make life miserable for almost everyone. How much of the budget is concerned with energy? The figure is 0.5%! Yes, folks, 0.5%! This figure is almost one (1) percent of the military budget. LET ME TELL YOU READERS SOMETHING! IF THE SITUATION WERE REVERSED WITH 0.5% OF THE BUDGET GOING TOWARD THE MILITARY AND 51% GOING TOWARD ENERGY DEVELOPMENT, THEN THINGS WOULD BE BETTER AND WE WOULD BE STEPS AHEAD OF A GLOBAL CATASTROPHE RELATED TO CLIMATE CHANGE AND GLOBAL WARMING!

During the Reagan Administration the total military budget of the world was over $1 trillion. Yes, a trillion is a one followed by 12 zeros. Let's see, 1,000,000,000,000 or put another way, one billion times one thousand. Lots of money, eh? Just think what would have happened if all that money was spent helping countries become friends instead of enemies like we did during the "Cold War." During this period I wonder how many people were killed because we weren't defending them. Good examples include: disease, muggings, drive by shootings, and other domestic attacks, which result in injury or death.

Yet, the military is responsible for pesticides, petroleum, lead, mercury and uranium and other wastes in the environment.[202] In fact according to the article by Feldman, the U.S. Military is the largest producer of waste, which even outweighs five major chemical companies combined. Just to give you an example, Washington's, Fairchild Air Force Base produced 13 million pounds of waste, which is more than the weight of the metal in the Eiffel Tower. Nice, huh?

WEAPON SYSTEMS

NUCLEAR WEAPONS

Let's see what types of weapons we are paying for in the name of defense. Well, for one we are trying to develop nuclear weapons and that requires testing. What do we release when we test nuclear weapons? Radiation. Yes, that's right, radiation, a poison, which can change our genetic structure leading to cancer and worse. Nuclear weapons are very expensive to develop, not only financially, but also ecologically. Who knows what mutations may be lurking our way in the future. Perhaps we have already encountered them. I know of one location where they may be hanging out. Yes, in the Rotunda in Washington D.C. Many of our Congressmen think with convoluted and perhaps mutated minds. Proof of this is that some congressmen are discussing a new class of nuclear weapons.

SONAR

There is something that does not appear in the local press and that is the fact that our military is using sonar in submarines which have an impact on cetaceans. Cetaceans are animals like whales, dolphins and porpoises. Submarines communicate with each other via sonar at frequencies of 5-11 kHz [203]at source levels of 180-200 db (decibels). Sonar works by emitting short pulses of sound which are designed to focus as much energy as possible in a narrow range. Loud sounds can be hazardous to ocean organisms. These sound ranges can be deadly for humans. It is possible that sonar may have caused the stranding of Cuvier's beaked whales in the Canary Islands and the Ionian Sea some years ago.

It appears that if the military conducts sonar tests in the marine environment they don't care about the health of the biota (life). This could have catastrophic effects on many organisms because it may affect the aquatic food chain. This could have a ripple effect on the world's fisheries, which could lead to starvation in developing countries which depend on food from the sea. Whales in particular depend on sound for communications. If we disrupt their behavior by the use of sonar, we could inadvertently interfere with their reproductive capabilities. This may in turn lead to extinction of the whales and a possible decline in the world's oxygen content. How might this be possible? This fact has to do with the food chain. Whales eat krill, *Euphasia superba* (a shrimp-like organism) tons at a time. Krill eat algae. Algae produce oxygen. If the whales become extinct, the krill will multiply and eat most of the algae. No algae means less oxygen. This is a possibility if we ignore the cause and effect of the military's actions.

Well, let us take a look at our defense budget. Can we make better use of our tax dollars? See Table 10.

183

TABLE 10

MILITARY AMOUNT IN U.S. DOLLARS	WHAT IT BUYS	WHAT IT COULD BUY-NON MILITARILY
100	11 HAND GRENADES	11 BLANKETS FOR REFUGEES
4000	ONE ROCKET LAUNCHER	TRAINING PROGRAM FOR PEACE FOR 160 PEOPLE
14,000	1 CLUSTER BOMB	ENROLL TWO NEEDY CHILDREN IN HEADSTART PROGRAM
40,000	1 HELFIRE MISSILE	PAYS FOR TWO HOME CARE HEALTH AIDS FOR DISABLED ELDERLY FOR ONE YEAR
145,000	1 BUNKER BUSTER BOMB	WILL TRAIN 29 NURSES (RN) FOR AN AA DEGREE
586,000	1000 M16 RIFLES	PAYS FOR RENT SUBSIDIES FOR OVER 1000 NEEDY PEOPLE
763,000	PAYS FOR 1 MINUTE OF WAR WITH IRAQ	ANNUAL SALARY FOR 15 REGISTERED NURSES
46, 000,000	1 HOUR OF WAR WITH IRAQ	CAN REPAIR 20 ELEMENTARY SCHOOLS IN USA

MILITARY AMOUNT IN U.S. DOLLARS	WHAT IT BUYS	WHAT IT COULD BUY-NON MILITARILY
130,000,000	7 UNMANNED PREDATOR DRONES	PAYS FOR WOMEN'S, Iinfant and nutrition programs FOR 200,000 CHILDREN
275,000,000	3 tests of missile defense system	Eradicate polio globally
35,000,000	6 trident missiles	Vaccination for 10 million Children worldwide
413,000,000	Pays for amphibious landing	68,000 with healthcare
494,000,000	Pays for military aid in Columbia	4000 needy Americans with housing
1.1 billion	One day war with Iraq	Prevent cuts to education for one year in USA
1.2 billion	2 months in Afghanistan	Fund Amtrak
2.1 billion	Pays for one stealth bomber	Annual salaries for 38,000 elementary school teachers
16 billion	One year nuclear weapons program	
12 billion	One year in Afghanistan	
38 billion	One month military spending	

204

I believe the above table says it all!

CHAPTER 23
TRADITION

Often, the less there is to justify a traditional
custom, the harder it is to get rid of it.
Mark Twain

In that the wisdom of the few becomes available to
the many, there is progress in human affairs; without
it, the static routine of tradition continues.
- Jospeh Jastrow

INTRODUCTION

When people talk about pollution, religion, education, and political celebrations, traditions associated with these are seldom mentioned. The world has continued with these traditions without regard for the environment. An incredible amount of damage to the environment, as well as the killing of animals, takes place because of tradition. Examples are given below.

CONCEPT

RELIGION

Much of religious practice in the U.S. is of an unconscious sort. By this I mean that we follow our rabbi, priest or minister's lead. These rituals are very similar to what our ancestors practiced. For example many of these traditions require burning incense. I would doubt that anyone would maintain that we do it to appease or honor a god who is physically present in the church and *not anywhere else*. Still the tradition is followed without consideration for asthmatics or respiratory illnesses. I, for one, can't stand being in a place where there is smoke not caused by water vapor. Many people are allergic to perfume and in any case there is only a tiny addition to the level of carbon byproducts to the air. This is not suggesting that incense is a cause of global warming. That would be like saying spitting into rivers causes flooding. Incense does cause distress to people, however, and the reason for it is long gone so why continue?

PLAIN PAPER, NEWSPAPERS AND OTHER PAPER

Waste paper is the largest component of a land fill. It actually makes up about 39% of our garbage. I teach at many schools so I see how much paper is wasted.(See figure 3.) People still make single page copies, when most copiers can make double sided copies. Being a teacher, I am familiar with tests. Multiple choice and fill in the blank tests can be taken on one sheet of paper for the whole semester. (See appendix VII for an example).

Newspapers, especially the Sunday newspapers are mainly composed of ads which use more ink and take lots of energy to produce. How many of those ads does the average person read? How many do you throw out? How many trees are killed to make this paper? Hundreds of trees are killed and processed into paper for each edition of a Sunday newspaper.

To me, one of the biggest abominations is the tradition of the Sunday newspaper. Very low prices, $12/month for seven editions per week encourage people to engage in this effort.. Do you know how many trees are cut down just to make the Sunday edition of the New York Times? Thousands! Those of you who get the daily newspaper as well as the Sunday edition of the Chicago Tribune know that it is filled with many sections, all of which are loaded with advertisements. The Sunday edition is the worst. In fact a great deal of the bulk is composed of advertisements trying to seduce the consumer to consume more of the advertised product. The newspapers themselves admit they make most of their money from advertising. The advertisers don't seem to care too much at all about the environmental price of cutting, chopping and digging for more paper to print their advertisements. They just care about the financial costs. It is true that certain newspapers use up to 50% recycled paper but the other 50% comes from real, once-alive, oxygen producing trees.

LAG BAOMER

When I was living in Jerusalem, Israel, I lived across from an area where there was a deep valley. On the other side of that valley were houses.

During the holiday Lag Baomer bonfires were built at night. I was able to smell the smoke all night. Why were the fires lit? Simple! Tradition! This is observed as a semi-holiday. The name Lag Baomer is composed of two Hebrew letters, Lamed and Gimel which signify 33 and this denotes the thirty third day in the counting of the omer, corresponding to the 18th day of the Jewish month of *Iyyar.* This holiday was set aside as a special holiday for children where they would go to nearby woods and spend the day picnicking and playing all sorts of games with an emphasis on archery.[205] Just think of the amount of smoke emitted when hundreds of fires are burning at the same time and in the same place. Just thinking of it makes me want to get a gas mask. Do, you the reader, smell the smoke as you read this?

GREETING CARDS

Another example of tradition is the sending of cards, especially during the Christmas season. I have seen just how elaborate the cards are that are being sent. Many are very expensive in gold toned envelopes, which while it does not add to the thought, it undoubtedly adds to the cost, but most importantly add to the waste stream. (The waste stream means the steady flow of varied wastes, from domestic garbage and yard wastes to industrial, commercial and construction refuse.).[206] I am sure that many of these two colored envelopes are not biodegradable or may not even be recyclable.

Sure it is nice to get these cards. When I was a youngster my parents used to receive close to a hundred cards. I thought it was nice to get so many cards. Of course this was before I became environmentally minded. My parents would place them on a string. If that happened now, however, I would be appalled because after the holiday season they would be thrown out. Guess where? That's right, in the garbage, just adding to the waste stream. Now, just add the number of cards that each person gets and sends; multiply that by millions and you can see how much waste we have generated. To be realistic, cards not only add a burden on the waste stream, but also for the mail carriers. Sure it's nice to be remembered by someone, but I think a less damaging way is a phone call. I remember once when I was in high school, I mentioned to a person that the mail rates keep going up. (In those days it cost less than a nickel, $.05, to mail a letter) and he told me jokingly that it soon will be cheaper to make a phone call. Now, as I write, stamps cost $.37 and a phone call is $.30, so he was right.

According to Robert Lilianfeld and William Rathje in their book, "Use Less Stuff", Americans send so many greeting cards each year that they would fill a ten story building the length and width of a football field. That's quite a bit of paper that is used for tradition only. Now in this day and age one can receive greeting cards through e-mail.[207] Some by the way are incredibly imaginative.

GIFT WRAPPING

Another tradition which is more prevalent during the holiday season is gifts. How many people would ever think of giving a gift without wrapping it? Why do people wrap gifts? There are many reasons which I will elaborate upon. Based on discussions with the students in my environmental classes, they gave these reasons: to surprise someone, employment, tradition, keeping the wrapping paper industry in business, to make children happy, and habit.

Reason 1: *To Preserve the Element of Surprise.* A student once said that people are surprised when a gift is wrapped. True, but, I told her that she should just think of the added surprise that people would get if you gave them an unwrapped gift. There would be the surprise of the gift and the added surprise of a paperless box.

If a child tells you what he wanted for Christmas and you agree to get the item for him, unless he just wants wrapping paper for Christmas, he will not be surprised. Even if you wrapped it and placed it under the tree all the child is interested in is the gift. The wrapping paper won't last more than a few seconds. He will crumple it up and throw it away which just adds to the waste stream. Why not just use the Sunday comics from the newspaper as wrap? Some people do this. That would be a lesser of two evils because as is discussed later on in this chapter, newspapers are a burden on the environment and wind up in the waste stream.

Reason 2: *Preserving Employment.* Keeping people employed is certainly a worthy goal. Every advance or shift in society can eliminate jobs. In most cases though, new jobs are created elsewhere. For example: The light bulb lessened candle making, but added jobs in the manufacturing area. Advances in medicine impacted the funeral industry, but also added jobs in hospitals. Perhaps eliminating paper will elicit some innovation as has actually happened. Let me explain. One day when I was returning to the train station from a hard day's teaching at Waubonsee College, I stopped at a grocery store to get some food for a lab that I was doing the same night at another school. Just when I was about to leave the owner came up to me and asked, "Hey, are you David Arieti?" I said yes. He said that he remembered me from ten years previously as his biology teacher at a local college I had been teaching at. He told me his name and I remembered it. He told me that because of my environmental stance, yes, even though I taught biology, I also mentioned the environment and ways to save it, he got inspired. His wife went into a business where she sells special cloth bags for gifts. These cloth bags can be brought to stores so that paper bags don't have to be used. He told me that business is just fine and that I was able to make a difference. I must admit that hearing this made me feel great.

Reason 3: *Children's happiness.* This, of course, is a goal that everyone should aspire to unless you are giving them a gift of just wrapping paper However, they should learn that wrapping gifts is a big waste of paper.

Reason 4: *Habit.* It is nice to hide what you are giving. In any case though, one can figure out what is being given by the shape and weight of the gift. When one is receiving a bottle of wine you can figure it out by the shape of the bag or box. The same is true of those who are receiving neckties. I have received many as gifts and I knew immediately what the gift was before unwrapping it. (Lately, those who know my stance on wrapping gifts give me gifts unwrapped). You see, they are learning.

CHRISTMAS TREES

This is another example of a waste of natural products. If Americans are so obsessed with Christmas trees, why not just use artificial ones which can be used over and over again. Tradition! We like the feel of the real tree and the fresh aroma of the decomposing pine. This good feeling lasts all the way to the New Year, when the object of our affection gets heaved out into the street. Talk about short term relationships: a month in our lives, but the end of the road for the pine. True, many people grind them up for mulch, but most just go to help fill up our abundance of landfill space. Why not leave the trees up and decorated all year round? Maybe it would remind us that the spirit of Christmas should be goodwill toward humanity, animals and all biodiversity including trees all year round.

CHRISTMAS LIGHTS

I wrote this section during the Christmas season. When nightfall comes, what do I see? I see millions of lights powered by electricity to celebrate Christmas. What's wrong with this scenario? Plenty! First of all, look at all the energy that is required to light the lights. (I saw many houses with fantastic Christmas lights and it is very nice that I don't have their electric bills).

What about all the cars that stop to look at the display? I know this is a free show but think of all the gasoline wasted. Now if there was another type of fuel in existence, other than fossil fuels, such as solar or fuel cells then cars could meander by without the effects of producing more CO_2.

What about the energy that went into making the lights in the first place? I like tradition as well as the next person (albeit not as much) but I feel that some traditions should be abandoned in the face of our growing dependence on foreign oil. Now of course some of these homes are exquisitely decorated but I believe that this is a little bit too ostentatious. Many homes are not as lavishly decorated with fewer lights, yet they express the Christmas spirit.

The fact of the matter is that, collectively, Christmas lights use lots of electricity. Don't forget that we went to war in 1991 to get Iraq out of the Kuwaiti oil fields. What has improved since the war on the energy front? Well, as far as I can see nothing. We still depend on oil both domestic and foreign, and we are still in Iraq with no end in sight.

BONFIRES

On November 18, 1999, a terrible accident occurred at Texas A & M University in College Station, Texas. A long standing tradition of building a tremendous bonfire before a football game ended in tragedy. During the construction of the 40 foot high structure (four stories tall) something caused the pile to collapse killing 12 students and injuring quite a few others. What was the purpose of this fire in the first place? Tradition! Why with global warming do we need traditions like this? Approximately 6,000-8,000 logs were used to build the bonfire. From looking at pictures in the newspapers the logs appeared to be just cut as they were virtually straight and new looking. Just think how much carbon in the form of carbon dioxide would have been released in the atmosphere if the unfortunate accident didn't happen. We already are suffering from global warming.

Our climate is changing drastically. On what do I base my conclusion? For one thing, in the Chicago area especially in November of 1999 snow and rain was a rare commodity. This just shows that tradition overrides common sense. Can't we use common sense to avoid disasters that are essentially accidents waiting to happen? An additional note: How many animals lost their homes because of this tradition? Many organisms undoubtedly lived in those trees that were cut down just so they could be used to pollute the air.

FIREWORKS

What is the function of fireworks? Well for one thing people seem to jump for joy when they see them. Fireworks: lovely colored lights in the sky followed by a big bang and lots of smoke. Fortunately for the birds fireworks only take place at night when birds generally do not fly. When we celebrate events like the Fourth of July (July 4th)[208] it seems that we need to light up the world. This may be considered a tradition as well but let's discuss why we feel good about fireworks. First of all, we mainly use fireworks on July 4th, America's Independence Day. Do we really have things to celebrate?

Well, let's take a look at the following: The rates of asthma are picking up, especially with children due to air pollution. We should also mention the fact that fireworks stress out animals within the radius of the Boom! Boom! Bang! Bang! We are helping the world to over-fish the oceans due to our advanced satellite technology. We drive inefficient cars many of which get less than 20 miles per gallon and add pollutants to the atmosphere. We encourage deforestation by our love for meat especially cows and pigs which contribute to water, air and land pollution. We have such an inept president, who because of his perceived ineptitude courages many authors to write books about his failings which contributes to deforestation by making paper to print the books. (This is one of them!), we are at war in Iraq and Afghanistan , we are over fishing the oceans, AIDs is on the rise in Africa, Marburg virus (similar to the Ebola virus) has just surfaced again etc, etc, etc. Really great things to celebrate, Huh?

Perhaps the next time you want to make a lot of noise buy a small paper lunch bag, fill it with air and pop it with your fist. That way you can make a loud noise without pollution.

Figure 29, shows fireworks over the Illinois skies during a
2003 Fourth of July celebration. (Photo by author)

AIR SHOWS LIKE THE ONE IN CHICAGO

Every August there is an air and water show along the lakefront of Chicago. The water show takes place in the mornings over a three day weekend. There are jets, jet skis and boats. However, the most interesting and polluting part takes place later on in the afternoon. This is the part where we see and hear both jet planes and propeller planes. During the show, smoke is spewed out from the engines of the planes. (See figure 30). That's all we need is more smoke which magnifies global warming. This is another example of how tradition affects the planet's climate. I bet that if I asked someone at the event if they would be willing to forgo the event because of the pollution they would say, "No!"

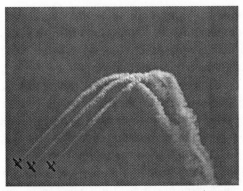

Figure 30. Here we see smoke coming from three planes for special effects, during the 2003, Chicago Air and Water show. (Photo by author)

COFFINS –KILLING LIVE TREES TO BURY DEAD PEOPLE

This section also appeared in Chapter 12 on Ignorance and Stupidity.

Perhaps one of the greatest injustices to befall nature is the human custom of burying people in caskets, formerly called coffins, generally made out of wood. Here, a live tree is cut down to house a dead person. Silly isn't it? Did you know that trees supply us with oxygen (O_2), and they also take away carbon dioxide (CO_2) from the air and serve as homes to animals, fungi and bacteria?

Another thing to be aware of is the fact that many people on this planet sleep on hard floors made of mud while dead middle class or rich people in America have a nice soft bed to rest on until they decompose. You know the word for that? It is called "dirt nap". Only on this planet do rich dead people sleep better than poor live people. Think about it!

Figure 31, here we see two typical caskets made out of trees that were once alive. (Photo by author. Courtesy of the Weinstein Funeral Home, Wilmette, Illinois.)

As can be seen by Figures 31, there are two caskets: one is totally finished and one is unfinished. Maybe the unfinished casket will remain unfinished even with a body in it. Whoever ordered it for their loved one may feel that he has an environmental responsibility by allowing natural decomposition. Perhaps one of the greatest indulgences I have ever seen is what takes place after a person's death. Why? Because some would like to be buried in expensive coffins or caskets as they are called today. Some people would be willing to pay thousands of dollars for caskets. I myself get upset when I see caskets of famous people or those killed by guns during funeral processions. I am amazed by the variety of caskets being carried. Most are expensive looking and made with wood from very nice formerly-living trees (many caskets, however, are made out of metal). All of those trees were destroyed just so some people could be buried and decompose in style. Just think. We kill live trees so that dead people can be buried in wood made from them. My! My! What have we become?

Figure 32. Another photo of coffin in a funeral home. It is made out of wood, glue and nails, paint and other substances. Remember most coffins were made from wood from trees in their prime. Just think, we get upset when people die in their prime years, so why shouldn't we get upset when a tree of perhaps 100 years or older gets cut down, just to bury dead people, who would decompose quicker with out a coffin. (Courtesy Weinstein Funeral Home, Wilmette, Illinois)

Traditions are nice if they don't instill pain or harm organisms or the environment. All too often we see that this is not the case. A good example of tradition is the bull fights in Spain where the **"Matador,"** which by the way means *killer,* is made into a hero. You may say that bull fights are Spain's equivalent to our (USA's) football Games. But in football no organisms are getting killed intentionally. Perhaps if we as a species really care about the environment then maybe we should try to do something to curb traditions if they cause harm to the environment.

THE CURE

CHAPTER 24
SOLUTIONS TO THE REAL CAUSES
OF ENVIRONMENTAL POLLUTION

The tourist got angry when Geronimo urged him not
to throw a beer can into the river. "Is this river yours?
"He asked." No," Geronimo replied, "it is ours"[209]

The leaders of the United States and of the entire West risk
ignoring humanitarian needs as the world passes into the age
of terror. But the lengthening lists of the dead and wounded
should remind those leaders that service to the humanitarian
conscience has become more essential than ever, not only for
the sake of others but also for the future of the West.[210]

The above sentence says it all. I live in America and have been here most of my life. Everyday I appreciate nature. However, you must understand that most city dwellers that I know forget that nature exists because they are so far removed from nature that it is really pathetic. When I was growing up in the middle of Manhattan (New York City) in the early 1950's I thought that the whole world looked like an urban environment until my parents took me out into the countryside. Unfortunately, this countryside, like so much of rural America, has become suburbia with its ubiquitous strip malls, housing developments, big shopping malls and highways. All of this is far removed from nature with the exception of trees neatly planted on the sidewalks and parks in the middle of a concrete jungle. (Is this nature?)

I always thank God that I have enough clean air, food and clean drinking water at will, basically from my sink. I know that it is basically clean and

I thank the planet for giving it to me. But most wealthy city dwellers are too busy trying to make a living and taking for granted the fact that nature exists. The tourist in the above quote does not realize that he himself is part of nature. We are all part of nature. This tourist doesn't realize that every bit of land is owned by every person, every bacterium, every fungus, every plant etc. Now you may ask how someone can say that he/she owns something thousands of miles from his or her home and who has probably never seen it.

The answer is simple. We all breathe the air from wherever it is made. We also need the ground to act as a home for the bacteria, plants and other living organisms as well as rocks, soil and dead logs from naturally fallen trees. The very first way to solve the pollution problem is to come to the realization that the WHOLE EARTH belongs to all of us. After all, it is both mother and home to us all. It is our recycling plant, our-converting dead-organisms- to- nutrient-factory,- our water- producing-factory, our nurturing-center. Mother Earth continues to give of her abundance but humanity's insatiable desire for more material and quest for profits are placing enormous burdens on our planet's life-support systems.

Upon writing this book, I have reflected on the ways we do things on this planet and I have come to the conclusion that the solutions to environmental pollution are relatively simple to implement. The only thing is that it needs cooperation and the *will* from everyone, and I mean *everyone* from politicians, the corporate world, religious leaders, and average citizens in both the United States and the rest of the world. We must realize that the planet is home not only to humans (*Homo sapiens)* but to all life as well as non-life (abiotic factors) such as mountains, deserts, rocks and air.

I have come up with some solutions. Granted some of them are unconventional but you know something, we have to begin somewhere.

SOLUTIONS

The solutions to most of these problems are many. I will list them and then discuss each one individually. I also would like to point out that most of the solutions that I propose are relatively simple and are not difficult to implement.

Solutions are as follows:
1. Implement the Earth Charter
2. Eliminate fossil fuels and solarize the planet
3. Encourage mass transit
4. Population Control
5. Environmental Education for everybody

6. Eat lower on the food chain
7. Curtailing greed (more or less)
8. Devalue or deemphasize money
9. End consumerism
10. Encourage recycling
11. Don't be lazy
12. Making other countries more livable by contributions from extremely wealthy people
13. Respect all life as if your life depends on it (because it does.)
14. Vote for environmentally friendly candidates (and honest)-don't believe what politicians tell you.
15. End warfare by making the military defend us
16. End the use of deadly chemicals like pesticides
17. Avoid using genetically altered and patented seeds
18. Encourage ecotourism
19. The American dream should be the world dream and attainable
20. Reprioritize

1. IMPLEMENTATION OF THE EARTH CHARTER

What exactly is the Earth Charter? "The Earth Charter is a declaration of fundamental principles for building a just, sustainable and peaceful global society in the 21st Century."[211] The Earth Charter was written by an international committee and approved at a UNESCO meeting in Paris in March of 2000. The Earth Charter was influenced by contemporary science, international law, indigenous cultures, and various religious and philosophical traditions.

According to the brochure the importance of the Erath Charter is that it

> ...challenges us to examine our values and to choose a better way. It calls on us to search for common ground in the midst of our diversity and to embrace a new ethical vision that is shared by growing numbers of people in many nations and cultures throughout the world.[212]

Finally I realized that I am not a minority of one who is out to save the environment. The fact that there are large UN based organizations should give one encouragement and the realization that all hope is not lost.

The following is a list of the 16 principles of the Earth Charter:

1. Respect Earth and life in all its diversity.
2. Care for the community of life with understanding, compassion, and love.

3. Build democratic societies that are just, participatory, sustainable, and peaceful.
4. Secure earth's bounty and beauty for present and future generations.
5. Protect and restore the integrity of Earth's ecological systems, with special concern for biological diversity and natural processes that sustain life.
6. Prevent harm as the best method of environmental protection and when knowledge is limited, apply a precautionary approach.
7. Adopt patterns of productions, consumption, and reproduction that safeguard Earth's regenerative capacities, human rights, and community well-being.
8. Advance the study of ecological sustainability and promote the open exchange and wide application of the knowledge acquired.
9. Eradicate poverty as an ethical, social, and environmental imperative.
10. Ensure that economic activities and institutions at all levels promote human development in an equitable and sustainable manner.
11. Affirm gender equality and equity as prerequisites to sustainable development and ensure universal access to education, healthcare and economic opportunity.
12. Uphold the right of all, without discrimination to a natural and social environment supportive of human dignity, bodily health, and spiritual well-being, with special attention to the rights of indigenous peoples and minorities.
13. Strengthen democratic institutions at all levels, and provide transparency and accountability and governance, inclusive participation in decision making, and access to justice.
14. Integrate into formal education and life-long learning the knowledge, values, and skills needed for a sustainable way of life.
15. Treat all living beings with respect and consideration.
16. Promote a culture of tolerance, non-violence, and peace.[213]

The importance of these principles cannot be ignored because they are the concern of many environmentally conscious people like me. I share all of these principles because they provide a foundation for solving the world's environmental problems in a practical manner. These principles are sound and can be practiced by everyone from corporate executives, politicians, and average people throughout the world in order to save the Earth.

The following is my list of solutions, many of which concur with the principles of the Earth Charter. Many of these require massive changes to our infrastructure, social behavior, and consumption patterns. By educating the world's public to be more environmentally conscious these solutions can be gradually implemented before catastrophic events which are now occurring become even more severe.

2. ELIMINATE FOSSIL FUELS AND SOLARIZE THE PLANET

Perhaps the greatest threat to the environment other than human overpopulation is the world's dependence on oil. Yes, that black, smelly, gooey stuff is the cause of both environmental degradation and political instability. Within the span of a decade the United States has gone to war twice in Iraq ostensibly for humanitarian purposes but actually to protect oil supplies. [214] The continual steady supply of petroleum is crucial to both the developed economies of the world as well as developing ones such as China and India. The sensible thing would be to develop alternate fuel sources from non-fossil material. However, as recent history has shown us this is not a priority of politicians or corporations since we are willing to go to war to secure current levels of crude oil to maintain our economic system.

It is not only the refinement of petroleum products and their transportation that endanger the environment but also their consumption. For example, one third of all CO_2 emissions come from transportation. So common sense would dictate that we should be encouraging smaller cars and eventually some other non-polluting source of energy to power our vehicles. A sobering statistic is the fact that for every gallon of gas burned 26 pounds of carbon dioxide are emitted into the atmosphere. Yes, you read correct, 26 pounds or 11.78 kilograms.

In the United States 3000 gallons of gasoline are burned every second which accounts for 60,000 pounds of CO_2.[215]

Figure 33 Rush hour. Look at all the cars. (Photo by author)

If we take in consideration the amount of gasoline wasted on large SUVs and light trucks we find that we Americans, in particular have wasted around 70 billion gallons of gasoline.[216] Seventy billion look like this, 70,000,000,000. Put another way it is the equivalent of 1.67 billion barrels of oil. (Each barrel of oil is equivalent to 42 gallons).

Another thing that people seem to forget is the fact that air pollution caused by burning fossil fuels can cause many discomforts such as asthma, lung damage, eye and throat irritations, nausea, dizziness, fatigue, confusion and headaches.

In addition to the massive amounts of pollution caused by our vehicles, 40 million acres of prime American soil have been turned into roads. Put another way that is equal to 62,500 square miles of land that is no longer productive either for farming or performing natural functions such as absorption of rainwater and supplying habitat for living organisms.[217]

In an editorial of the Chicago Tribune M. Herron made a brilliant connection between our dependence on foreign oil and how this threatens our national security. Herron's main point is that "Regardless of ones belief about the relationship between automobile fuel economy and global warming, there simply is no question that an American consumer's purchasing of gasoline harms the ability of the U.S. to conduct its foreign policy in a way that best protects American interests"[218]

Herron also mentions that every gallon of gasoline purchased in the United States contributes to dependence on Middle Eastern states like Saudi Arabia which is a dictatorship. Of course, consumption of fossil fuels contributes to such devastating effects such as global warming as well as pollution of the world's oceans and atmosphere. Herron rightfully emphasizes the need for our politicians to stress the importance of conservation and mass transit use. Of course in a Bush Whitehouse, whether papa or son, we shouldn't expect conservation measures since both are oil-men.

SOLARIZING THE PLANET

Perhaps the most efficient way to eliminate fossil fuels as an energy source is to replace them with solar energy. There are lots of ways to use solar energy for everyday needs such as heating water, cooking food, making electricity, and heating homes during the winter. Many of these solar devices are currently being used with great success such as the device called a "Dude Shemesh" invented in Israel. Israeli law dictates that every new home must have such a unit.

The "Dude Shemesh" heats water for showering, washing kitchen dishes and for other domestic uses. The words "Dude Shemesh" in Hebrew means a solar powered water heater (See figure 34). If a small country such as Israel can produce such an efficient device as the "Dude Shemesh" why don't other countries such as the US have the same will?[219]

Figure 34 A picture of the "Dude Shemesh" water heater. Here is a picture on top of a home in Israel. The sun beats down on the glass covering the pipes and the hot water gets pumped and stored in the cylinder on top. (photo by the author)

Solarizing is my term for placing photovoltaic cells on rooftops in order to generate electricity. Photovoltaic cells are composed of wafers made out of silicon, a common element on the planet, then treated with other chemicals. When sunlight comes in contact with these cells, electricity is created. We use this phenomenon in calculators and in satellites sent into space. Rooftops are the biggest waste of space on the planet and it is time that we come to realize this and use this fact to our advantage by installing solar panels on them. Kenya, a country in Africa, already has thousands of homes electrified with photovoltaic cells. If they can do it, why not us? Some smart individuals, even in the United States are solarizing most of their appliances which include stoves, cars and lawnmowers.[220] Yes that's right, lawn mowers. Politicians tend to ignore these facts, especially in election years because it conflicts with current energy policy (do we really have a policy?).

I have been advocating solar energy use for years but many people claim that it is too expensive. However, if solar voltaic cells are mass produced, the price will eventually come down making this energy source affordable for all. As a matter of fact there is a magazine out called *Solar Today* published by the American Solar Energy Society with articles explaining the benefits of solar energy, purchasing residential units and providing new information about emerging solar technologies.

Another use for solar power is the solar cooker. This is especially useful in countries like those located in northern Africa such as Ethiopia, Sudan, Egypt and Somalia where much of the land is desert. In order for people of these countries to cook they need to hunt for wood which is scarce and leads to deforestation. This in turn leads to the creation of deserts by the process of desertification. The obvious solution to this dilemma is for the people of these countries to get solar cookers which only need the sun and which are relatively inexpensive. By building solar cooker factories in these countries not only would local people be employed but also indoor air pollution from cooking would be eliminated entirely. This would also greatly reduce the incidences of air pollution problems such as emphysema and other respiratory ailments. This is especially true for those who live in one room houses where smoke from cooking permeates throughout the room and into the lungs. (See figure 35.)

Figure 35 This is a solar oven. Solar ovens reduce pressure on the forests, they reduce health hazards such as indoor air pollution. They also improve women's conditions since they do most of the cooking and hunting for wood. **(Courtesy of Paul M. Munsen of Sun Ovens International, Inc. www.sunoven.com)**

3. ENCOURAGE MASS TRANSIT (Avoid driving cars)

The human population is around 6.4 billion and the number of cars worldwide is 531 million.[221] Half a billion automobiles is equivalent to one twelve (1/12th) the world's human population. The United States has around 124 million vehicles. This means that there are 0.6 cars per person in the US.[222] Put a better way, for every two people in the United States there are approximately 1.2 cars. Too many cars on the road create several serious problems such as air pollution, higher insurance rates, congestion, accidents, injuries, deaths, high repair costs, expensive parking fees and road rage.[223]

Not only is road rage a problem but cities are very dangerous because of cars. Let's cite two examples - Detroit and Mexico City. According to W. Ellwood [224] Detroit is synonymous with two things: cars and violent death. As of 1989 Detroit had the highest murder rate of any city in the West. This is because everything has been removed from the streets (trees, grass etc.) and replaced by hoodlums. Mexico City is another example. The Zocolo, the main square in Mexico City was a nice place to walk in. Now, however, it is noisy and filled with blue smoke from cars. It appears that walking may be more dangerous than driving.

This situation continues to grow worse and demands *immediate* attention. Part of the solution would be to encourage mass transit to make it a more viable option for people who drive to work. Mass transit is wonderful especially in any metropolitan area because it reduces the numbers of cars, and it's efficient in both travel time and fuel usage. It's obvious that mass transit is the best approach to alleviating many of the problems associated with automobiles.

Curitiba, Brazil was planned with these very ideas in mind. Under the leadership of its mayor, Jamie Lerner, the city was transformed into a commuter paradise.[225] While mayor he instituted a wonderful mass-transit system which easily allowed the average person to get to work without driving. Bus stops became very commuter friendly and relatively affordable. It is unfortunate that local governments in the United States don't copy Mayor Lerner's ideas.

Another solution would be to build offices, schools, stores and other places nearer to where people actually live. If this solution is not practical then car-pooling should seriously be considered. Perhaps one of the most brilliant solutions espoused by Paul Hawken[226] is to build homes without parking spaces and give the owners a perpetual mass transit pass. [227] This will encourage living near work or taking mass transit. Of course not everyone can live near work, especially factory workers because factories that make heavy equipment are usually built far from residential areas or near minority areas. In this case, there should be some form of meeting place where workers can drive to and be met by a company van or bus to pick up the workers.

Bicycling is another alternative to automobile commuting. Holland with its emphasis on bicycling is a prime example of a country which depends on a connection between residential areas, bicycle use and mass transit. (See figure36.)

Fig. 36. This is a bicycle parking lot by The Hague's Train
station in Holland. This is typical of the European common
sense attitude toward conserving energy and resources through
bicycling and use of public transit. (Photo by author)

INCREASE THE PRICE OF GASOLINE

Surely the most unpopular way to encourage mass transit is to raise the price of gasoline by as much as four times the current price. Politicians no matter what persuasion are hesitant to anger their constituency with proposals to increase both fuel efficiency and gasoline prices. Predictably, politicians are more concerned with being elected and continuing their careers instead of protecting the environment. Raising prices, which is actually the ethical solution, would encourage fuel conservation and the development of alternate non-fossil forms of energy. However, such measures threaten the enormous profits of oil companies as well as employment and therefore do not get the attention they deserve from government bodies. From an environmental point of view this is a very logical solution because it will lead to an increase in better air quality and a decrease in respiratory ailments.

Figure 37. Perhaps this is the best solution for our automobiles. The location is 22st and Harlem near Chicago. .(Photo by author)

Another obstacle preventing better fuel economy and protecting our environment are the automobile manufacturers. Large vehicles such as SUVs and Hummers are highly profitable for these companies and thus purchasing of such vehicles is encouraged instead of smaller more efficient cars which have a lower profit margin. As a result, fuel economy has continued to plummet over the last decade instead of improving. For example, between 1987 and 1997 fuel efficiency decreased from an average of 26.2miles per gallon (mpg) to 24.4 mpg.[228] How many Iraqi , American and Afghani deaths have been attributed to the fact that we still depend on oil for gasoline and drive cars with low gas mileage?

Figure 38. The author is holding a bottle of water at a gas station selling gasoline for around $2.10 per gallon. Buying water in this size bottle (591 ml) sells for the equivalent of $7.61 per gallon. As the reader can see this price is over three times the price of a gallon of gasoline in the US in 2004. So how come we don't complain about the cost of bottled water? (Photo by M. Schwartz)

4. POPULATION CONTROL

Overpopulation contributes to increased erosion of the Earth's environment, further depletion of precious natural resources and increased poverty. Al Gore's book *The Earth in the Balance* states that population control is the major solution to the global environmental crisis.[229] This is just common sense because the majority of environmental problems are caused by people. An historical milestone occurred when the sixth billionth person was born on October 12, 1999.[230] This number is symbolic because it brings further emphasis on the strain on Earth's carrying capacity. Carrying capacity is defined as the maximum population an area can sustain without bringing in outside resources.

Solving this problem requires a more responsible action guided by common sense, something which is lacking in government circles. Countries such as the United States can make a major contribution to alleviate overpopulation in the developing world. Yet, instead of common sense dictating policies toward these goals such decisions are often made by ideology based on certain religious beliefs that will ensure reelection. Developed countries like the United States should strive for a far more humane approach that would encourage birth control, family planning, sex education, employment, and access to medical care in many parts of the world.

Perhaps one of the best ways to stop population growth is to only have one child as China has tried to implement. In his wonderful book, *Maybe One*, author Bill McKibben[231] suggests that maybe one child is enough. He maintains that only children are in fact psychologically stable and not necessarily as spoiled as previously thought. Having one child makes sense from an economic standpoint because of less stress on the environment. This is essentially a numbers game which benefits the Earth by less consumption (at least in theory), less pollution and more chance of a sustainable ecosystem.

In contrast to McKibben's thesis is that of the Pope. He has taken a stance against many sensible solutions to alleviating overpopulation. One such stance is denouncing birth control. It is obvious that he , the Pope, never took a class in environmental science with me. It appears that the Pope is out of touch with many of his members who suffer from his teachings regarding reproductive rights. This is mostly because adequate birth control is not easily available in their countries. Instead of preventing such measures the Pope should encourage birth control as a humane solution which alleviates health problems, early death of the baby, death of the mother during child birth and poverty.

It is for these very reasons that birth control is a necessity for the developing countries. Unfortunately, it is not only limited access that prevents birth control from becoming a reality in these regions but also the lack of health and environmental education. Also associated with this problem is illiteracy and a strict adherence to religious doctrine.

5. ENVIRONMENTAL EDUCATION FOR EVERYBODY

Perhaps the best way to help end the environmental crisis with its associated problems is education. Children as well as adults *must* be educated on this topic in order to assure the future of humanity. This education must be a priority all over the world. If people understand that there is more to life than just eating, sleeping, being entertained and going to the store to buy things then they will have a better environmental consciousness. First they must realize that everything they buy is manufactured from raw material that comes from nature even human made items such as plastics and synthetics. Then people must learn how everything in nature is not only connected but fragile and finite. Courses in ecology and biology will lead to a greater understanding of humanity's role in nature and the importance of preserving our planet instead of destroying it.

Even now without the benefit of widespread environmental education, many children are aware of the importance of recycling, wasteful consumerism (culturally influenced), and depletion of natural resources. Occasionally I encounter this awareness with young adults while teaching my classes. Children have been known to educate their parents on environmental matters. It is this attitude that must be further encouraged and incorporated into our education system even as early as grade school.

6. EAT LOWER ON THE FOOD CHAIN

Essentially this means becoming a vegetarian. Animals that consume plant material contribute to the depletion of land by adding manure and methane gas to both soil and air. In addition, cattle grazing decimates large areas of rainforest (essential to the world's climate and oxygen content), poisons waterways with added nutrients (causing the growth of toxic aquatic organisms such as *Pfiesteria picicida and other species*) and contributes greatly to the greenhouse effect. Other than carbon dioxide (CO_2) methane (CH_4) is the second most common gas involved in the greenhouse effect.

Food is essential to human survival but consider the consequences of consuming meat products which have been a staple of wealthy nations for many years. In order to gain one pound of you, you have to eat 10 pounds of food. If you eat this food in the form of vegetable material such as grains then all you need is 10 pounds. However, if you eat 10 pounds of cow you are eating the equivalent of 100 pounds of grain. Thus if we would eat plants (vegetables) directly we can save 90% of the grain or plant material for human consumption and possibly alleviating starvation throughout the world.

By eating lower on the food chain we save fuel, electricity, seeds for crops, labor, valuable land, and other important limited resources. An extra added benefit is a reduction in diseases such as heart attacks and cancer. See the food chain below. Since the picture below is more of an aquatic food chain the primary producer is the algae but it is still a plantlike organism.

HUMAN FOOD CHAIN

Tertiery Consumer

Secondary Consumer

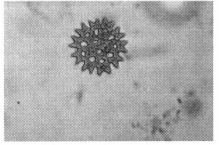

Primary Consumer

Primary Producer

7. CURTAILING GREED (MORE IS LESS)

Greed is a basic genetic trait found in humans. People are inherently greedy and our economic system, to a certain extent, uses that greed to profit by. The competition factor for a myriad of items from cars to homes to fashion encourages greed between people. Until people realize that material objects are simply that with no particular utilitarian value greed will continue on the scale that it is today.

However, in this world with an ever increasing population and wealth, and poverty, people want more, simply because there are more and more things. Therefore, people will do whatever it takes to get these things even if it means destroying their own planet. This parallel attitude is found throughout the world whether it is developing countries that continue to destroy their land by cutting, chopping and digging or the developed world which is consuming natural resources at an unprecedented rate.

People have to come to some sort of realization that we're not only endangering the planet's ecosystems but also threatening our standard of living by over consumption. As citizens of the world we have an obligation to nurture the Earth as it has nurtured us for so many centuries and not be persuaded by advertisements, media, politicians and business people. Although greed cannot be entirely eliminated it can be controlled if people only reflected on how this emotion is ruining our world.

8. DEVALUE OR DEEMPHASIZE MONEY

Now let's discuss why we have to either devalue or deemphasize money in the world. It is obvious that we always hear of crimes committed in the name of money whether it be murder, embezzlement, campaigning for contributions, land deals, drug production (cocaine, hashish etc.) or whatever. It almost always involves money. In the year 2002, one of the biggest scams was Enron's disastrous bout with bankruptcy. Enron reportedly overstated its profits while simultaneously allowing energy shortages and service disruptions, especially in California. This resulted in a recall of its democratically elected governor, Grey Davis, who was a democrat and replaced by Arnold Schwarzenegger, a Rebublican.

It is our perception that if we don't have money, especially those who live in wealthier countries, then we are insignificant. This goes beyond mere survival for basic necessities and is directly connected to the value placed on money, especially in a market economy. This form of behavior is pathological and is found in all strata of our society from ordinary folks to corporate executives.

Of course, this also impacts the environment because "natural capital" which includes raw materials such as trees, gorillas, plants, fossil fuels, bacteria and fungi (used for various medicines), are valued as commodities.

Devaluating or at the very least deemphasizing money is problematic in a world society based on its accumulation. For this very reason a solution is difficult to propose but what is urgently needed is a change in mindset or paradigms which include consumerism, culture, social interaction, and governance.

9. END CONSUMERISM

There was a cowboy who lived out in the wilderness for 20 years. One day he goes to a big city and winds up in a K-Mart. He says to himself, "Boy, how did I live without so many things?"

What exactly is consumerism? It is the idea that we must have more and more things whether we need them or not. The media continues to saturate the public with messages aimed at encouraging consumption on an ever-increasing scale. As a result, the average Western person has more of everything from clothes to cars to electronic equipment to excess food. We in America are conditioned to consume at increasing levels regardless of need or ability to pay; hence the proliferation of credit cards.

Consumerism, on the scale that it is practiced, results in huge environmental destruction by building malls on prime farmland which contributes to biodiversity loss. This also adds to suburban sprawl, which increases air pollution and congestion in once pristine ecosystems.

Not only do malls initially take a toll on the land but also the very items that are sold there deplete "nature's capital" in the manufacture of such items.

In his book, *Maybe One* Bill McKibben shows that exaggerated consumerism is alive and well. He points out that people are still willing to pay $4000 for a Kelly Bag, (and I thought that Louie Viutton stuff was bad), $75,000 Jaguars (the car ,not the animal), but the clincher is a watch that costs an unbelievable $44,500. That's right over $44,000 just to tell time.[232] Other items which are mentioned include: large 64 inch TVs, luxury SUVs (Sport Utility Vehicles), two-seater sport cars, large private yachts, diamond and gold rings, etc, etc. Not only do these extravagant items waste natural resources but the money spent on them could be put to better use to alleviate poverty, disease and environmental degradation.

The difficulty in finding a solution to this problem is that consumerism is such an ingrained part of our society because business depends on it. Millions of people are employed at every stage of our consumer-driven society from acquisition of raw materials to manufacture and distribution to their sale and eventual dumping into landfills.

In addition, media advertising contributes to increased consumption. So does television and radio commercials, print ads, billboards, sky writing and other forms of advertising. These help convince people to accumulate more of everything.

In the good old days, when the air was clean and sex was dirty, it appeared that we had values which were demonstrated by the sensible shopping patterns of citizens. They would get the necessities and not splurge on needless items. Such a mindset is possible even today if we rethink progress as consuming less, saving more and de-emphasizing the social patterns of modern shopping behavior. In other words, people should be happy with what they have and not fixated on the newest and larger goods. Unfortunately, this will be difficult to achieve especially with ubiquitous media slogans such as "Shop till you drop" and "Shop like you mean it."[233]

10. ENCOURAGE RECYCLING
AND THE PERCENTAGE PARADOX

The trend in recent years of recycling is a positive step in the right direction. Yet, somewhat paradoxically its success has brought upon itself a number of problems, mainly an over- abundance of recycled material. A good example of this is the accumulation of newspapers to be recycled; more is being collected than the facilities can handle. Of course one should recycle but don't use it as an excuse to buy more stuff like newspapers which can be shared. Purchasing newspapers encourages the production of waste that ultimately winds up in landfills. Using less not only conserves resources but produces less waste which increases the life of landfills. This particular situation illustrates a dilemma defined as the "percentage paradox."

What exactly is the percentage paradox? The best way to explain it is in an example. In 1960 the total waste that was generated in the United States was 88 million metric tons of which 7% was recycled. In 1995, 209 million metric tons was produced of which 27% was recycled. The 7% recycled represented 6 million metric tons and in 1995 the 27% represented 56 million metric tons, however, the amount of waste discarded in landfills was 82 million metric tons in 1960 and in 1995, 152 million metric tons.[234] This means that even though there was a higher percentage of waste that was recycled three decades later there was a lot more discarded in landfills. To put it bluntly, percentages don't mean much when we are talking about the amount of waste generated.

Everyday items such as plastic milk containers can have many post-consumer uses. One example in particular comes to mind. Many park benches are made out of wood but now we can make them out of milk containers (See figure 39). Yes, Number 2 plastic also known as High Density Polyethylene (HDPE) can me used to make decks in homes, furniture and even a marina such as the Jackson Park Marina in Chicago.

Figure 39-A milk container (Number 2 plastic) is sitting on top of
a park bench made out of number 2 plastic. (Photo by author)

11. CONSUMERISM AND LAZINESS (DON'T BE LAZY)

Some people are lazy and they just don't want to take the time to recycle
or take a stance on the environment. It is very easy to be lazy in today's
world because of the plethora of consumer items such as plastic and paper
products. We are so inundated with these materials that we forget that they
come from nature. This is yet another example of the attitude that many
people have that "nature doesn't exist." It is easier to buy and use new items
and discard them later rather than recycling them or finding alternate uses.
A good example of this idea is using strong, reusable plastic plates instead
of paper on picnics. Theses plates can be washed and used over and over
again. The only effort on the consumer's part is to take the time to clean
them in water. Remember, the water used is recycled by Mother Nature.

12. MAKING OTHER COUNTRIES MORE LIVABLE BY
CONTRIBUTIONS FROM EXTREMELY WEALTHY PEOPLE

If we are to have a survivable planet the extremely wealthy must donate
even more of their personal wealth to the world's poor in order to assure the
survival of humanity. As we have seen extreme poverty and extreme wealth
result in planetary destruction. This eventual reality can be avoided if the
extremely wealthy become more aware of it and how it impacts their lives.
All people regardless of economic status need clean water, air and food as
well as shelter. A destroyed planet will not only be the result of negligence
by the wealthy but also unlivable for all living creatures.

13. RESPECT ALL LIFE AS IF YOUR LIFE DEPENDED ON IT
(BECAUSE IT DOES)

As we saw in chapter 1 there are seventeen functions that the world's
ecosystems perform in order for life to continue. Every organism has an
ecological function—even those that we may not be aware of. Nature put
everything here for a purpose from the much-maligned cockroach[235] to

the "dreaded" bat to the beautiful but tiny copepod to the giant whales and redwood trees. Every organism, even those that humans perceive as annoyances or ugly, still deserve to live and function in their proper way within their respective ecosystem... By killing weeds with chemicals or unwanted insects by bug zappers we do not know the main extent of the damage that was done to the ecosystems.

In his wonderful book, *Medical Quest,*[236] Mark Plotkin writes of the astonishing and extraordinary medical properties of insects, fungi, spiders, leeches, marine organisms and other organisms. Children as well as adults should learn about the properties of organisms found in areas of the world such as the Arctic or tropical rainforests. One example is the most famous drug yet (next to Viagra) and that is aspirin. That's right aspirin, which originally came from a plant, is the world's most commonly used drug. Many organisms such as the Rosy Periwinkle (*Catheransus roseus*) have been shown to have many medicinal properties and show promise in treating certain forms of cancers and other disorders More than 50% of drugs now in use are derived from nature's bounty and that is why all life deserves respect.

14. VOTE FOR ENVIRONMENTAL FRIENDLY CANDIDATES (AND HONEST)—DON'T BELIEVE WHAT POLITICIANS TELL YOU

For citizens of the 29 or so countries on the planet that have elections for their leaders it is imperative that the people vote for candidates that have proven environmental friendly records. If all the candidates talk about is how a vote for them insures economic prosperity with total disregard for the environment then citizens should not vote for them. Remember, if there is no environment then there can't be existence, therefore, no edible food, oxygen or other life support systems or an economy to worry about. Without an environment, there won't be any politicians either.

The best solution is to vote for candidates with a proven environmental record and, if possible, some form of environmental education. If this option is impractical (as it is most often with (republicans), then candidates should be pressured or educated to be more sensitive to the planet's care instead of being preoccupied with business interests like the Bush Boys.

A good example of this environmentally unfriendly attitude was the proposed drilling in the Arctic National Wildlife Refuge (ANWR) which essentially pitted Democrats against Republicans.

The reason for this mindset is the insatiable appetite for oil, especially our love affair with the automobile. Securing a steady supply of oil has become a mantra for politicians to please their Constituents despite the known environmental consequences. Politicians that advocate conservation measures, continued research into alternate fuels, and more environmentally sound policies are assured of either no political career or at the very most a very short career.

This ongoing battle to secure fossil fuel energy has been accelerating for at least the last three decades, despite oil "shortages" and petro-wars with massive environmental damage. Yet, paradoxically, increases in alternative technologies that utilize solar power and wind energy continue to be improved and offer practical solutions to our energy problems.

15. END WARFARE BY MAKING THE MILITARY DEFEND US

Having a strong military is not the answer to a strong defense. What is the purpose of a military? I assume its purpose is to defend against foreign invasion. Yet instead of defending its citizens it's creating situations which are endangering the world's populations by the production of armaments, their storage and eventual use. The military uses vast amounts of resources and as a result of this, continues to pollute the Earth at an alarming rate. These resources, both material and monetary can be better spent *to really defend citizens by investing in their futures.*

Much of the wasted resources that the military consumes can be better spent on the environment as well as its inhabitants which include bacteria, animals, plants, fungi, protists, and viruses. In addition to protecting the environment these vast resources could be used to defend people's lives against debilitating or incurable diseases. Deaths due to cancer, respiratory ailments such as asthma, heart disease and other fatal diseases continue to occur due to inadequate funding to find cures. For poor people these situations are even worse because of the unavailability of expensive and necessary care. If a foreign enemy killed this many people per year it would be a cause for war.

Despite these social and environmental problems the military continues to spend at an alarming rate on planes, ships, submarines, tanks, bombs, guns, bullets, missiles, and other implements of both human and environmental destruction.

What forms of defense should all countries have? The following list offers some solutions to this major problem:

1. Spend a great deal of the military budget on providing a sustainable economy that is environmentally friendly throughout the whole world.
2. Alleviate poverty by funding agricultural education, water treatment plants and homebuilding in the developing world.
3. Provide universal heath care and increase research funding for medicine.

4. Make education either low cost or free from grade school to graduate school.
5. Assure that everyone has such basic needs as clothing, food, shelter and clean water and mass transit. These are the things that governments should be defending us against. These are the threats which come from within and not from without.

16. END THE USE OF DEADLY CHEMICALS LIKE PESTICIDES

The continued use of pesticides poses an immense threat to the biota of the planet because these chemicals tend to bioaccumulate and biomagnify. This means that such chemicals accumulate in individual organisms as well as move up the food chain. These can cause allergic reactions as well as diseases such as cancer. It is obvious that pesticides need to be eliminated even if this means difficulty for agribusiness.

What do we use pesticides for? To kill pests such as fungi and insects that eat our crops before, during and after harvest. However, there are now alternatives such as biological, genetic, cultural, and integrated pest management (IPM) controls of pests. Biological control involves using natural predators of pests such as insects which eat the target pest and may have some other anti-pest effect. Genetic controls involve placing the natural predator's DNA into the host organism, thus making it naturally deadly to its pest. A good example is the insertion of the BT gene, *(Bacillus thuringiensis- a bacterium)* inside a crop such as corn, which causes the attacking insect to die. Cultural controls consist of harvesting crops at certain times before pests can get to them, as well as crop rotation. Crop rotation means planting one crop one year and planting another crop the following year such as corn followed by soybeans. This discourages the proliferation of a crop-specific pest. IPM means applying some chemical pesticide, some biological and some cultural control thus allowing less chemical pesticide. These practices appear to be very successful in controlling pests and lessening dependence on chemical pesticides. If we humans can put our heads together and use common sense we can solve most of our problems without destroying our environment and ourselves as well.

17. AVOID USING GENETICALLY ALTERED AND PATENTED SEEDS

Genetically altered seeds are seeds that have been genetically modified so that they yield more crops and impart other desirable qualities. They are displacing centuries-old seeds that have been the mainstay of the world's food source. This means in plain English that these seeds, many of which are hybrids, do not have natural resistance to pests or adverse environmental conditions that native seeds have. As of 1970 only six seed types make up 71% of the domestic corn crop.[237]

Currently, a new form of seed called the **terminator** is being developed by the Monsanto Corporation. Essentially this seed is developed with the intention of only being planted once, thus forcing farmers to buy seeds every year instead of planting seeds from their own crops. Farmers were able to save some of their crops for seeds for planting but terminator seeds can't be planted more than once. This will be especially devastating to small farmers in poor nations thus leading to possible starvation for millions of people worldwide. In addition, pollen from these crops can pollinate non-genetically altered crops, thus imparting sterility and threatening every crop on the planet.[238]

Genetically altered seeds can vastly diminish biodiversity of food crops worldwide. The value of biodiversity can best be exemplified by the famous Irish Potato Famine which was caused by the fungus, *Phytophthora infestans,* more commonly known as Late Blight. The cause of the blight was that the Irish planted one type (variety) of potato which was attacked by this specific fungus. If they had a polyculture (many varieties) this blight would not have wiped out all the potatoes because the fungus is specific to only one variety. By 1850, when the blight was over, Ireland had over one million dead and many more emigrated to the United States and other countries.

Biodiversity is needed in agriculture as well as everywhere else because it insures a wide gene pool which allows wide genetic diversity and survival of species. Genetically modified seeds lower the gene pool by standardizing crops and making them less diverse and thus more prone to diseases and crop failure. Sometime in the future this can be a *worldwide* problem.

18. ENCOURAGE ECOTOURISM

Costa Rica is one of my favorite countries because they have something that most countries should have and that is ecotourism. Ecotourism is tourism specifically designed to see the natural sites that countries have such as trees, animals, soil and ecosystems in general. The opposite of ecotourism is ecoterrorism, which is the deliberate destruction of ecosystems. We see this when trees are being bulldozed to make tree plantations (such as monocultures) or to use the wood for fuel as in Africa or the use of trees to earn income by selling them.

Trees are worth more standing than by cutting them down. A tree, if it is cut, is only worth the intrinsic value of the wood. A tree standing is worth millions of dollars because it exists. The trees contain animals, plants as well as bacteria, and fungi which are part of the ecosystem. These are the things that tourists come to see. Hence, no trees, no ecotourism. Ecotourism, however, must be regulated so that too much tourism in these spots doesn't damage the ecosystem.

19. THE AMERICAN DREAM SHOULD BE THE WORLD DREAM AND ATTAINABLE

The American dream should be applicable to everyone in the world. This does not mean living in bigger homes, driving gas-guzzling, CO_2 producing cars and having an extravagant lifestyle that is almost obscene. Applying the American Dream on a worldwide basis means that everyone should have access to decent housing, sanitary conditions, clothing, shelter, education, healthcare and peace. These measures would assure the longevity of the planet by preventing the needless destruction of ecosystems for people to make a living.

Sharing our wealth and distributing our resources at a more equitable level will not only protect the environment but alleviate much of the poverty that is so common in many places of the world. Perhaps the best example of people subsisting at the lowest level of society are those found living and working in a garbage dump called Smokey Mountain outside of Manila in the Philippines. In the book, *Biohazard: The Hot Zone and Beyond*[239] there is a picture of Smokey Mountain. This picture boldly illustrates the daily reality that these people experience looking for any useful item that can be resold. Such an environment is a breeding ground for disease-bearing mosquitoes, respiratory ailments and other physical disorders. Unfortunately, this site is common throughout most of the world where people just manage to survive and can never achieve their full potential.

Making the American Dream applicable on a worldwide basis is possible only if we take a sensible approach that would encourage ecological conservation, preserve local economies, and educate people. Both sides need to have a change of mindset and come to the realization that all share the same planet. For the developed nations this means consuming less so that the rest of the world can have more.

20. REPRIORITIZE

Throughout this book I have attempted to show how the activities all over the world threaten the planet's existence. To assure the continuance of all life on Earth we humans must change our priorities. This involves changing our mindset to be more aware and sensitive to environmental issues. The Earth's ecosystems are deteriorating at an alarming rate while people in wealthy nations are more concerned with sports, entertainment, sex, partisan politics and maintaining an affluent lifestyle. On the other hand, the Earth's poor ignore the environment because they depend on its bounty to maintain even a subsistence level of existence.

Changing our priorities begins with the more affluent doing more to help the less fortunate of the world. By showing the destitute that there are better ways of living and working along with care of the environment, it will assure the longevity of this planet. One thing is certain and that is that we can no longer consume in a manner that we have become accustomed to no matter where on this planet we may live. As is the case of global warming, it is better to err on the side of caution by assuming it is a human made problem rather than a natural phenomenon. The consequences either way are too grim to even contemplate.

We have to act as if the world is

not only my patient, but our patient.

APPENDIX I
GLOSSARY OF COMMON
ENVIRONMENTAL TERMS

ACID RAIN- Rain with a pH below 5.6.

ATMOSPHERE- The technical name for the part of the biosphere containing air. The major components of an unpolluted atmosphere are nitrogen gas (N_2) accounting for 79.08% and Oxygen (O_2) are accounting for 20.84% of the atmosphere and Carbon dioxide accounting for roughly .036%. The atmosphere is composed of five main parts differentiated by altitude. They are in order starting from sea level: Troposphere, stratosphere, mesosphere, thermosphere and exosphere.

BARREL OF OIL (bbl) = 42 GALLONS

1 BECQUEREL = 1 radioactive decay per second, 1 gram of radium is equivalent to 0.037 TBq

BIOACCUMULATION: This means the buildup of chemicals in bodies of organisms. Example: DDT accumulates in fatty tissues of humans. See Biomagnification.

BIOMAGNIFICATION: This is similar to bioaccumulation except that chemicals tend to move up the food chain. An example is the fact that a chemical may be found in a small algae cell. The algae cell is then eaten by a zooplankter,a little animal, then a fish will eat the zooplankter then a bigger fish will eat the other fish and so on.

BIOME- A large geographical area that has a similar climate, soil, vegetation and animal life.
Examples are the tropical rain forest, deserts and grasslands.

BIODIVERSITY- This term includes the wide variety of genes, species and ecosystems. As of 2001 there are approximately 1.8 million known species of organisms which include bacteria, single celled organisms (mainly protists), plants, animals and fungi.

BIOSPHERE- The area of the planet which includes the land, water and air where most life survives. Technical names are the lithosphere, hydrosphere and atmosphere.

BOD- The term means Biochemical Oxygen Demand. It is used to describe the cleanliness of waste water before and after treatment. It is expressed as milligrams of oxygen per liter of water.

BYCATCH- Aquatic animals that are caught by mistake in nets and are usually thrown away and left to die. These include birds, sharks, starfish, and a host of other organisms.

CDC-Centers for Disease Control and Prevention, located in Atlanta Georgia

CARRYING CAPACITY- The maximum population that an area can sustain without importing outside resources.

CLEAN AIR ACT- The first attempt to reduce air pollution. It was first established in 1963 but was amended in 1970 to reduce emissions of cars and industries.

CURIE- (Ci) 37 billion disintegrations per second. A unit of radiation exposure.

DEMOGRAPHIC FATIQUE-The growing inability of poor governments with burgeoning populations to cope with new threats to society...such as aids, malaria, tuberculosis, land degradation , warfare and other miseries.

ECOSPHERE- Same as biosphere.

ECOSYSTEM- The area where there is an interaction between the living and non living. Living meaning organisms and non-living meaning air, water, atmospheric pressure etc.

ECOTONE- A sharp boundary between two different types of communities. An example is sharp difference between where a forest ends and a grassland begins.

ENDEMIC- Found only in one location on the planet. This refers to plants, animals and other organisms which are native to specific parts of the planet. An example is the large tortoise found on the Galapagos Islands.

ENVIRONMENTAL POLLUTION-1) The contamination of Mother Nature by Human Nature
2) The effluence of Affluence 3) The contamination of an ecosystem by the addition or removal of something.

ENVIRONMENTAL SCIENCE- The study of the environment to include all aspects of the environment and their interactions.

EUTROPHICATION- The term used when a body of water, especially a lake, has too many nutrients causing growth of aquatic plants and algae which eventually die and decompose. The body of water will eventually turn into dry land.

HYDROSPHERE- The area of the planet that contains water.

INORGANIC CHEMICALS- These are chemicals that are composed of elements other than carbon. Examples include sodium chloride (NaCl) table salt, H_2SO_4, Sulfuric acid and
H_2O (water)

LEACHATE- the liquid containing dissolved chemicals. Leachate is formed when water dissolves chemicals which are usually from landfills or from rain in contact with dissolvable substances.

LITHOSPHERE- The term used to describe the land mass of the planet.

NEMATODA- This is a (phylum) group of worms which range in size from less than a mm to more than a meter. They are very important in maintaining the proper functioning of ecosystems. Some are parasitic on plants, animals and humans but the majority are beneficial to the planet. There are around 12,000 known species.

NICHE- The role that an organism plays in its environment.

NOX This is the term used to identify oxides of nitrogen. There are three main gases: N_2O, nitrous oxide; NO, nitric oxide and NO_2, nitrogen dioxide

ORGANIC CHEMICALS- These are chemicals consisting of carbon and hydrogen in covalent linkage. Examples are sucrose (table sugar), ethyl alcohol and starch.

PAN-Peroxyacylnitrate-A form of photochemical smog.

pH-Measure of the acidity of a substance. ph ranges between 0 to 14. ph below 7 is acidic ;ph above 7 is alkaline or basic.

PHOTOCHEMICAL SMOG- Pollution in the atmosphere where many chemicals such as gases and hydrocarbons react together using the sun as an energy source. PAN is an example.

PRION-A piece of protein responsible for Mad Cow Disease. The human form is called Creutzfelt-Jakob disease.

SALINIZATION- The buildup of salt in soil due to too much irrigation of fields.

SYNERGISM- The multiplicative effects of two substances taken together rather than each taken separately. Put in another way one could make the statement 1+1=5. An example is the health effects of smoking and working with asbestos. If one smokes he may have a 15% chance of developing lung cancer. If a person works with asbestos and doesn't smoke he may have 12% chance of getting lung cancer but if the person smokes and works with asbestos his chances of getting cancer can shoot up 92 times.

TRANSPIRATION- Evaporation of water from leaves of trees. They supply water to the atmosphere which falls as rain.

VECTOR- Something that spreads a disease. A good example are mosquitoes which can spread Malaria.

VIROID- A piece of RNA implicated in some plant diseases.

VIRUS- A structure that has a core of either RNA or DNA and a protein coat. Many are disease causing agents.

ZOONOSIS- Diseases that can be transmitted from animals to humans.

APPENDIX II
BOOKS ABOUT G.W.BUSH

Below is a list of books written about G.W. Bush. Never in the history of the United States has there been a presidency of such perceived ineptitude, which has inspired scores of authors to express their concerns about the global culture, politics, the world's peoples, terrorism and the environment. G.W. Bush's ineptitude has caused many trees to be destroyed in order to create paper to print these books, and of course, this book is one of them.

1. 9-11 by Noam Chomsky NY: Seven Stories Press, 2001

2. Against All Enemies: Inside America's War on Terror by Richard A. Clarke: Free Press, 2004

3. Alice in Wonderland and the World Trade Center Disaster by David Icke Wildwood MO: Bridge of Love, 2002

4. American Dynasty; Aristocracy, Fortune and Deceit in the House of Bush by Kevin Phillips NY: Viking, 2004

5. America's Secret Establishment; An Introduction to the Order of Skull and Bones by Antony C. Sutton Trine Day 2002

6. Behind the War on Terror: Western Secret Strategy and The Struggle for Iraq by Nafeez Mosaddeq Ahmed Gabriola Island, B.D.: New Society Publishers, 2003

7. Big bush Lies: The twenty most telling lies of President George W.Bush by Jerry Politix Barret. 2004

8. Big Lies: The Right Wing Propaganda Machine and How It Distorts the Truth by Joe Conason. 2003. Thomas Dunne Books 2004

9. Bush on the Couch by Justin A. Frank Regen Books. 2004

10. Bushwacked; Molly Ivins and Lou Dubose, Random Press, 2003

11. Bushwomen: Tales of Cynical Species by Laura Flanders. Verso 2004

12. Bushworld: Enter at your own Risk. by Maureen Dowd by Putnam Publishing Group G.P. Putnam 2004

13. Crimes Against Nature; **How George W. Bush and His Corporate Pals Are Plundering the Country and Hijacking Our Democracy** by <u>Robert F. Kennedy Jr.</u> Harper Collins 2004.

14. Cruel and Unusual: Bush Cheney New World Order by Mark Crispin Miller. Norton.2004

15 Dark Majesty: The Secret Brotherhood and the Magic of a Thousand Points of Light by Texe Mars Austin , TX: Living Truth Publishers, 1992

16. Dreaming War: Blood for Oil and the Cheney-Bush Junta by Gore Vidal NY: Thunder's Mouth Press/ Nation Books, 2002

17. Dude, Where's My Country by Michael Moore NY: Warner Books., 2003

18. Move On's Fifty Ways to Love Your Country: How to Find Your Political Voice and Become a Catalyst for Change compiled by Moveon.org. Maui, HI; Inner Ocean Pub, 2004

19. Forbidden Truth: U.S. Taliban Secret Oil Diplomacy, Saudi Arabia and the Failed Search for Bin Laden by Jean Charles Brisand, et al. NY city: Thunder's Mouth Press, 2002

20. Fortunate Son: George W. Bush and the Making of an American President. By J.H. Hatfield and Mark Crispin Miller NY: Soft Skull Press, 2000

21. Frontier Justice: Weapons of Mass Destruction and the Bushwhacking of America by Scott Ritter NY: Context Books., 2003

22.. George W. Bush Coloring Book by Karen Ocker and Joley Wood Garrett County Press, 2004

23. George W. Bushisms: The Slate Book of the Accidental Wit and Wisdom of our 43rd President by G.W. Bush and Jacob Weisberg, Editor. NY: Fireside, 2001

24. Had Enough: A Handbook for Fighting Back by James Carville NY: Simon & Schuster, 2003

25. House of Bush, House of Saud; The Secret relationship between the world's Most powerful Dynasties by Craig Under N.Y: Scribner, 2004

26. How Much Money did you Make on the War, Daddy? A quick and dirty guide to war, profiteering in the Bush Administration. By William D. Hartung NY: Nation books., 2003

27. Iraq: From Sumer to Saddam by Geof Simons NY: St. Martin's Press, 1994

28. Is Our Children Learning by Paul Begala NY: Simon & Schuster, 2000 NY: W.W. Norton, 2002

29. Lies and the Lying Liars who Tell Them: A Fair and Balanced Look at the Right by Al Franken . Dutton, 2003

30. Losing America: Confronting a Reckless and Arrogant Presidency : By Robert Byrd. W.W. Norton and Co. NY: Thomas Dunne Books., 2003

31. Perpetual War for Perpetual Peace: How we got to be so hated. by Gore Vidal NY: Thunder's Mouth Press/ Nation Books, 2002

32. Plan of Attack by Bob Woodward NY: Simon & Schuster, 2004

33. Secrets of the Tomb: Skull and Bones, The Ivy League, and The Hidden Paths of Power by Alexandria Robbins Boston, Little Brown, 2002

34 Shrub:The Short But Happy Political Life of George W. Bush by Molly. Ivins and Lou Dubose Vintage Books, 2000

35. Strategic Ignorance by Carl Pope and Paul Rauber, Sierra Club Books, 2004

36. Stupid White Men by Michael Moore: And other sorry excuses for the State of the Nation. Regan Books, 2001

37. War Plan Iraq: Ten Reasons against War with Iraq by Milan Rai, with Noam   Chomsky   Verso Books   2002

38. The Best Democracy Money can Buy: An Investigative Reporter Exposes the Truth about Globalization Corporate Cons and High Finance Fraud busters by Greg Palast NY: Plume, 2003

39. The Bush Dyslexicon: Observations on a National Disorder by Marl Crispin Miller . W.W. Norton 2001

40. The Bush-Haters Handbook: A guide to the most Appalling Presidency of the Past 100 Years by Jack Huberman   NY: Nation Book, 2003

41. The Franklin Coverup: Child Abuse, Satanism, and Murder in Nebraska by John W. Decamp Lincoln, NE; AWT, 1992

42. The Great Unraveling: Losing our Way in The New Century by Paul Krugman NY: W.W. Norton, 2003

43. The Iron Triangle: Inside the secret world of the Carlyle Group by Dan Briody NY: J. Wiley, 2003

44. The Lies of George W. Bush: Mastering the Politics of Deception by David Corn NY: Crown Pubs., 2003

45. The Price of Loyalty: George W. Bush, the White House and The education of Paul O'Neil by Ron Suskind NY: Simon & Schuster, 2004

46. The Very Hungry Caterpillar by Eric Carle   NY: Philomel Books, 1979 This was one of the first books that Bush

remembers reading. Maybe he is fond of it now because it is written for his present reading level. !!!

47. The W Effect: Bush's War on Women by Laura Flanders. Feminist Press at the City University of New York. 2004

48. The War on Freedom: How and Why America was Attacked, September 11, 2001 by Nafeez Mosaddeq Ahmed, John Leonard Joshua Tree, CA: Media Messenger, 2002

49. Thieves in High Places: They've Stolen Our Country and Its Time to Take it Back by Jim Hightower NY: Viking, 2003

50. War and Globalization: The Truth Behind September 11 by Michael Chossudovsky Shenty Bay, ONT: Global Outlook, 2002

51. Worse than Watergate by John w. Dean : Little Brown & Co. 2004

52. *If The Gods had Meant us to vote they would have given us Candidates.* by Jim Hightower. Perennial. 2001

In all fairness, to G.W. Bush, I did once read an article praising his environmental stance. According to Christine Todd Whitman, the former U.S. Environmental Protection Agency Administrator, "President Bush has crafted the strongest, smartest and most practical climate- change program the U.S. ever had...For the first time our strategy establishes a specific and realistic goal: to reduce America's greenhouse gas emissions relative to the size of our economy 18% over the next ten years..."[240] This is the only time in four years that I heard something positive about Bush's environmental policies. It could be that Ms. Whitman was talking about a President Bush on a parallel planet (ala the Parallel, from the Twilight Zone television show, which aired in March 14, 1963).[241] Or...she may have had too many secretary-of-agriculture-cocktails (a secretary of agriculture cocktail is made with rum, in such a way that when you drink two you get plowed).

APPENDIX III
GLOSSARY OF COMMON DISEASES CAUSED BY ENVIRONMENTAL CHANGES BROUGHT UPON BY HUMANS

(This section was compiled by Dr.Jacob Nieva and David Arieti)

With global warming and other environmental changes new diseases as well as old diseases normally relegated to the tropics could appear in other regions of the world including the United States and other previously unaffected areas. This is because the climate will accommodate mosquitoes and other vectors of diseases. These vectors such as mosquitoes, flies, ticks and rodents like warm climates and may increase due to global warming. The following are lists of diseases and the organisms which cause disease now, but, in the future may become even more horrific worldwide.

PARASITES
1) Malaria
2) Giardiosis
3) Cryptospirodiosis

BACTERIA
4) Cholera
5) Leptospirosis
6) Shigellosis
7) Salmonellosis
8) Escheichia coli 0157:H7
9) Lyme Disease

VIRUS
10) Dengue Hemorrhagic Fever
11) Hantavirus Pulmonary Syndrome
12) Hepatitis A

OTHERS
  13) Red Tide
  14) Pfiesteriosis
  15) Non-infectious conditions
      A. Malignant melanomas
      B. Non melanoma skin cancers
      C. Sunburn
      D. Other conditions
  16) Asthma

PARASITES

1. MALARIA [242]

Malaria is of great concern today. In spite of the advancement in medicine and the invention of new drugs it is still a major problem especially in the tropical countries in Asia, Africa, and Latin America. Try traveling to these areas and the travel agent or local authorities will give you chemoprophylatic drugs before you step on these lands. Moreover, you will be advised to bring with you insect repellant, mosquito coils, aerosol spray, protective clothing and mosquito nets.

How is malaria affected by change? Well, temperature and surface water are factors for the breeding of the mosquitoes. The higher the temperature and humidity the better it is for the mosquitoes to breed. Another factor is rainfall, the greater the rainfall (especially in The El Nino Phenomenon), the greater the breeding of the mosquitoes. However, very hot and very dry conditions can reduce mosquito survival.

VECTOR: Female Anopheles mosquito (male mosquitoes do no not bite).

CAUSATIVE AGENTS:
Plasmodium falciparum, found throughout Africa, Asia and Latin America
Plasmodium vivax, found worldwide in tropical and semi-tropical climate
Plasmodium ovale, found in West Africa
Plasmodium malariae, found worldwide but very patchy distribution

TRANSMISSION: When a mosquito bites a person with malaria, the mosquito ingests the blood containing the malarial parasites. Then the parasites multiply and migrate to the salivary glands of the mosquito. When the mosquito bites another person, it injects saliva and parasites. The parasites multiply exponentially in the liver then invade the red blood cells, where they multiply again until the red blood cells ruptures causing widespread parasitemia. This is clinically manifested with high grade fever and chills.

SYMPTOMS
The three most important symptoms of malaria are high grade fever, moderate to severe headache, and chill with drenching sweats. The chills correspond to the episode of parasitemia and it is repeated every 2-3 days depending on the specimen of the parasites. -*Plasmodium vivax, Plasmodium ovale* -repeated every 2-3 days
-*Plasmodium malariae* -repeated every 3 days
-*Plasmodium falcifarum* -not periodic but at times every 2 days.

Infected RBCs are circulated systemically and may block smaller arteries of the vital organs like the brain causing cerebral malaria which render the patient comatose and may lead to death.

DIAGNOSIS: A patient with a history of travel from an endemic area complaining of high grade fever, headache, and chills is highly suspected of having malaria. The diagnosis, however, rests on the identification of the parasites on the peripheral blood smear. It is important to identify the specimen of the parasites because each of them has their recommended treatment.

PREVENTION: Vector control measures must be done such as doing away with stagnant water in your backyard (in pots, in low lying areas, in old tires, in marsh land), and use of insecticide spray, mosquito nets, and insect repellants.

Chemoprophylaxis is given if exposure is very likely.These include Chloroquine alone or in combination with Proquanil, Mefloquine, Doxycycline. Take note, however, that no prophylaxis drug can give 100% protection.

2. GIARDIASIS[243]
This infection occur worldwide especially in those areas with poor sanitation. During the past two decades, Giardiasis is one of the most common waterborne diseases in the United States. The incidence is high among the travelers to other countries and in promiscuous homosexuals.

CAUSATIVE AGENT: *Giardia lamdia* also known as *Giardia intestinalis*

TRANSMISSION: Transmission like other diarrheal disease is by the fecal-oral route. Once the microorganisms lodge in the intestinal lumen they firmly attach to the mucosa of the duodenum and proximal jejunum and multiply by binary fission. Then Giardia cysts are released and passed out with the stool. Millions of these cysts are released in every bowel movement. So you can find the microorganism in soil, water, food or surfaces that has been contaminated with feces of infected humans or animals. This infection is easily spread in areas with a greater concentration of people such as mental institutions, day care centers and among homosexuals.

SYMPTOMS: The symptoms usually appear one to three weeks after ingestion of the microorganism. These are watery diarrhea, abdominal cramps and distention, abdominal pain and flatulence. The character of the stool is greasy, tending to float. Usually there is absence of mucus and blood.

Some individuals are asymptomatic but being infected they continue to pass out the *Giardia lamdia* with the stool so they need to be treated.

DIAGNOSIS: The diagnosis is mainly by isolating the parasites from the stools. Since the excretion of the parasites is intermittent, chances are the parasites cannot be seen in one specimen alone. Your doctor may ask you to send several specimens for several days. Immunofluorescent Assay and ELIZA can be done to determine the parasite or the parasite antigen in the stool.

TREATMENT: There are several drugs that are effective for Giardiasis. These are: (1) Metronidazole which is given for 5-7 days. This is contraindicated in pregnancy. (2) Oral quinacrine is highly effective but may produce gastrointestinal symptoms. (3) Oral furaxolidone is available but not as effective as the metronidazole and quinacrine.

PREVENTION: Again good hygiene is very important. Hand washing before and after eating and thoroughly washing after using the toilet. Avoid drinking recreational water and refrain from swimming if you are suspicious by having diarrhea.. When traveling, refrain from drinking untreated water or ice. Preferably bring bottled mineral water or canned carbonated drinks.

3. CRYPTOSPORIDIUM INFECTION OR CRYPTOSPORIDIOSIS[244]

Cryptosporidiosis or "Crypto" is another diarrheal disease that can be attributed to heavy rainfall and contaminated water. This disease is common worldwide. Travelers to foreign countries, immunocompromised patients and health care providers who are treating or caring for patients with this condition are highly vulnerable to acquire the disease. During the past two decades, there were several outbreaks or Cryptosporidiosis in the United States mainly occurring in day care centers and in the hospitals as a nosocomial infection. The parasites were found in the drinking water and recreational water in every region of the United States. It has been estimated that Cryptosporidiosis is responsible for 5% of gastroenteritis in the developing and industrialized countries.

CAUSATIVE AGENT: A protozoan of genus *Cryptosporidium*

TRANSMISSION: This diarrheal disease can be acquired by accidentally putting something into your mouth or swallowing something that is contaminated by fecal matter of persons infected with Cryptosporidium. These may be recreational water (swimming pools, hot tubs, jacuzzis, fountains, rivers. springs, and ponds), contaminated water, uncooked food and raw vegetables or fruits. It can also be accidental swallowing of the protozoan picked up from the surfaces such as bathroom fixtures, toys and tables. Once the protozoa enter the body they stay on the brush border of the mucosa of the small intestine and release oocytes that pass out with the stool. One unique feature of this protozoan is its protective shell covering that allows it to survive outside the body for a longer period of time and be resistant to chlorine-based disinfectants. These oocytes may be ingested again by other vertebrates. In the intestine of the vertebrate these oocytes are transformed to sporozoites which eventually become trophozoites that inhabit the brush border of the intestinal mucosa. Here they replicate and after a period of 12 days form oocytes which are released again as the cycles go on.

DIAGNOSIS: Symptoms of cryptosporodiosis start at 2-10 days (average 7 days) after ingestion. There are frequent passages of watery stools. Patients may develop dehydration, nausea and vomiting, stomach cramps and pain, fever and, if prolonged, leads to weight loss. These symptoms may last for 1-3 weeks after which the patient is in remission. Ordinary stool examinations are unreliable. Using the formalin-ethyl acetate sedimentation or the sugar flotation concentration procedure enhances the identification of the oocytes. Other methods of identification are by phase-contrast microscopy or by staining with Kinyoun modified acid-fast reagent. Fluorescein-labeled monoclonal antibody test or ELIZA (enzyme-linked immunoassay) provides excellent detection of the oocytes.

TREATMENT: There is no specific treatment for Cryptosporidium. People with a good immune system spontaneously recover even without medications. It is, however, important to know the possibility of dehydration that should be managed right away by fluid and electrolyte replacement.

In the case of small children and infants, dehydration and electrolyte imbalance are common complications which must be promptly treated. Addition of antidiarrheal drugs may be necessary. Nitazoxanide has been approved for treatment of Cryptosporidiosis in children less than 12 years old.

PREVENTION: The most reliable decontamination method is boiling water or the use of a filter that has the absolute pore size of at least one micron or those filters that have been rated as "cyst removal". Chemicals and disinfectant (chlorine or iodine) are not a reliable method of removing the parasites because of their protective shell covering.

Good hygiene must be practiced, such as thoroughly washing of hands after using the toilet, before and after handling and eating food, before and after caring for a patient with the disease.

For swimmers, do not drink recreational water. On the other hand, protect the others by not going to the pool if you are having diarrhea.

For travelers, do not use untreated ice or water. Better bring with you bottled mineral water, canned carbonated soft drinks or non-carbonated soft drinks and fruit juices that do not require refrigeration. Avoid eating uncooked food and raw vegetables or fruits. If you want the fruit, wash it thoroughly and peel it by yourself.

BACTERIA

4. CHOLERA[245]

One of the diarrheal diseases linked to heavy rainfall and contaminated water supply is Cholera. This disease is seasonal suggesting sensitivity to climate change. In the US and other industrialized nations cholera is very rare because of the advancement of water treatment and sanitation systems. However, in other parts of the world especially in the Indian subcontinent and sub-Sahara Africa this condition is still very common. In 1998, there was an outbreak of Cholera in Africa where more than 400,000 people suffered from the disease. An outbreak however was reported in South America also in 1991.

CAUSATIVE AGENT: A bacterium called *Vibrio cholera*

TRANSMISSION: The *Vibrio cholera* bacteria live in an aquatic environment attached to a particular alga. People get the infection by ingesting water and food contaminated by the bacteria. These bacteria are returned back to the environment in the human stool. With improper waste disposal, poor sanitation, poor sewerage and improper treatment of drinking water, these bacteria are easily spread and eventually cause an outbreak.

In the human intestine, the bacteria produce exotoxins that stimulate the mucosal cells of the intestine to secrete enormous amounts of fluid (water and electrolytes) rendering the person severely dehydrated. These bacteria, however, are very sensitive to acid such that they are inhibited in the stomach. So individuals with less acid in the stomach (children and old people) are more prone to Cholera.

SYMPTOMS: The typical symptom of cholera is the so called "painless diarrhea".

The person does not feel any abdominal pain in spite of frequent watery stools occurring almost every 15 minutes. In serious cases it can amount to one quart of watery stool per hour. This enormous loss of water and electrolytes can cause severe dehydration clinically manifested as sunken eyeballs, washer woman's hands (severely wrinkled hands) and leg cramps. If not immediately treated it can cause renal failure, hypovolemic shock, and death. Confirmatory diagnosis is done by recovering the bacteria from the rectal swab or fresh stool.

TREATMENT: Treatment is initially geared to the prompt replacement of water and electrolytes to maintain an adequate fluid volume in the body. Isotonic intravenous fluids are given at once. At times, it is even necessary to put 2-3 intravenous fluid lines at the same time. After recovering the normal fluid volume of the body, treatment is directed to the causative microorganism by giving Tetracycline. It is also helpful to test for kidney function by requesting BUN and creatinine level in the blood because at times with the enormous amount of fluid lost the kidneys may fail.

PREVENTION: Sanitation is important in the prevention of Cholera. Proper disposal of human excreta, proper purification and treatment of water supplies are essential in eradicating the bacteria. Avoid inadequately cooked fish and shellfish, and unboiled water because they

carry the bacteria. For those traveling to endemic areas the following are recommended:
- Avoid drinking water if you are not sure of the source. Always bring with you bottled mineral water or carbonated drinks.
- Avoid drinking tea, coffee with unboiled water or carbonated drinks with ice.
- Avoid eating salads or raw or uncooked vegetables and fruits
- Eat only well cooked fish and vegetables preferably still hot when served.
- If you want to eat fruit, preferably you be the one to peel it.

As the saying goes "Boil it, cook it, peel it or FORGET IT"

5. LEPTOSPIROSIS[246]

In temperate countries following wet winters or in tropical countries following monsoon rains, flooding usually occurs. Rodents proliferate in these flooded areas. They serve as reservoirs for leptospirosis and other disease. Animals like cattle, pigs, dogs, and other wild animals can be reservoirs too. Usually the bacteria are transmitted on the soil or flood water through the urine of the rodents. People who make contact with the water, soil, food may acquire the disease.

CAUSATIVE AGENT: *Leptospira sp.*

VECTOR: Rodents, pigs, dogs, cattle, and wild animals.

TRANSMISSION: Epidemics of leptospirosis are usually caused by exposure to water contaminated with the urine of infected animals which serve as their vector. These animals may be sick or asymptomatic. Exposure may be made by swallowing the contaminated food or water or through skin contact, especially the mucosal surfaces such as the eyes. Once the bacteria are in the body system they will affect some organs like the liver and the kidney (Weil's Syndrome or Hepatorenal Syndrome) and lead to Septicemia.

SYMPTOMS: About 10% of the infections are potentially fatal, while 90 % have only a mild disease. The incubation period is usually one week but may range from 2-29 days. Patients experience fever, chills, headache and severe muscular ache. Conjunctival suffusion is characteristic, usually appearing on the 3rd or 4th day. Spenomagaly and hepatomegaly are uncommon. In severe cases the patient develops jaundice (liver involvement) and dark colored urine (kidney involvement).

DIAGNOSIS: A person is suspected with leptospirosis if he has the typical symptoms plus a history of wading in flooded waters and contact with soils potentially infested by rodents. Confirmatory tests, however, are done to identify the bacteria itself in blood culture, urine culture and by detecting antibodies against the *Leptospira*.

TREATMENT: Penicillin and Ampicillin are given parenterally for the patient with the disease while oral Doxycycline is given prophylactically for persons exposed to the bacteria. Preventive measures may include avoidance of swimming and wading in the water that might be contaminated with urine of rodents. For workers, protective clothing and footwear should be worn.

6. SHIGELLOSIS (BACILLARY DYSENTERY)

In the United States, about 18,000 cases of Shigellosis are reported yearly. This infection is common in child care settings and families with small children where hygiene is poorly practiced. Shigellosis is more common in summer and winter seasons. In the developed countries, Shigellosis accounts for 5-10% of diarrheal illness.

CAUSATIVE AGENT:
- *Shigella sonnie*, also known as "Group D" *shigella*. This species accounts for more than 2/3 of Shigellosis in US
- *Shigella flexneri*, also known as "Group B" *shigella*. This species accounts for the rest.
- *Shigella boydii* is very rare in US
- *Shigella dysenteriae* is also rare in US but common in the developing countries. This species can cause deadly epidemics.

TRANSMISSION: It is spread by the fecal-oral route. The usual source of infection is the excreta of an infected people. Seldom do they come from water. Indirect transmission can be attributed to contaminated food and inanimate objects. Flies contribute to the spread of the bacteria by breeding in the infected feces and contaminating food. Once inside the intestinal lumen, the bacteria penetrate the mucosa of the small intestine. In there they produce enterotoxin that causes hyperemia, edema and ulceration of the mucosal cells. Moreover, this enterotoxin stimulates the mucosal cells to produce secretions leading to watery diarrhea. Outbreaks occur frequently in overcrowded populations with poor water disposal and inadequate sanitation.

SYMPTOMS: The most distinguishing clinical presentation of Shigellosis is bloody stool with some pus and mucus. Other symptoms are fever, abdominal pain and cramps, nausea, vomiting and tenesmus. The incubation period (period from the ingestion of the bacteria to the appearance of the first symptoms) is 1-4 days and lasts for 5-7 days.

DIAGNOSIS: Diagnosis is established by high index of suspicions during epidemics. Proctoscopy can be done to see the mucous membrane of the colon. Usually the mucosa of patient with Shigellosis is erythematous with numerous small ulcers. A swab specimen from the ulcers and fresh stool specimen must be smeared and cultured. In acute cases, differential diagnosis includes Amoebiasis, Salmonellosis, E. coli infection and other viral diarrhea.

TREATMENT: Aside from fluid and electrolyte replacement, antibiotics may be given to shorten the course of the illness. These are Ampicillin, Trimethoprime/Sulfamethosazole combination (Bactrim, Septra), Nalidixic Acid and Ciprofloxacin. Antidiarrheal drugs such as Lomotil or Imodium are contraindicated because they make the illness worse. Persons with mild infections usually recover quickly without medication.

PREVENTION: Similar to the other diarrheal diseases, practicing proper hygiene is a must. Hand washing before and after eating, handling food after handling paraphernalia of an infected person must be followed. Basic food safety precautions, regular water treatment, and proper disposal of waste prevent the spread of the bacteria.

At swimming beaches and pools, there must be enough restrooms for the public. This is a way of preventing water from contamination.

7. TYPHOID FEVER[247]

Typhoid fever is a life-threatening disease. It is common in most parts of the world. In the developing countries it affects around 125 million people annually. In the United States and other industrialized nations (Canada,

Australia, Japan, Western Europe) this condition is rare. In the United States only about 400-500 cases of typhoid fever are reported annually and 70% of these cases are acquired while traveling abroad.

CAUSATIVE AGENT: *Salmonella typhi*

TRANSMISSION: The *Salmonella typhi* bacteria live only in humans. It is transmitted to human beings by fecal-oral route. Once the organisms enter the gastrointestinal tract, they gain access to the blood stream through lymphatic channels. Inflammatory reactions occurs within the lamina propia or the Payer's patches (lymphoid tissue in the intestine), in the ileum and some portion of the colon where local tissue necrosis is common. In severe cases, these intestinal inflammations can cause ulceration with intestinal bleeding. In the worst scenario it can lead to intestinal perforation. Patients with active disease pass out the microorganism through the stool and urine. Health care providers are vulnerable to this disease especially if they do not practice proper hygiene. A certain percent of the population who have better immune systems are asymptomatic, thus do not seek consultation and are therefore untreated. These people continue to shed the bacteria in their stool as long as one year after infection. If these people carelessly use the toilet and you happen to use the same toilet without practicing hygiene, you are vulnerable to acquire this infection.

In areas with poor sanitation, the microorganism is transmitted more frequently by water than food. Flies contribute to the spread of these microorganisms by transferring it from stool to food. Unhygienic sexual practices can also spread the disease by anal-oral route.

SYMPTOMS: The incubation of typhoid fever is 8-14 days. Barring complications, the average course is 2-3 weeks. Patients usually have a sustained fever as high as 104 F. Aside from the fever they usually complain of headache, myalgia, anorexia, and abdominal pain. In some cases, patients may have the so called "rose spot" which are flat colored spots on the chest and abdomen. These spots usually appear on the second week of the disease and resolve after 3-5 days. In severe cases, patients may have bradycardia, signs of central nervous system infection like delirium, stupor and coma. If left untreated, they may have intestinal ulceration which may lead to bleeding and worse perforation. These complications are usually manifested by severe abdominal pain with abdominal muscle rigidity.

DIAGNOSIS: Initially a patient with typhoid fever can have his blood tested for the Widal Agglutination Reaction. This laboratory test determines the rise of antibodies titer against the antigen of the typhoid bacilli. A fourfold rise in the antibody titer is indicative (but not confirmatory) of typhoid fever.

The best way to diagnose this infection is to identify the *typhoid* bacilli in cultures. On the first week of illness, the typhoid bacilli can be isolated from blood and bone marrow. On the third and fifth week, the microorganism can be isolated from the stool.

TREATMENT: There are many antibiotics that are very effective for typhoid fever. One is Chloramphenicol. The oral route of this drug is as effective as the intravenous route. Other antibiotics are the cephalosporins (Ceftriaxone, Cefoperaxone) and the Quinolones.

Steroids are added to the antibiotic in severe cases. These are those with central nervous system symptoms (delirium, stupor and coma) and those with gastrointestinal complications (ulcerations, bleeding and perforation)

PREVENTION: Basically prevention refers to the avoidance of risky food and drinks. Avoid drinking water from an unknown source. Better take with you bottled mineral water or canned carbonated drinks. Avoid taking ice unless the ice is made from sterilized water or from bottled water. Avoid uncooked food, raw vegetables and fruits. If you want to eat fruit, peel it yourself. Avoid food from the street vendor because it is difficult for a food to be kept clean on the street.

If traveling to areas endemic for typhoid fever, ask the doctor for a vaccination against typhoid fever. These vaccinations are given one week before travel.

8. *ESCHERICHIA COLI (E. Coli)* INFECTION [248]

Some food borne diseases are well recognized but are considered emerging because they have become more common. One of the pathogens of these food borne diseases is Escherichia coli. Infection of E.Coli serotype 0157: H7 was first described in 1982. Subsequently it has emerged rapidly and has been considered as one of the causes of bloody diarrhea and acute renal failure. Most illnesses are associated with uncooked and contaminated ground beef. Other foods implicated in this illness are alfalfa sprouts, unpasteurized fruit juice, lettuce, game meat and butter.

CAUSATIVE AGENT: *Escherichia coli* serotype O157:H7

TRANSMISSION: The microorganism can be found in cattle farms and can live in the intestine of healthy cattle. During slaughter and meat processing (ground meat), the bacteria are mixed with the meat. Some bacteria present in the cattle's udders can get into the raw milk. Eating uncooked beef meat (especially ground meat) is one way of acquiring the infection. In the intestine, the bacteria produce high level of toxin that causes direct mucosal damage. At times it extends deeper up to the blood vessels where they damage the endothelial cells of the vessels causing intestinal bleeding. The bacteria are shedding off with the stool up to two weeks after the illness is resolved. The bacteria now are ready to infect other individuals. Usually toddlers are vulnerable because they are not yet toilet trained.

SYMPTOMS: The clinical manifestations of E.coli infection are abdominal pain, abdominal cramps and watery diarrhea that may be grossly bloody. Some would describe the diarrhea as "all blood, no stool" which gives rise to the word hemorrhagic colitis. The diarrhea may last for 1-8 days in uncomplicated cases. Patients may be afebrile or febrile as high as 39 C.

In 15% of cases, complications set in such as Hemoytic-Uremic Syndrome (HUS) which is characterized by hemolytic anemia and acute renal failure. These complications usually occur in the second week of illness.

9. LYME DISEASE[249]

Ticks, like rodents, are also affected by climate change. The deer ticks serve as reservoirs for the Lyme disease bacteria. Lyme disease was initially reported in an area in Connecticut that gave its name (Lyme, Connecticut) in 1977. In that year health authorities were concerned with the increased incidence of arthritis in a group of children in and around Lyme, Connecticut. Further studies discovered that this disease was caused by ***Borrelia burgdorferi***, a bacterium and it was transmitted by the deer ticks.

Lyme disease is common in summer and early fall. Children and young adults who live in the wooden areas or persons who are camping on these areas are prone to infection. In 2002, more than 23,000 reported cases of Lyme disease were reported in the United States. As reported by the CDC about 99% of these cases were from the state of Connecticut, Delaware, Rhodes Island, Maine, Maryland, Pennsylvania, New Hamsphire.

CAUSATIVE AGENT: *Borrelia burgdorferi*

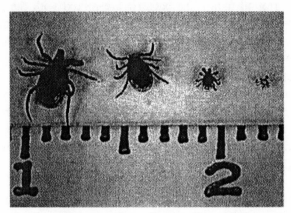

Figure 40. Ticks that cause Lyme disease. If you get bitten by a tick you may become "Ticked off". (Photo Courtesy of the CDC)

VECTORS:
- Black-legged ticks (*Ixodes scapularis*) usually found in the North-eastern and North-central United States.
- Western black-legged ticks (*Ixodes pacificus*) usually found in the Pacific coast.

(These Ixodes ticks are smaller in size no bigger than the size of the pinhead.)

TRANSMISSION: The immature ticks (nymph) feed on the blood of small rodents, especially the white footed mouse which is considered as a carrier of these bacteria. These ticks, once becoming adults feed on blood of the deer. In the deer the bacteria do not cause the disease. They are simply another food source for the adult ticks. How are they transmitted to people? It is through the bite of the adult ticks that are present mostly on the ground. Children and young adults who live in wooded areas or people, who are camping on these areas, are prone to infection. The bacterium, ***Borrelia burgdorferi***, is not transmitted from person to person through kissing or sexual contact or by health workers who care and treat patients infected with the disease.

SYMPTOMS: The clinical manifestation of Lyme disease varies. The person may be asymptomatic (confirmed by serologic tests) or may have a large red spot at the site of the bite usually on the trunk, buttocks, thigh or armpit. The spot called erythema migrans may extend up to 5 inches in diameter with an internal clearing called a "bull' s eye" lesion. It may not itch or hurt but is warm to touch. Once the bacteria are disseminated throughout the body from initial sites the person experiences non- specific symptoms like fever, fatigue, myalgia, and headache. Sometimes the signs of disseminated infection occur days or months after the appearance of erythema malgrans.

If left untreated, it may affect the nervous system, the heart and the musculoskeletal system. The neurologic symptoms may be manifested as more severe headache, stiff neck and hemiparesis (like Bell's palsy). Heart involvement may be presented as arrhythmia (irregular heart beat) or pericarditis (inflammation of the sac that covers the heart) causing chest pain especially on deep breathing. The musculoskeletal manifestation is migratory pain and swelling of big joints, especially the knee. The joints are warm to the touch and at a rare instance, reddish. bursitis (inflammation of the sac that surrounds the knee) may develop. This bursitis may rupture causing severe knee pain. These arthritic knees may recur for several years. Lyme disease morbidity maybe be severe, disabling and rarely, if ever, fatal.

TREATMENT: Some doctors do not give antibiotics right away to persons who were simply bitten by the ticks and have no symptoms. Early treatment is effective in preventing the disease. Penicillin, Amoxicillin, Erythromycin, Doxycycline are effective treatments. They may relieve the person of the arthritic symptoms because of bacterial eradication; however, some people persist to have the arthritis necessitating analgesic/ anti-inflammatory drugs like NSAID (Non-steroidal anti-inflammatory drugs) and aspirin.

PREVENTION: Whenever possible, avoid wooded areas with leaf litter, low lying vegetation, brushy or overgrown grassy habitat. These areas are likely to be infested with ticks, particularly in spring and summer. If it is necessary to go to infested areas wear light colored clothes so that the ticks can be easily spotted and removed. Cover your body as much as possible by wearing long sleeve shirts with pants tucked into the socks or boot tops to prevent the ticks from approaching your skin. The embedded ticks transmit the bacteria, *Borrelia burgdorferi* 36 hours after attachment, so daily checking and removal of ticks will be enough to prevent acquiring the infection. Use fine tipped tweezers, hot match, or nail polish to remove the embedded ticks.

VIRUSES

10. DENGUE AND DENGUE HEMORRHAGIC FEVER[250]

Dengue fever is a common disease in the tropical and subtropical regions. The Pacific-based El Nino Southern Oscillation (ENSO) was noted to have a positive relationship with the incidence of dengue. This is because of changes in household water storage practices and water pooling. Between 1970 and 1995, the incidence of the dengue epidemic in the South Pacific was positively correlated with La Nina condition (i.e. warmer and wetter).

Dengue is endemic throughout the tropics and subtropical areas. In 1969, an outbreak occurred in the Caribbean including Puerto Rico and US Virgin Island. According to WHO, the disease is now endemic in more than 100 countries in Africa, America, Eastern Mediterranean, Southeast Asia and Western Pacific. Some 2500 million, about 2/5 of the world population are at risk of dying. The current estimate of the WHO is 50 million cases of dengue infection are contacted every year.

CAUSATIVE AGENT: Virus'of 4 distinct families: arenavirus, fibrovirus, bunyavirus, flavovirus.

TRANSMISSION: A female mosquito acquires the virus while feeding on the blood of an infected person. The incubation period of the virus in the mosquito is 8-10 days after which the mosquito is capable of transmitting the virus during probing and blood feeding to the humans. The humans are the main amplifying host of the virus although in some parts of the world monkeys can be infected and a source of the virus for uninfected mosquitoes. A rise in urban population would mean a greater number of individuals in contact with the vectors especially in areas that are favorable for mosquito breeding.

SYMPTOMS: The virus circulates in the blood of infected humans for 2-7 days at approximately the same time as with the appearance of the constitutional symptoms. The fever may be mild or as high as 40-41 degrees Celeius with or without febrile convulsion and hemorrhagic phenomena. Other symptoms include severe headache, pain behind the eyes, muscle and joint pains, and rashes. In severe cases, the patient may deteriorate after a few days of fever. This stage is noticed by signs of circulatory failure which are low blood pressure, weak or fast pulse, absence of urine and paradoxically low temperature. If still unattended, may lead to a critical state of shock and eventually die.

On the other hand, some individuals may manifest only mild febrile syndromes with or without rashes. In these cases, constant monitoring of blood volume and platelet count until the end of the course of the disease is necessary to prevent hemorrhagic shock.

DIAGNOSIS: The WHO has established criteria for the diagnosis of dengue hemorrhagic fever which is the fever lasting for 2-7 days, hemorrhagic manifestation including at least a positive tourniquet test, petechiae, purpura, ecchymmosis, melena, hematemesis. These hemorrhagic manifestations are due to thrombocytopaenia (diminished platelet count) which occurs in the course of the disease. Serologic tests, however, may be done by hemagglutination inhibiting and complement fixation test.

TREATMENT: There is no specific treatment for dengue. It is just a plain symptomatic treatment like antipyretic, analgesic (except aspirin because it may cause bleeding).

The mainstay in the management of Dengue is prevention of the complication which is bleeding due to thrombocytopaenia. This should be carefully monitored by requesting frequent platelet count (every 2-4 hours if necessary) until the end of the disease which is usually 7-10 days. Once the platelet count is down to 100,000/mm^3, a platelet transfusion must be given.

11. HANTAVIRUS PULMONARY SYNDROME[251]

Another disease transmitted by rodents is Hantavirus Pulmonary Syndrome. This disease first appeared as a mystery illness in Southwest US in the spring of 1993. By the end of the year, 53 cases had been reported from 14 states. As of May 2003 a total of 336 cases of Hantavirus Pulmonary Syndrome have been confirmed. These cases occurred chiefly in summer. 75% of cases are traced to inhabitants of rural areas. In those cases the male to female ratio was 60:40. The average age was 37 years old. White Americans accounted for 76% of the cases while American Indians accounted for 21 % of the cases. The remaining percentage was in other races or ethnic groups.

CAUSATIVE AGENT: A specific virus from the group of hantavirus

VECTOR: Sigmodotine rodents (especially the deer mouse)

TRANSMISSION: The virus is usually acquired by inhaling airborne excreta, through broken skin, and possibly through contaminated food and water. The infected animals, however, do not become ill.

SYMPTOMS: Patients with Hantavirus Pulmonary Syndrome initially experienced the usual constitutional symptoms of fever, body malaise, muscle ache, and headache. He may have also gastrointestinal symptoms such as diarrhea, vomiting and abdominal pain. The virus may concentrate late in the lungs to cause Acute Respiratory Distress Syndrome (ARDS) which severely impairs the external respiration (gaseous exchange between the alveoli and the lung capillaries). The virus may concentrate also in the skin to cause renal failure clinically manifested by anuria (no urine output) or oliguria (scanty urine output).

TREATMENT: Treatment is mainly supportive like giveng symptomatic treatment such as an antipyretic, an analgesic, and O_2 inhalation. Patient with ARDS however require hospitalization possibly with a respirator. Those with renal failure necessitate dialysis.

12. HEPATITIS A [252]

Hepatitis is an inflammation of the liver characterized by diffused or patches of necrosis affecting all acini (small sac like dilations in a gland). There are six types of viruses that cause hepatitis (A, B, C, D, E, and G) but we will limit ourselves to Hepatitis A only because this is the type that is transmitted by fecal-oral route. According to the CDC, it is estimated that there are between 125,000-200,000 cases of Hepatitis A yearly in the United States and between 84,000-135,000 experienced symptoms while the rest are asymptomatic. Approximately 100 people die of Hepatitis each year.

CAUSATIVE AGENT: A single -stranded RNA picoma virus

TRANSMISSION: Hepatitis A virus is transmitted by fecal-oral route; that is, putting something in the mouth that has been contaminated with stool of patient with Hepatitis A virus. It can be water borne or food borne. Once the virus reaches the liver, it induces inflammatory reactions leading to diffuse or patchy necrosis. These viruses are later on passed out together with the stool. The fecal shedding of the virus occurs in the incubation period until a few days after the appearance of the symptoms; usually the patient is not infective anymore at the time of the diagnosis.

This fact makes Hepatitis A the least infective among the Types of Hepatitis. Transmission is common in areas with poor sanitary conditions and overcrowded conditions. Most of these infections result from contact with household members or sex partners who have the original disease. Casual contact, as in the usual office, factory, or school setting does not spread the virus.

SYMPTOMS: Symptoms of Hepatitis varies from a minor flu-like illness to fatal liver failure depending on the type of etiologic virus and the immune system of the of the other person. For Hepatitis A, symptoms occur abruptly. These may include fever, tiredness, loss of appetite, nausea, abdominal discomfort and the universal signs of hepatitis which are jaundice (yellowish discoloration of the skin and eyes) with dark or tea colored urine. In a milder form the person may not have symptoms at all. The symptoms may last for 1-2 months and the average incubation period for Hepatitis A is 28 days.

DIAGNOSIS: In the early phase of the disease the diagnosis may be difficult because all types of hepatitis present the same clinical manifestations (flu-like symptoms). So the history of the patient is important to rule out the other causes of Hepatitis like Alcoholic Hepatitis or Drug Induced Hepatitis. Liver enzymes level test (AST ~ ALT) may be requested. These enzymes are indicative of liver injury. Other tests that may be requested are the Prothrombin Time (indicative of liver injury and function) and Alkaline Phosphatase (indicative of cholestasis). The confirmatory test is the Serologic test for the presence of IgM anti HA. These are the antibodies that appear early in the disease.

TREATMENT: There is no cure for Hepatitis A. In most cases, no treatment is required. Most people with severe infection will have a short term illness that will resolve completely. Patients need not be confined in the hospital, instead advised to rest for 1-4 weeks to avoid intimate contact with others. Some doctors recommend a high protein , low fat diet during recovery. They are also advised to avoid alcohol, sedatives and narcotics. Once recovered, the patient is immune for life. He can return to work after the resolution of the jaundice.

PREVENTION: Personal hygiene is important in the prevention of Hepatitis A. The stool of a patient with Hepatitis A must be considered infectious. Always wash your hands after using the toilet, changing diapers, and before and after preparing or eating food.

As for prophylaxis, there are two vaccines that are available. (1) The immunoglobulin (passive immunity) which provides a short term protection against Hepatitis A and is for patients with active disease. This must be given within two weeks after the exposure to a virus to have maximum protection. (2) Hepatitis A vaccine (Havrix, Vaqta) provide active immunity. It is recommended in people two years and older. This is given to people who are more likely to get Hepatitis A virus infection or to people who will more likely become seriously ill if infected with Hepatitis A.

OTHER TYPES OF ILLNESSES

13. RED TIDE (Phytoplankton-related Disease)[253]
Phytoplankton are microscopic plants that live in the upper part of the water column. They are normal components of all aquatic environments. Because of some environmental and climate changes, they bloom in significant numbers and produce a biotoxin that have deleterious effects on both aquatic life and those who depend on the water for their subsistence.

Phytoplankton stretches from the North Pole to the South of the equator; along the Pacific coast on the Asian side especially the Philippines, where they are considered a real problem, while on the opposite side of the Pacific coast (US, Canada), Phytoplankton are not a problem. Other areas where these microscopic plants are a problem are Northern Spain, Ireland, and Mediterranean/Adriatic seas.

HOW IS IT AFFECTED BY CLIMATE CHANGE?
Environmental conditions such as nutrients, sunlight and temperature are factors for blooming of the phytoplankton called Harmful Algal Blooms (HAB). Global processes like the El-Nino Southern Oscillation (ENSO) causes higher than average rainfall, aquatic and temperature increases. These factors have an impact on the frequency and magnitude of HABs.

CAUSATIVE AGENTS: Dinoflagellates (Pyrrhophycophyta)
1. *Alexandrium catenella,* isolate from shellfish, produce toxins which causes Paralytic shellfish Poisoning.
2. *Saxidomus giganteus,* isolated from Alaska butter clams, produces saxitoxin which causes Paralytic Shellfish Poisoning

3. Rhodophyta or red algea, *Chondria armata. Digenea simplexes* are isolated from fish, shellfish, producing Domoic Acid which causes Domoic Acid Poisoning

4. *Dinophysis sp. Dinophysis acuta, Dinophysis acuminata,* isolated from shellfish, producing okadaic acid and other related compounds called dinophysis toxin which causes Diarrhetic Shellfish Poisoning.

NATURAL RESERVOIR: Shellfish, mussels, clams and other marine fishes.

TRANSMISSION: There are many types of phytoplankton two of which are described: (1) dinoflagellates with a flagella or a whip like tail that can move through the water column. (2) diatoms, which have no flagella and do not move with water columns and are dependent on ocean currents for transport. The phytoplankton are considered microscopic plants in the sea. Once the right set of environmental factors occur they bloom in enormous numbers. These factors are nutrients (usually human inputs like treated and untreated sewage, farming and gardening products such as fertilizers). Rainfall, sunlight and high temperature increase the ocean currents favorable for the diatoms to bloom and spread out. These phytoplankton in enormous numbers produce a biotoxin (one of most toxic compound known to man) which has deleterious effects on marine environments. During the HAB, fish, and shellfish consume the phytoplankton without apparent harm. Any marine mammals, birds and humans who consume these fish can acquire the toxin and may develop poisoning.

These algae also produce slime that can emit noxious odors which are carried by the air to coastal communities causing severe eye, nose, and throat irritations.

SYMPTOMS:
There are 3 types of poisoning related to Red Tide:
1. Paralytic Shellfish Poisoning which is usually caused by *Alexandrium catenella, Saxidomus giganteus*, is acquired by eating contaminated shellfish. Persons experience paresthesia (burning and tingling sensation) of the lips, gum, tongue, face and gradually extending to the arm and fingertips. It may further extend to the legs and toes. The paresthesia leads to numbness, motor weakness and paralysis. It may also restrict the throat causing difficult breathing, motor incoordination and aphasia (loss of speech). In severe cases, respiratory paralysis and death may ensue within 12 hours after ingestion. If patients survive the first 12 hours, chances of recovery are great.

2. Domoic AcidPoisoning (See Appendix VI)) is caused by Rhodophyta or red algae, *Chondria armata and Digenea simplex*. This is acquired by eating fish and shellfish. The toxin interferes with peripheral nerve conduction and may enter the brain which may result in permanent brain damage or at higher doses, death.
3. Diarrheal Shellfish Poisoning is caused by *Dinophysis sp. (Dinophysis acuta, and, Dinophysis acuminata.* This is the mildest form among the poisoning caused by Red Tide. It is only manifested as diarrhea. There are some reports claiming that the toxin enhances tumor agents.

PREVENTION: Since Red Tides are due mainly to natural causes that we cannot avoid, prevention is more a passive program. Monitoring programs should be planned with the aim of preventing exposure on these areas. For example, monitoring the movement of the organisms in the Gulf Steam, as well as temperature monitoring by remote sensing of infrared radiation can give information about the bloom.

Health authorities in the affected areas must be well aware of the pathogenesis (course of the disease), symptoms, diagnosis, and treatment of Red Tide poisoning.Surveillance of people who are at risk must be done. Health information must be available to the public especially to the recreational water users. This information must be disseminated by mass media, schools, and on-site notices.

The following are guidelines that must be followed by water users in the affected areas:
1. Avoid areas with visible algal concentration on the sea as well as shore.Direct contact or swallowing of the biotoxin may be fatal.
2. Avoid sitting on algal materials drying on the shore because it may emit noxious odor.
3. After coming from the shore, bathe yourself to remove all the algal material.
4. Consult health authorities at once for any signs and symptoms of Red Tide.

There were some attempts to develop practical methods of controlling Red Tides. (use of clay, herbicides. metal chelators. artificial turbulence, dinoflagellates, parasites and zooplankton) but these were not practical and causes adverse ecological side effects. Minimizing the nutrient input from land-based sources (nitrates, phosphate) may be done to control the blooming of the phytoplankton.

14. PFIESTERIOSIS-
NO NEUSE IS GOOD NEWS-YES NEUSE IS BAD NEWS

Yes, reader you read the above correctly. The Neuse River is a river in North Carolina. It's existence was not widely known (at least by me) or to much of the world's population prior to 1996. It was known to those who lived near it or to those who were interested in doing research on North Carolina's rivers. Since then it has become famous or should I say infamous because of a microscopic resident nicknamed *"The cell from Hell"*. This sounds like the introduction of a Twilight Zone episode, doesn't it?

The Neuse River has the widest mouth of any river in the United States and is part of the second largest ecosystem in the continental US. It is also on the top 20 list of the most threatened rivers in North America. The Neuse River flows approximately 200 miles from its headwaters in Orange and Person counties in North Carolina to its mouth at Pamlico Sound. The Neuse contains over 3000 stream miles. The drainage area of the Neuse River basin is 6,234 square miles which is 8.8% of the state. Agricultural land use comprises 35% of the river basin.

The river has many hog (pig) farms near it. Pig farms, which are so huge that now they are considered factories, produce tons of fecal waste.

Pigs produce between four and ten times the amount of fecal waste as humans do. The waste is stored in lagoons. Sometimes the lagoons collapse releasing the waste into the Neuse River. This river then becomes a gourmet restaurant for the little monsters or cells from hell called *Pfiesteria piscidida*. *Pfiesteria* belong to the phylum of algae called Pyrrhophycophyta or dinoflagellates. This literally means fire-algae-plants. In fact the situation became so severe on the Neuse that even a book was written about this incident. The title, which has a biblical sounding name, is "And the Waters Turned to Blood" by Rodney Barker. 1997 (Simon and Schuster).

CAUSATIVE AGENT- *Pfiesteria piscicida*

SYMPTOMS: Eye irritations, long term vision problems, brain damage, respiratory, liver, kidney and immune problems, nausea, memory loss, confusion, skin lesions that don't heal, rashes, headaches, irritability and mood swings. [254]

TREATMENT: There is no specific treatment at this time.

15. NON-INFECTIOUS CONDITIONS

INTRODUCTION: Strictly speaking, stratospheric ozone depletion is not a part of global climate change. However, there are recently described interactions between ozone depletion and greenhouse-gas-induced warming. We know that sunlight contains ultraviolet radiation (UVR). These are short wavelength radiation which is potentially damaging to the human cells and tissues. We are, however, protected from these harmful rays by the ozone layer in the atmosphere. Because of our ignorance of this fact we carelessly dispose of chemical wastes which produce gases that destroy the ozone layer. These chemical wastes are the industrial halogenated chemicals called chlorofluorocarbons (CFC- used in refrigeration, insulation and spray-can propellants- See Appendix VI) and methyl bromide. The gas produced by chemical wastes is inert at ambient temperatures at the surface of the earth but react with the ozone layer in the extremely cold polar stratosphere. These atmospheric phenomena usually occur in late winter and early spring.

In 1980 scientists had estimated that the decline in ozone concentrations was approximately 5-6% and likely to peak by the year 2020 with an estimated 10% increase in effective ultraviolet radiation relative to 1980 levels. In the mid 1980s the world was concerned with this emerging threat. The Montréal Protocol of 1987 was adopted and the phasing out of major ozone destroying gases began. If the provisions of the protocol are strictly implemented, scientists predicted a near complete recovery of this stratospheric ozone layer by 21st century.

How does UVR affect humans? Excess UVR causes abnormality in cell reproduction such as decrease rates of cell mitosis, and slow synthesis of cell DNA. This will produce dysplasia (abnormality in the development, size, and shape of cells) which may lead to carcinogenesis . Studies have shown that the UVR from the sun can cause skin cancer in fair-skinned humans especially white Caucasians of Celtic descent. Furthermore, behavioral changes such as sun-bathing and skin tanning cause higher UV exposure.

The following are conditions are caused by ultraviolet radiation.

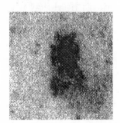

Figure41 Malignant melanoma on skin.(Courtesy of CDC)

I. MALIGNANT MELANOMA

Malignant melanoma is a tumor arising from pigmented areas of the body. About 40% to 50% of Malignant Melanoma develops from pigmented moles while the rest arises from melanocytes in the normal skin. This skin cancer is the leading cause of death. Studies showed that the risk of malignant melanoma correlates with the genetic make-up of the person and his exposure to UVR. The following are risk factors for Malignant Melanoma

1. A large number of atypical nevi (mole) are the strongest risk factor for Malignant Melanoma in fair-skin population,
2. Malignant Melanoma is more common in people with pale complexion, blue eyes, and red or fair hair.
3. Incidence of Malignant Melanoma in white populations increases with decreasing latitude, with the highest recorded incidence occurring in Australia, where the annual rate is 10 and over 20 times the rate in Europe for men and women respectively.
4. Several studies have shown a direct relationship of Malignant Melanoma to the history of sunburn, particularly sunburn at an early age.

DIAGNOSIS: Skin lesion with variegated colors (e.g. brown, black with shade of red, blue, white), irregular elevation that are visible or palpable and borders with angular indentation and notches are highly suspicious of Malignant Melanoma. This lesion necessitates early biopsy. A typical lesion enlarges at a fast rate with ulceration and bleeding points. The diagnosis is mainly based on biopsy. The degree of lymphocytic infiltration (representing the immune system) correlates with the degree of invasion and progress.

TREATMENT: The treatment is surgical excision. For a lesion 1 mm. thick, the line of excision must be extended 1 cm. from the border of the lesion. Thicker lesions may have larger area for excision plus nodal dissection. Those with distant metastasis are treated by chemotherapy.

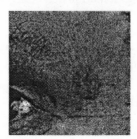

Figure 42. Basal cell carcinoma (Courtesy of CDC)

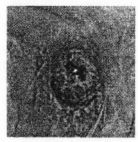

Figure 43. Squamous cell carcinoma (Photo courtesy of CDC)

II. NON-MELANOMA SKIN CANCERS

Basal cell carcinoma and squamous cell carcinoma are the non-melanoma skin cancers. These are common to people exposed to sunlight like sportsmen, outdoor workers, and sunbathers. The frequent sites of this carcinoma are the parts exposed to sunlight such as the ear, forearm, face and neck. There is a positive relationship between increased incidences of non-melanoma skin cancer with decreasing latitude. Studies in Australia, Canada, and US indicated that between 1960-1980, prevalence of non-melanoma skin cancer increased more than twice.

DIAGNOSIS AND TREATMENT: The clinical manifestation of basal cell carcinoma and squamous cell carcinoma are highly variable. It can be mistaken as psoriasis or localized dermatitis. The diagnosis is basically based on the biopsy result of any suspicious lesion. The best treatment is surgical excision. Other treatment modalities are curettage, cryosurgery, and X -ray therapy.

III. SUNBURN

Sunburn results from brief (acute) overexposure to UV rays. Its formation depends on the person's pigmentation and ability to produce melanin. This substance is produced by the melanocytes in the epidermis and protects the underlying tissue from damages caused by the UVR.

Sunburn may produce painful erythema of the skin but in severe cases can cause swelling and blisters. The symptoms may start one hour to one day post exposure lasting 2-4 days after which peeling of the skin occurs which may be painful and itchy.

TREATMENT: Application of a cold compress can soothe raw and hot areas. Skin moisturizers can also be applied. For painful conditions, NSAIDS (non-steroidal anti-inflammatory drugs) can be taken orally. Burn cream and ointment with or without antibiotics can be applied if blisters appear. Steroids and anti-inflammatory drugs are given for severe sunburn. Healing processes may take days to weeks.

PREVENTION: The most obvious prevention is to stay away from direct sunlight, particularly between 10am-3pm on sunny days. If exposure is necessary, sunscreen creams.and ointment should be used. These topicals contain para-aminobenzoic acid (PABA) and benzophenone that absorb UV rays. They must be applied 30-45 minutes before exposure. Other topicals contain zinc oxide or titanium dioxide. They almost block all the sunlight and can be used on small, sensitive areas such as the nose and lips.

IV. PHOTODERMATOSIS
Photodermatoses are immunological reactions triggered by sunlight. They are sometimes called solar uticaria or sun allergy. Certain diseases, however, like Systemic Lupus Erythematuses and Porphyrias can predispose the skin to photodermatosis once it is exposed to sunlight.

DIAGNOSIS, TREATMENT AND PREVENTION: There is no specific diagnostic test for Photodermatosis. Doctors mainly suspect a person to have the condition if rashes appear in areas exposed to sunlight. Persons with a severe form (polymorphous light eruption) may benefit from hydroxychloroquinone or oral steroids. As a prevention, a person sensitive to sunlight should wear protective clothing, avoid exposure to sunlight as much as possible and use sunscreen.

V. MISCELLANEOUS CONDITIONS
(Other effects of UVR on human health)

EFFECTS ON THE EYE
-   **Acute photokeratitis**[255] also called Radiation keratitis or snow blindness (burning of the cornea which is the clear front surface of the eye by ultraviolet light-UV B)
-   **Photoconjunctivitis**-inflammation of the conjunctiva-surface tissue on the white of the eye.

- **Climate droplet keratopathy**-blinding degeneration of the cornea
- **Pterygium**-[256] A pterygium is a wedge-shaped fibrovascular growth of conjunctiva that extends onto the cornea. Pterygia are benign lesions that can be found on either side of the cornea.
- **Cancer of the cornea and conjunctivae**
- lens opacity (cateract)
- **Uveal melanoma**- The uvea is the part of the eye, consisting collectively of the iris, the choroid of the eye, and the ciliary body.[257]
- **Acute solar retinopathy**-disease of the retina by exposure to short wavelengths of light. Is common after viewing a solar eclipse.[258]
- **Macular degeneration**-Macular degeneration is caused by the deterioration of the central portion of the retina, the inside back layer of the eye that records the images we see and sends them via the optic nerve from the eye to the brain. The retina's central portion, known as the macula, is responsible for focusing central vision in the eye, and it controls our ability to read, drive a car, recognize faces or colors, and see objects in fine detail.[259]

EFFECTS ON IMMUNITY AND INFECTION
- **Suppression of cell mediated immunity**-This is a form of immunity helped along by T-cells in the human body. T cells are lymphocytes and are called white blood cells along with other cells.
- **Increased susceptibility to infection**
- **Impairment of prophylactic immunization**-Prophylactic immunity is the artificial establishment of immunity with vaccines.
- **Activation of a latent virus infection**. Latent viruses are those that lie waiting to cause a problem. They are dormant until activated by something.

16. ASTHMA
Asthma is a chronic lung condition that is characterized by difficulty in breathing. Asthma appears to be increasing in once pristine areas such as Trinidad because of dust storms in the continent of Africa, yes Africa. This could be due to the effects of global warming.

SYMPTOMS OF ASTHMA
Wheezing, coughing, shortness of breath and chest lightness

TREATMENT

Treatment involves the use of anti-inflammatories (corticosteroids) and bronchodilators.

PREVENTION

Avoid pets with fur or feathers; wash bedding often with hot water, encase mattresses and pillows and other bedding in dust proof covers, replace upholstered furniture with leather or vinyl, use hardwood floors and keep humidity in the house low.

APPENDIX IV
A POSSIBLE SOLUTION TO THE MIDDLE EAST PROBLEM-THE ARAB-ISRAELI-PALESTINIAN CONFLICT

Since the establishment of Israel in 1948 there is nothing but bad news about death and destruction on both sides of the Arab-Israeli-Palestinian conflict. The United States fought three wars within the last 14 years (1991-2004) in that violent part of the world, one in Afghanistan and two in Iraq. [260] I believe the wars were fought mainly because of oil. The world is too dependent on oil for its energy needs even though there are better and less polluting sources available if only we had the will to use them. Oil is both politically and environmentally terrible for the world.

The fact that the Arab countries depend on oil based revenues for their livelihood and the fact that the whole Middle East is essentially in turmoil opens up an opportunity to help solve the crisis both environmentally and politically. How can we use this situation in a positive manner to make peace and protect the environment? Simple!!!!

This is what I propose. Since the Israelis have a very good scientific community and since they were responsible for the "Dude Shemesh" or solar water heaters I believe that they can design solar energy producing equipment which will solarize the planet and which can be made with the help of the Arab countries. Many Arab countries such as Saudi Arabia have an overpopulation problem as well as an employment problem which may lead to political instability in that country if the problem continues to fester. Thus we should encourage the goodwill of the international community including that of the United States if there is any good will left, to pursue this effort to solarize the planet.

Using fossil based fuels (oil, coal and gas) into the foreseeable future does not bode well for the health of the planet and its residents. If we succeed soon, and I mean very soon, such as two to three years rather than decades then we will all be better off.

APPENDIX V
A POSSIBLE SOLUTION
TO END TERRORISM IN BOTH
THE UNITED STATES
AND THE REST OF THE WORLD

It is obvious that since terrorism hit the United States on September 11, 2001, the whole world has been on a heightened state of alert. Instead of taking military action as we have done in Afghanistan and in Iraq (even though it appears that no Iraqis were significantly involved in September 11) maybe we should find out why there is terrorism directed against us. Instead of killing first in the name of retaliation as we did in Afghanistan, we should have asked the simple question" ***Why do they hate the United States so much***?" How can we answer this question so that a catastrophic event like the destruction of the World Trade Center (WTC) does not happen again?[261] To me the answer is simple. **Have a worldwide conference in a neutral country like Switzerland and invite representatives from every country and representatives from terror organizations as well. Yes, invite the terrorists themselves. How can you solve a problem without the major players involved?** [262] World meetings have been held quite frequently such as the Kyoto Conference on Global Warming (1997), the Conference on Development and the Environment in Rio De Janeiro (1992) and the worldwide conference on AIDS in Bangkok, Thailand (2004) to discuss global issues; so why not a conference on 'Why they hate the U.S."? It makes sense to me!!!!!!!

APPENDIX VI
STRANGE COMPOUNDS
FOUND IN THE ENVIRONMENT

The following is a list of chemicals which have been implicated in both human and environmental problems. I consider them strange because they are all human made or made naturally by microorganisms. Below is a list of some of the most interesting ones.

POPS-PERSISTENT ORGANIC POLLUTANTS[263]

All of these chemicals persist in the environment and can bioaccumulate through the food chains. They can also cause long term health effects in humans and travel great distances by wind. They all contain chlorine (Cl).

1) Aldrin-This is a pesticide used on corn, potatoes, cotton and for termite control
2) DDT-An insecticide used for vector control such as on mosquitoes
3) Endrin-An insecticide used on field crops as well as against rodents such as mice, rats etc.
4) Dieldrin-Insecticide used on cotton, certain vegetables and as a control for termites
5) Chlordane-Insecticide used on food crops and cotton.
6) Toxaphene-A mixture of chemicals used for insect control, mites and ticks on livestock and as substance for fish eradication.
7) Dioxins-By-products of chlorinated compounds and their incineration.
8) Furans-By-products of chlorinated chemical production and incineration.
9) Hexachlorobenzene-Fungicide (kills fungi) used on seeds and as an industrial chemical.
10) Mirex-Insecticide used to combat fire ants, other insects and as a fire retardant
11) Polychlorinated Biphenyls (PCBs)- Industrial chemicals used as insulators in electrical transformers, solvents, and other products.
12) Heptachlor-Insecticide used on soil insects.

AGENT ORANGE, AGENT BLUE AND AGENT WHITE

Agent Orange is the chemical associated with the Viet-Nam War and it's after effects. It was implicated in causing cancer in veterans of that war. The reason why it is called Agent Orange is because the barrel containing the substance had an orange stripe. Agent White and Agent Blue have white and blue stripes around their respective barrels. Below is a list of their contents:

Agent Orange: 2,4-D and 2,4,5-T
Code name for a 1:1 mixtures of n-butyl esters of 2,4,5-T (2,4,5.-trichlorophenoxyacetic +acid) and 2,4-D (2,4-dichlorophenoxyacetic acid). It is used against forest vegetation.

Agent White: 2,4,-D and Picloram
Code name for a 4:1 mixture of 2,4-D (2,4-dichlorophenoxyacetic acid) and Picloram (4-amino-3,5,6-trichloropicolinic acid in water) Trade name from Dow is Tordon-101. It is used against forest vegetation.

Agent Blue: Cacodylic Acid
Code name for a 6:1 mixture of dimethyl arsenate and dimethyl arsenic acid in water. Known as Cacodylic Acid or Phytar-560G from the Ansul Co. Its use is against rice and other food crops.

DOMOIC ACID.

This is a toxin produced by certain algae.[264] This toxin has been implicated in Amnesic Shellfish Poisoning (ASP). It is produced by a marine diatom called Pseudo-*nitzschia multiseries* which is a form of algae. .(See Appendix III))

CFCs- CHLOROFLUOROCARBONS

These are compounds that are used in refrigeration. CFCs have the chlorine which is implicated in the destruction of the ozone layer. They have trade names such as CF-12, which was the CFC that was used in older car air conditioners and was a main destroyer of the ozone layer. Newer cars have air conditioners which contain 134-A which do not have any chlorine and is believed to be safer for the environment.

HFCs stands for hydroflurocarbons. They contain hydrogen, fluorine, and carbon atoms only. An example is 134A

HCFCs contain hydrogen, chlorine, fluorine and carbons. Example are CF-22. and R-123

CFCs contain Chlorine, fluorine and carbon. Examples are R-11 and R12

PLASTIC RECYCLING CODES

There are seven types of plastics encoded for recycling purposes. The codes and symbols are as follows:

#1-PET	Polyethylene terphthalate	Soda bottle
#2-HDPE	High density polyethylene	Milk containers
#3-PVC (V)	Polyvinyl Chloride	Pipes, shampoo bottles
#4-LDPE	Low density polyethylene	Bread wrappers
#5-PP	Polypropylene	Yogurt containers
#6-PS	Polystyrene	Styrofoam cups, printers
#7-Other		Juice containers, chocolate syrup bottles

APPENDIX VII
SAMPLE ANSWER SHEETS FOR TESTS

This is an example of a test sheet. Instead of giving out tests which waste literally tons of paper throughout the US and the world teachers can give the tests on the overhead projector or directly from the computer as I do. One answer sheet such as this is especially good for multiple choice questions where all that is needed are one letter answers.

TEST ONE				
1.	11.	21.	31.	41.
2.	12.	22.	32.	42.
3.	13.	23.	33.	43.
4.	14.	24.	34.	44.
5.	15.	25.	35.	45.
6.	16.	26.	36.	46.
7.	17.	27.	37.	47.
8.	18.	28.	38.	48.
9.	19.	29.	39.	49.
10.	20.	30.	40.	50.

TEST TWO				
1.	11.	21.	31.	41.
2.	12.	22.	32.	42.
3.	13.	23.	33.	43.
4.	14.	24.	34.	44.
5.	15.	25.	35.	45.
6.	16.	26.	36.	46.
7.	17.	27.	37.	47.
8.	18.	28.	38.	48.
9.	19.	29.	39.	49.
10.	20.	30.	40.	50.

TEST THREE				
1.	11.	21.	31.	41.
2.	12.	22.	32.	42.
3.	13.	23.	33.	43.
4.	14.	24.	34.	44.
5.	15.	25.	35.	45.
6.	16.	26.	36.	46.
7.	17.	27.	37.	47.
8.	18.	28.	38.	48.
9.	19.	29.	39.	49.
10.	20.	30.	40.	50.

TEST FOUR				
1.	11.	21.	31.	41.
2.	12.	22.	32.	42.
3.	13.	23.	33.	43.
4.	14.	24.	34.	44.
5.	15.	25.	35.	45.
6.	16.	26.	36.	46.
7.	17.	27.	37.	47.
8.	18.	28.	38.	48.
9.	19.	29.	39.	49.
10.	20.	30.	40.	50.

ENDNOTES

1   Unknown author in the Philippines. Awake, Wallkill, N.Y., November 22, 2003, p.3

2   Unknown, Smart Alecs (New York: Ballantine, 1987) 218.

3   Wilson, E. O. Vanishing before our eyes. Time Magazine April-May 2000.p29-30

4   R.Costanza, R. d''Arge,R.de Groot, S. Farber, M.Grasso, B. Hannon,K.Limburg, S.Naeem, R.V.O'Neil,J. Paruelo,R. Raskin, P. Sutton and M. van den Belt, "The Value of the World's Ecosystem Services and natural capital," Nature 385 (May 1997): 253-262.

5   Dick Thompson. Asphalt Jungle. Time. April-May 2000. Pp. 50-51.

6   Hindrich,R. and M. Kleinbach. Energy: Its use and the Environment. Brooks/Cole p.264

7   P. Raven, L. Berg and G. Johnson, Environment 1995 Version, Saunders, Fortworth; P520

8   This reminds me of the T.V. commercial where Roach Motel, the pesticide, is being advertised. In the commercial it is mentioned that the cockroaches check –in but don't check out! Ha! Ha! This is analogous to the fact that yellow wave lengths of light come in through the clouds of carbon dioxide, and then are trapped when they change to the red wave length which does not escape thus, leaving the heat in.

9   L. Brown, Michael Renner and Christopher Flavin. Weather Damages Eases. Vital Signs 1998.p80 W.W. Norton Press.

10   Keaten, Jeremy. Heat wave kills 3000 in France. Truthout August 14, 2003. www.truthout.org <viewed August 15,2003

11   McKibben, Bill. Maybe One. 1998. Simon and Schuster P.120

12   W. Cunningham and B. Saigo, Environmental Science- A Global Concern (Boston: McGraw-Hill, 2001) p194.

13   M. L.McKinney and R.M. Schoch, Environmental Science: systems and solutions (New York: West, 1996) 311-351.

14   Peter Raven and Linda Berg, Environment 3rd Edition (Fort Worth: Harcourt, 2001) 375.

15   www.apex-environmental.com/CoralHealthIndicators. htlm#BB.Viwed Dec. 12,2000.

16   Mastny, Lisa A worldwatch Addendum Worldwatch May/June 2001.

17   P. Raven, L. Berg, Environment 3rd edition (Fort Worth: Saunders, 2001) 335.

18   Bright, C. Life Out of Bounds. W.W. Norton 1998. Pp.156-157

[19] Ibid .p97
[20] Associated Press, "Japanese desperately fight slick," Chicago Tribune January 7,1997: 14.
[21] Sandra Steingraber, Living Downstream (New York: Addison-Wesley, 1997) 248-251.
[22] Postal, Sandra. Pillars of Sand. 1999. P.92. W.W. Norton Press, New York
[23] www.environmentaldefense.org/clickable_gcan/d_news.html-Viewed May 16,2001
[24] Prugh, Thomas and E. Assaudourian. What is sustainability Anyway. Worldwatch September/Octobere 2003. p.16-17.
[25] Brown, M. The Toxic Cloud.1987 Harper and Row.p65-70.
[26] Jacobson, Jodi L. Environmental Refugees: A yardstick of Habitability. Worldwatch paper 86. November 1988
[27] Epstein S. L. Brown and C. Pope. Hazardous Waste In America. 1982. pp90-132. Sierra Club Books.
[28] Nierenberg, D Toxic Fertility in WorldWatch Magazine March/April 2001. p.32.
[29] Bush, Mark B. Ecology for a changing planet. End ed. Prentice Hall. 2000. p93-94
[30] Nadakavukaren, A. Our Global Environment: A Health Perspective. Waveland Press 1995   P.135
[31] http://ran.org/info_center/factsheets/04b.html. Viewed March 15,2003
[32] Op Citum Nadakavukaren.p.240
[33] Between 1945-1992 there were 1,051 nuclear explosions for testing purposes. 210 in the atmosphere, 5 underwater and 836 underground. Russia on the other hand conducted around 713 tests.
[34] Op Citum Nadakavukaren, p.383
[35] Stone, Richard. The hunt for hot stuff. 2003. Smithsonian. Pp.58-65.
[36] Winston,Mark L. Nature's War. 1997.Harvard University Press.p118
[37] www.exn.ca/stories/1997/01/06/03asp < viewed May 26, 2003
[38] www.copa.org/men/finsperm.html <viewed May 26,2003
[39] Lyman, Howard, Mad Cowboy: Plain Truth from a Cattle Rancher who won't eat Meat. 1998. pp. 65-66
[40] G.Tyler Miller, Environmental Science (Belmont, California: Wadsworth Publishing, 1995) 26.
[41] Lester R.Brown, Who Will Feed China (New York: W.W. Norton, 1995) 1.
[42] Lewis Regenstein, America the Poisoned (Washington D.C.: Acropolis, 1983) 1-365.
[43] Chris Bright, "Matters of Scale," Worldwatch Magazine 1998: 39.

[44] Lester Brown et. al, Vital signs (New York: W.W. Norton, 1994) 93.

[45] Bernard Nebel, Richard T. Wright, Environmental Science (Upper Saddle River, N.J.: Prentice Hall, 1998) 279.

[46] Weir.D. The Bhopal Syndrome. 1987. Sierra Club Books P143

[47] Ware, George. W. Pesticdes: Theory and Application. 1983. p 19

[48] Op Citum Weir 1987,. P.21

[49] 1 KG IS EQUAL TO 1000 GRAMS OR 2.206 POUNDS.

[50] B.J. Nebel, R.J. Wright, Environmental Science (Upper saddle River, N.J.: Prentice Hall, 2000) 413.

[51] Insects and other organisms become resistant by a process called directional selection. In this case if a pesticide is sprayed and most insects die, but not all, the remaining ones that survive may mate making superbugs.

[52] Morgan, Donald. Recognition and management of pesticide poisonings. United States Environmental Protection Agency. EPA -540/9-88-001. March 1989. pp.13,19, 57,58

[53] Lewis regenstein, America the Poisoned (Washington, D.C.: Acropolis, 1983) p. 79.

[54] Surgeoner, G.A and W. Roberts in. The Pesticide Question: Environment, Economics and Ethics. D. Pimental et al Editors. P.224.

[55] Mike McKinney,Robert M. Stoch, Environmental Science-Systems and solutions (Minneapolis/St. Paul: West, 1996) 425.

[56] Op Citum Weir, pp. 1-11.

[57] The formula for methyl isocyante is: CH3NCO

[58] Op Citum Weir 1987. p44

[59] Hawken, Paul. The Ecology of Commerce. 1993. Harper Business. P.116

[60] Culliney, T, D. Pimentel and M.Pimentel. Pesticides and Natural Toxicants in Foods. Pp127. In Pimentel ed. The pesticide Question. Chapman and Hall. 1993

[61] Brown,L. Vital Signs 2001. Norton Press. P.32-33

[62] Daniel Chiras, Environmental Science (Belmont Ca: Wadsworth, 1998) 170.

[63] Lester Brown, Gary Gardner, and Brian Halweil, Beyond Malthus (New York: Norton, 1999) 63.

[64] One hectare is equal to 2.47 acres .

[65] Jamieson, Bryan Z. A Warning Shot. http://www.zeppscommentaries.com/Science&Environment/warningshot.htm; viewed August 8/12/03

[66] Arthus-Bertrand, Yann. Earth From Above. Harry N. Abrams, Publisher. 2002. p.412

67   Dixie Lee Ray, Lou Guzzo, <u>Trashing the Planet</u>
(Washington, D.C.: Regnary/ Gateway, 1990) ix.

68   Lichens are organisms that belong to the fungal kingdom. They consist
of fungi and algae cells. They are very sensitive to air pollution.

69   The rosy periwinkle (*Catharanthus roseus*) is one of these
organisms. It is a plant found in Madagasgar and has
properties against aids, cancer and other diseases.

70   Nierenberg, D. Correcting Gender Myopia;
Worldwatch paper #161. September 2002. P.24.

71   There are over 1.8 million known organisms on the planet.
Many are incredibly beautiful. Without them our lives
would be non existent or certainly less interesting.

72   What a way to start out being president of the US
knowing that the world is overpopulated .

73   Op citum Arthus-bertrand p.412.

74   http://www.enviroweb.org/issues/enough08.
htm-page 1 of 10.Viewed Jan. 3,2001.

75   http://www.enviroweb.org/issues/enough11.htm-viewed Jan. 3,2001.

76   Emelda Marcus is known as the shoe lady because she had over
2,000 pairs of shoes. According to Johnny Walker, a Baltimore
radio host, the reason why Emelda had that many pairs of
shoes was because she was the reincarnation of a millipede.

77   Michael L. McKinney and R.M.Schoch, <u>Environmental Science:
Systems and Solutions</u> (New York: West, 1996) p.425.

78   R.C. Longworth, "America's Rally Cry:Buy,Buy," <u>Chicago
Tribune</u> Friday, March 12,1999, . First Section: 1,22.

79   http://www.enviroweb.org/issues/enough/index.html-
viewed Jan. 2, 2000.

80   From CNN's The People Bomb. 1992 Turner Educational
Service. A series of two VHS video tapes.

81   http://www.geocities.com/CapitolHill/Lobby/1818/3_1suv.html
Viewed Jan. 1,2000

82   http://salon.com/news/1997/12/08news.html Viewed Jan. 1,2000

83   Our soldiers are killing and getting killed in Iraq in order to
supply these Hummers and SUVs with cheap gasoline.

84   http:/www.howard.net/ban-suvs.
html#SUVEnvironment, Viewed Jan. 1,2000

85   Many of my students are adults because I teach at night
also and the older students take night classes.

86   Paul Hawken, <u>Ecology of Commerce</u> (New
York: harper-Collins, 1993)

[87] <u>Dead Ahead</u>, The video. 1992. Paul Seed, director

[88] www.radisol.com/cows/political.htm: < viewed November 6, 2005

[89] Chernobyl was the site of the worst nuclear accident in history.
To this day effects of the disaster are still lingering.

[90] Vovk, V. and T. Prugh. Red Past. Green Future? In
World-Watch.July/August 2003. p. 14-15

[91] Gary E McCuen and Ronald P. Swanson, <u>Toxic
Nightmare: Ecocide in the USSR &Eastern Europe</u>
(Hidson Wisconsin: GEM Publications, 1993) 14.

[92] Donald Kaufman, Cecelia Franz, <u>Biosphere 2000</u> (New
York: Harper Collins, 1993)p310 and p 384.

[93] Eastman Kodak Company, <u>One Earth</u> (City:
Kodak Company, Year) pp.84-89.

[94] Lee Davis, <u>Environmental Disasters</u> (New York: Facts on File, 1998) p.97.

[95] Gary Gardner, "Why Share?" <u>Worldwatch</u> July/August 1999: 10.

[96] David Ibata, "Imagine dawn of never-Ending rush
hour," <u>Chicago Tribune</u> Dec 1,1999: 1,20.

[97] America the Congested by Geraldine Sealey from
http://abcnews.go.com/sections/us/DailyNews/
ontheroad1_991119.html. viewed Nov.23,1999

[98] http://en.Thinkexist.com/dictionary/meaning/corruption;
Viewed November 20, 2004

[99] Associated Press online 7/17/2000 viewed 2/14/02

[100] Runyan, C. Indonesia's Discontent. Worldwatch May/June 1998.p20

[101] Schmetzer, Uli. Haze fading ,but fires will cloud
Asia's future. Chicago Tribune October 2,1997.p1.

[102] Mike Edwards, "Lethal Legacy," <u>National
Geographic</u> August 1994: 70-99.

[103] Al Gore, <u>Earth in the Balance</u> (Boston ,New
York: Houghton/Miflin, 1992) 1.

[104] Ibid, 287

[105] One person once suggested that the reason why Imelda
Marcos had so many pairs of shoes was due to the
fact that she is the reincarnation of a millipede.

[106] Randomhouse Dictionary. 1980 Ballantine Reference. P.384

[107] El Nino refers to the periodic warming of the Pacific
Ocean, which causes weather problems worldwide.

[108] Weir, David, M. Schapiro, Circle of Poison. 1981.
Institute for food and Development Policy. P.63.

[109] Broad, Wm. J. "Export of Hazardous Goods Raises
Congressional Ire . Science 27 March, 1981

110 Record of Redd Fox, "You Gotta Wash Yor Ass"

111 McKibben, Bill. *Maybe One.1998.Simon& & Schuster p.85*

112 Lyman, Howard. F. *Mad Cowboy.*1998. Scribner.pp 41-42

113 Ibid p.42

114 Lester R. Brown, <u>The Agricultural Link:How Environmental Deterioration Could Disrupt Economic Progress#136</u> (City: Worldwatch Society, 1997) Pages.

115 Lester brown, "Worlwatch paper #136,"

116 Internet. www.abcnews.com viewed Oct. 14,1999

117 George B. Schaller, <u>The Last Panda</u> (Chicago and London: University of Chicago Press, 1993) Front jacket.

118 M. McKinney and R.Scoch, <u>Environmental Science: Systems and Solutions</u> (New York: West, 1996) 327.

119 See the internet for metric conversions

120 Kerry A. Dolan, "The World's Working Rich," <u>Forbes Magazine</u> Vol. 166-Number 1 (July 3, 2000): pp.258-260.

121 Jennifer Loven, "Army Corps found rigging data," <u>Chicago Sun Times</u> Dec 7,2000, sec. Metro: 24.

122 Edited by Lewis and Faye Copeland, <u>10,000 jokes, toasts and Stories</u> (Garden City and New York: Doubleday and Company, 1965) p.674.

123 The American heritage Dictionary. 4th edition. Houghton Mifflin, 2000.

124 Bats are very efficient in pollinating plants and planting trees by dropping seeds with their waste products. For more information on bats, check out the organization: Bat Conservation International.

125 G. tyler Miller, <u>Environmental Science</u> (Belmont Cal.: Wadsworth, 1995)pp 384-7.

126 Peter Brimblecommb, <u>The Big Smoke</u> (London: Methuen, 1987) p49.

127 William Neikirk, "Nuclear Test ban Treaty Fails," <u>Chicago Trbune</u> October 14,1999: 1.

128 Allan Durning, <u>How much is Enough</u> (New York, London: W.W.Norton & Company, Year)

129 Estimated number of AIDS cases about 40 million worldwide. (National Institute of Allergy and Infectious Diseases). Estimated number of malaria cases about 300-500 million according to the World Health Organization (WHO). According to Cambridge University the estimated number of people with Schistosomiasis is more than 200 million.

130 It should be pointed out that during the last couple of weeks of the 2004 election, John Kerry was out in hunting gear ready to bag a bird. This is an aspect that I find quite shameful.

[131] Richard Preston , <u>The Hot Zone</u> (New York: Random House, 1994) Front Jacket.

[132] http://members.aol.com/ramola15/funfacts.html#paper viewed April 20, 2004

[133] Dealey, Sam. Sheila Jackson Lee, Limousine Liberal. Does she think the ethics rules don't apply to her? Weekly Standard 2/11/2002 volume 007, issue 21.

[134] Hartman, Tom, The Last Hours of Ancient Sunlight, 1998, Mythical Books, p. 133

[135] Nierenberg, Danielle. Correcting Gender Myopia. Worldwatch paper Number 161. September 2002

[136] ibid. p.39

[137] A word probably coined by that great Republican commentator, Paul Harvey

[138] The French were notorious for this with their underwater nuclear tests in the South Pacific islands a few years ago.

[139] Gerald Ford and Theodore Roosevelt were not elected but followed their predecessors.

[140] A running story tells of a mayor of a famous city who wanted tourists. He had the local chamber of commerce put up a sign saying: Come to our wonderful city and see the air.

[141] This also fits into the problem of the Aral Sea . (See chapter 8)

[142] www.wilderness.net/nwps/legis/nwps_act.cfm <viewed May 3,2003

[143] This is the same as earning $100,000 a year and spending $100,000 a year instead of spending only $50,000 and have some left for a rainy day.

[144] http://www-popexpo.ined.fr/eMain.html viewed April, 27,2004

[145] Doubling times of populations are calculated according to the following formula: 70 is divided by the percent growth rate. For example: If a country has a growth rate of 2%, the doubling time is calculated as 70/2, which equals 35 years. For those of you who are interested in investing money, you can figure out the amount of time that it would take to double by using the same formula. It is obvious that you would want a growth rate, which is very high on your income when it comes to investing, but when it comes to population increase, you would want the smallest percent growth rate as possible.

[146] Paul R. Ehrlich, Anne. H Ehrlich,The <u>Population Explosion</u> (New York: Simon and Shuster, 1990) 190-195.

[147] This was on a bumper sticker that I noticed one day.

[148] Lester brown, G. Gardner and B. Halweil, <u>Beyond Malthus,Nineteen Dimensions of the Population Challenge</u> (New York: W.W. Norton & Company, 1999)

[149] Daniel D. Chiras, <u>Environmental Science:Action for a Sustainable Future</u> (Redwood city, California: Benjamin Cummings, 1994) p.114.

[150] Fish and chickens require less than a ten to one ratio of food to body mass.

[151] Dick Thompson, "Asphalt Jungle," <u>Time</u> April-May 2000: 50-51.

[152] From www.plannersweb.com/sprawl/define. html. Viewed Dec 16,2000.

[153] Jane Jacobs, <u>The Death and Life of Great American Cities</u> (New York: Random House, 1961) Back Cover.

[154] The Worldwatch Institute ,Vital Signs. 2001, p.56

[155] J.Stein and L.Urdang Ed., <u>Random House Dictionary of the English Language</u> (New York: Random House, 1966) 1045.

[156] "Developer" is the dirtiest word in the environmental dictionary according to me.

[157] See appendix I for definition of bioaccumulation.

[158] Weisberg, Gary Ed. Ecocide in Indochina. 1970. Canfield Press p. vi.

[159] Lash,J.K. Gillman and D. Sheridan. Season of the spoils. Pantheon Books. 1984. p.6-7

[160] John B. Judis, <u>The Paradox of American Democracy</u> (Pantheon Books: Random House, 2000) p.185.

[161] Mosley, Ray "Climate change debate has US in Minority, Chicago Tribune March 31,2001 p. 3

[162] The New Republic, May 13, 1991 p. 7; The Nation, April 22, 1991 v252, n15, p511(1): Viewed on the internet during a search on Oct. 18, 2004.

[163] Provey, Joe, Plugging the Sun, The Taunton Press. http://www. taunton.com/finehomebuilding/pages/h00114.asp> Viewed June 8, 2004

[164] Lester Brown,M. Renner and B. Halweil, <u>Vital signs</u> (New York, London: W.W. Norton, 1999) 116-117.

[165] The total number of nuclear weapons represented are those of the United States, Russia, United Kingdom, France, and China.

[166] Steve Croft, <u>60 Minutes</u>, CBS, Channel two (Chicago), Chicago, July 23,2000.

[167] J.Lash,K. Gillman and David Sheridan, <u>A season of Spoils</u> (New York: Pantheon Books, 1984) 6.

[168] Op citum Lash p.184

[169] Weir, David and M. Schapiro, Circle of Poison. 1981 Institute for food and development policy (publishers)

[170] Ibid Weir, 1981.p.62

[171] Ibid Weir 1981 p.63

172 There was a joke going around when Watt was the Secretary of the Interior. How much power does it take to destroy the environment? Answer: One Watt.

173 H.W. may stands for Herbert Walker or Hazardous Waste.

174 Marcia D. Lowe, Back on Track: The Global Rail Revival Washington D.C.: Worldwatch, April 1994 p.5.

175 This is from a video tape called: Advertising and the end of the World.

176 Dixie Lee Ray, Trashing the Planet (Washington D.C.: Regnary Gateway, 1990) 1-172.

177 Do you know why the ocean roars? Because you would roar too, if you had crabs on your bottom.

178 Daniel Chiras, Environmental Science Action for a Sustainable Future (Redwood City California: Benjamin Cummings, 1994) 114

179 Ibid, Chiras, p.114

180 David Day, The Environmental Wars (New York: St Martins Press, 1989) 84-86

181 Prugh, T. and E.Assadourian. 2003. Worldwatch Magazine, September/ October 2003 p.18

182 http://www.uct.ac.za/general/monpaper/99-no28/wbaims.htm viewed 5/29/01

183 Roodman, David. Still Waiting for the Jubilee: Pragmatic solutions for the third world debt crisis. Worldwatch paper #155. April 2001. P.6

184 http://www.cid.harvard.edu/sidinthenews/articles/sf9108.htlm, Viewed August 26, 2004

185 Garret, L. The Coming Plague. Penguin Books. P.205. 1994.

186 www.nikewages.org

187 Roodman, David. Still waiting for the Jubilee. #155. Worldwatch 2001 p.6

188 Ibid. Roodman p.6

189 http://ciesin.org/IC/wri/chap3.html   viewed June 9,2001

190 Wm. Cunningham and B. Saigo. Environmental Science. 1992. Page 201. WC Brown.

191 McKinney, M and R. Schoch. Environmental Science: Systems and Solutions page.425. Jones and Bartlett 1998

192 Cunninham, Wm, M. Cunningham, and B. saigo. Environmental Science; A Global Concern. 2003. p433-435

193 This reminds me of a story that fits here perfectly. Someone just asked , "David, did you just take a shower?" I reply, "Why? Is one missing?"

[194] Op citum. Cunningham

[195] Brewer, G. On a Beam of Light. 2001.p.260.

[196] P. Hawken and A. Lovins. Natural Capitalism. 1999. Little, Brown and Company. p50

[197] Ibid p. 50

[198] Goering, L. Orphans a tiny hint of Africa's AIDS apocalypse. Chicago Tribune , Aug. 28, 2002. P1.

[199] Personal communication from William Klarman, plant pathologist. 1978

[200] Worldwatch publication... 199

[201] Agrios, G.N. Plant Pathology. Academic Press 1969. p.7 , 209.

[202] Feldman, Bob, The U.S.. military's war on the earth. www. Alternet.org. < viewed June 6,2003

[203] Parsons, E.C.M. The Possible impacts of military activity on cetaceans in West Scotland. 2000. European Research on Cetaceans. 14 p.185

[204] Mike Malloy Radio Show, May 9, 2003

[205] Hymen E. Goldin, A Treasury of Jewish Holidays (New York: Twayne, 1952) p.188-191.

[206] Wm. Cunningham and B. Saigo, Environmental Science (Boston, New York: McGraw Hill, 1999) p.626.

[207] Lilienfeld, R. and Wm. Rathje. Use Less Stuff. 1998.p.169-170

[208] I believe Disneyland shoots off fireworks everyday.

[209] Awake Correspondent in Brazil, "The Pantanal," Awake Sept. 8,1999: 15.

[210] Smyser, W.R. The Humanitarian Conscience.2003. Palgrave Macmillan. P.282

[211] The Earth Charter Brochure from the Earth Charter International secretariat . n.d. San Jose Costa Rica

[212] Ibid .

[213] Ibid. For more details about these environmental principles see www.earthcharter.org or write to them at The Earth Charter Fund, P.O.B 648, Middlebury, Vt 05753.

[214] Isn't it ironic that both George Bushes had a W as a middle initial. Could it be that the W may stand for War?

[215] Op Citum p16 Lilenfeld

[216] Op Citum Lilienfeld p14

[217] Op Citum Lilienfeld. p.45

[218] Herron, Michael. Guzzling gas may threaten our national security. Chicago Tribune p.20. 4,Nov 2001.

[219] Some people in the US suggest that we don't have enough sunlight for these devices. My answer to that is even a few months of summer in northern states is enough to heat water using these devices.

[220] Brandon, Karen. Cutting the cord. <u>Chicago Tribune Magazine</u> July 9,2001. 12-28.

[221] Renner, M. In Vital Signs. 2003 W.W.Norton. p.56-57.

[222] Lillianfeld, r. and W. Rathje. Use Less Stuff. 1998.Fawcett Books. P.45

[223] Parking fees can be as much as $24 a day in a large metropolitan area like Chicago which is more than the cost of a cheap motel.

[224] Ellwood, Wayne. New Internationalist- issue 195-May 1989

[225] Daniel Chiras, <u>Environmental Science</u> (Belmont Cal., N. Y.: Wadsworth, 1998)

[226] Op citem Hawken

[227] Op citem Hawken

[228] www.w-rabbit.com/fote/environ.html

[229] Al Gore, <u>Earth in the Balance</u> (New York: Houghton/Mifflin, 1992) p.307.

[230] Bradley, Keoun. "Of Earth's 6 Billion, 0.11% call this Home-As world population beefs up, Chicago's shoulders not so big." <u>Chicago Tribune</u> 12 Oct. 1999: p1,p12.

[231] McKibben, Bill: <u>Maybe One.</u> Simon and Shuster 1998

[232] Op Citum Mc Kibben. p116.

[233] <u>Chicago Sun-Times</u> of Nov. 23, 2001. Front page headline.

[234] Op Citum LilienfeldP.36

[235] Is it possible that the cockroach may even have a substance which can be used to treat cancer?

[236] Mark J.Plotkin, <u>Medicine Quest</u> (New York: Viking, 2000) 3-224.

[237] Weir, D andM. Schapiro. Circle of Poison. Institute for food development Policy. (Publishers) p45-46.

[238] http://www.ethicalinvesting.com/monsanto/terminator.shtml< viewed Aug 10, 2004

[239] Brookesmith, Peter. Biohazard : <u>The Hot Zone and Beyond</u>: Barnes and Noble, Inc. 1997. P135

[240] Whitman, Christine Todd, A Strong Climate Plan in Time Magazine , August 26,2002. p.A48

[241] Zicree, M.S. The Twilight Zone Companion. 1982.p.349

[242] www.who.int/tdr/diseases/malaria/diseaseinfo.htm; viewed October 2004

[243] www.cdc.gov/ncidod/dpd/parasites/giardiasis/factsht_giardiasis.htm; viewed October 2004

[244] www.cdc.gov/ncidod/dpd/parasites/cryptosporidiosis/factsheet_cryptosporidiosis.htm

245 www.cdc.gov/ncidod/dbmd/diseaseinfo/cholera_g.htm;
     viewed October 2004
246 www.cdc.gov/ncidod/dbmd/diseaseinfo/leptospirosis_g.htm;
     viewed October 2004
247 www.cdc.gov/ncidod/dbmd/diseaseinfo/typhoidfever_g.htm;
     viewed October 2004
248 www.cdc.gov/ncidod/dbmd/diseaseinfo/escherichiacoli_g.htm;
     viewed October 2004
249 www.cdc.gov/ncidod/dvbid/lyme/prevent.htm; viewed October 2004
250 www.who.int/mediacentre/factsheets/fs117/en/; viewed October 2004
251 www.cdc.gov/ncidod/diseases/hanta/hps/noframes/;
     viewed October 2004
252 www.cdc.gov/ncidod/disease/hepatitis/a/faga.htm;
     viewed October 2004
253 www.nwfsc.noaa.gov/hab/HABs_Toxins/Marine_
     Biotoxins/PSP/index.htm; Viewed October 2004
254 http://home.mtholyoke.edu/~akpeters/humans.html;
     viewed November 26,2004
255 www.medterms.com/script/main/art.asp?articlekey=19394 - 24k
     viewed Nov.11, 2004
256 www.djo.harvard.edu/site.php?url=/patients/pi/426
     viewed Nov.13, 2004
257 www.medterms.com/script/main/art.asp?articlekey=9888
     Viewed Nov. 14, 2004
258 www.mrcophth.com/ ophthalmologyonstamps/phototoxicity/b1.html
     Viewed Nov. 14, 2004
259 www.macular.org/ Viewed Nov. 13, 2004
260 Both Iraqi wars can be called: Operation Iraqi
     Liberation (OIL). Coincidence?
261 I would like to point out that when I was living in New York City I
     saw the WTC being built. I was born and grew up in New York.
262 How can you study the AIDS virus without having an actual
     sample to work with? The same is true with terrorism. Ask the
     terrorists directly why they hate us with the stipulation of course
     that they will not be arrested if they attend the conference.
263 Cunningham, Wm, Mary Ann Cunninham and Barbara
     Saigo. Environmental Science. 7th Edition.2003. p 264
264 http://www.cfsan.fda.gov/~mow/domoic.html;
     viewed November 20, 2004.

About the Author

David Arieti has been an environmentalist for over 30 years. Mr. Arieti graduated from the University of Denver in 1967 with a degree in Science. He also received an MS degree in Marine Science from Long Island University (LIU). Since graduating from LIU, Mr. Arieti was the research director of the Baltimore Environmental Center working on hazardous waste issues, did environmental research on both the Hudson River and Chesapeake Bay, consulted on environmental issues as well as lecturing, and as an adjunct professor in various colleges in the Chicago area where he is now. Mr. Arieti won three Best-Teach-Of-The-Year-Awards at Columbia College, Chicago (1996); Oakton Community College in Des Plaines, IL (2002) and at Richard J. Dailey College, Chicago (2005).

Printed in the United States
39426LVS00003B/90

9 781420 832273